The Politics
of Defeat

The Politics of Defeat

Campaigning for Congress

Robert J. Huckshorn and
Robert C. Spencer

THE UNIVERSITY OF MASSACHUSETTS PRESS

This book is dedicated to

Carolyn and Edith

Copyright © 1971 by the
University of Massachusetts Press
All rights reserved
Library of Congress Catalog Card Number 71–123538
Printed in the United States of America

Preface

Early in the fall of 1962 the authors met in the lobby of the Sheraton-Park Hotel in Washington, D.C. From that meeting there grew common concerns and interests, and finally the joint effort which produced this book.

During 1962 and 1963 each of the authors was a division head of one of the national party committees in Washington. Holding fellowships cosponsored by the two national committees and the National Center for Education in Politics, Spencer was Research Director at the Democratic National Committee, while Huckshorn was Director of the Division of Arts and Sciences of the Republican National Committee.

Both authors were interested in those nonincumbent candidates in each party who, over the summer of 1962, were beginning to campaign in earnest for seats in the U.S. House of Representatives. Most of these men were seeking to challenge and defeat incumbent congressmen or to win contests in new districts heavily weighted in favor of the opposition. It seemed to us that defeat was predestined for most of these candidates.

Aware on the one hand of the low turnover of seats in the U.S. House of Representatives and on the other hand of the vigor with which the seats were being contested by these candidates, we were curious as to why they sought these offices, and we were fascinated by the magnitude of the problems they faced in their lonely crusades.

Scholars have devoted much time and effort to the U.S. Congress in recent years, but few have systematically studied the electoral system which produces its members. The roles of the candidates—their relationships to their parties and personal organizations—have remained largely a matter of conjecture. To be sure, some candidates have analyzed their own campaigns, but seldom have these studies become available to the community at large.[1] Congressional campaigns present the difficulty of understanding a variegated multicellular structure by analysis of a single cell. More often than not, these personal accounts have become a part of political folklore rather than an addition to scholarly literature.

What motivated these men and women to seek high public office when the chances of victory were so remote? What led them to extensive personal and political commitments when for most the yield was certain to be small? What unique problems were encountered during their short tenure as candidates, and how were they resolved? Were these candidates self-starters or were they "recruited" by the officials of their respective parties? What relationships were developed between the challenger candidates and the national, state, or local party organization? What ends were served by these contests: for the candidates, for the party, for the House, for the country? Was it possible that, in the words of Montaigne, there were "some defeats more triumphant than victories"? The congressional elections of 1962 presented a unique opportunity for us to systematically explore some of these questions.

After discussing the perplexing problems of the probable con-

1. A candidate occasionally attempts to explain his campaign, election, or defeat to his constituents through privately circulated statements. His purpose ordinarily is to justify his campaign strategy, inform those who worked in his campaign, or consolidate support for a future effort. Several candidates furnished copies of such personal analyses in 1962. Even so, very few published materials exist. A few candidates have published case studies of their own campaigns, and others have been produced by scholars. Joseph P. Lyford described his campaign for a congressional nomination in the Connecticut Democratic Convention in *Candidate* (New York: Holt, 1959). Stephen K. Bailey and Howard D. Samuel described the campaigns of three members of Congress in short case studies in 1953 in *Congress At Work* (New York: Holt, 1953). *On Capitol Hill* by John Bibby and Roger Davidson (New York: Holt, 1967) contains two brief descriptions of the campaigns of Senator Abraham Ribicoff and Congressman Clark McGregor. John W. Kingdon, in *Candidates for Office: Beliefs and Strategies* (New York: Random House, 1968), presents much useful information on campaign strategies for a variety of offices in Wisconsin. David A. Leuthold, *Electioneering in a Democracy: Campaigns for Congress* (New York: Wiley, 1968), is a study of congressional races in the San Francisco area in 1962. Other materials on campaigns from the candidate's perspective are included in Stimson Bullitt, *To Be a Politician* (New York: Doubleday, 1959), and Clem Miller, *Member of the House* (New York: Scribner, 1962). On the whole little attention has been paid to political campaigning either by those who have taken part or by scholars who have observed it.

gressional losers of 1962 with a number of political scientists, candidates, and party officials, we decided to concentrate our efforts in two general areas: the phenomenon of political defeat; and the congressional campaign as a manifestation of a unique universe in American politics. The first of these has not been studied at all, while the second has not been explored in depth. As our investigations progressed, it became apparent that the two were closely intertwined—were, in fact, inseparable. The causes of defeat were inextricably tied to the uniqueness of the congressional contest. These contests were exceptional because of their place in the total political setting. Congressional districts rarely fit within the established party framework at any organizational level—national, state, or local. This situation places the candidate in the role of political entrepreneur. Starting with the primary and continuing through the general election campaign, he must run as an individual with a highly personal organization. Furthermore, because of the nature of many districts and the isolation of his efforts, the nonincumbent, to a greater extent than any other candidate, must engage in a campaign which, despite his best efforts, is very likely to end in his defeat.

Accumulation of data for a study of this kind must include as large a part of the total universe as possible. With over 800 candidates representing the two major parties in all the contested congressional districts, personal interviews were out of the question. Neither would a reliable representative sample of congressional races accomplish our purpose. We concluded, therefore, that a properly timed questionnaire mailed to all candidates, plus selected interviews and our own observations, would constitute our major investigative tools.

A thirteen-page questionnaire was then designed for distribution to the defeated candidates. A shorter ten-page questionnaire was sent to nonincumbent winners, while one of seven pages went to the successful incumbents. The latter two questionnaires contained fewer of the questions than the one furnished the defeated candidates, but the questions remained the same.[2] The differences were based upon an assumption, which proved valid, that newly reelected incumbents would have less time and interest in completing the questionnaire than would the defeated candidates or the new win-

2. See Appendix A for the questionnaire sent to all defeated Democratic candidates. The GOP questionnaire was identical except for particular references to parties, issues, and opposition.

ners. Furthermore, the two national committees—the bases from which we operated—were most actively serving the causes of the nonincumbent candidates, both those who won and those who lost. The incumbents, having the advantages of their own staffs and personal organizations, in addition to the assistance of the National Congressional Campaign Committees of each party, felt little need for help from the "downtown" party committees, whose role traditionally has been directed toward the presidential party and national conventions.

Republican National Chairman William E. Miller and Democratic National Chairman John M. Bailey both cooperated fully to secure as wide a response as possible to the questionnaire while at the same time leaving the authors completely free in its design. In this respect the authors were inhibited only by the possibility that some questions might dampen the rapport between the national committee staff and the candidates. It would have been fruitless to probe for answers which might have added insult to the keen disappointment felt by most of the defeated candidates.

During the week following November 6, 1962, the day of defeat or victory, both National Committee Chairmen sent letters to all candidates in their respective parties urging their cooperation in the study. Reproduced on electric typewriters, these letters also bore the chairman's signature. They were followed a few days later by another letter from the appropriate author, on National Committee letterhead, enclosing the questionnaire, requesting a prompt and thoughtful response, and assuring respondents of the confidential nature of the inquiry.[3]

It should be noted that the Republican Congressional Campaign Committee, when apprised of this study, readily agreed to forego its usual postelection survey to gather information from the candidates. Interim reports were filed with the chairmen of each National Committee a few months after the election. No party official was privy to any material from this survey which dealt with the other party or its candidates.

The response to the questionnaire was heartening and resulted in a total return of 60 percent from the defeated candidates; 64 percent from the new winners; and 50 percent for the incumbents.[4] Members

3. See Appendix B for copies of the letters sent to each candidate by the Republican National Chairman and by one of the authors.
4. The House of Representatives in the Eighty-Sixth Congress had 437 members: 263 Democrats and 174 Republicans, including (since 1958) one

of both parties responded to the questionnaire in nearly equal proportions. In nearly all instances the defeated candidates and new winners took the time to complete the questionnaires themselves. In the case of incumbents, acknowledgment was often in the form of a letter from the congressman or his assistant, indicating that most of the questionnaire was not applicable, since each incumbent tended to feel his situation to be unique.

The generally low response of incumbent winners can be explained in part by the success of their established personal organizations and the other well-known advantages of incumbency. It may further be explained by the fact that most of them held seats in the less competitive districts, where little support or interest from the national party committees was apparently needed or wanted. However, because the Republican Congressional Campaign Committee traditionally has been more active in these campaigns than has its Democratic counterpart and, further, because National Chairman Miller was himself a member of the House of Representatives at the time,[5] the Republican incumbent winners responded more generously to the survey than did the Democrats who were reelected.

The authors also concluded that the incumbent winners' questionnaires were less reliable, since many had turned them over to campaign or administrative aides. One result was a much greater number of "no response" and "don't know" answers than was the case with other groups of respondents. It was of more importance

---

extra member each for the new states of Alaska and Hawaii. The number of seats contested for the Eighty-Seventh Congress returned to 435, after the Congressional apportionment of 1961–62. Because of uncontested seats in the South and a handful in the North, there were only 398 nonincumbent candidates for the 435 seats: 223 Republicans and 175 Democrats. Of the 398 losers, 238 responded to this questionnaire: 110 Democrats and 128 Republicans. This was a response of 63 percent for the Democratic losers, and 57 percent for the Republicans.

The response from the "new winners," among the 398 contestants for house seats in 1962, was better. Sixty-seven won election and forty-three responded to this questionnaire, a yield of 64 percent. This included twenty-four Democrats and nineteen Republicans, a party response of 66 percent and 61 percent respectively.

Of the 222 incumbent Democrats who held on to their seats, ninety-four, or 42 percent, responded. Of the 145 incumbent Republicans retaining their seats, eighty-nine, or 61 percent, replied.

5. Miller was also the immediate past chairman of the Republican Congressional Campaign Committee; William S. Warner, Executive Director of the RNC, had formerly been with the Hill Committee.

that the information culled from these questionnaires frequently did not reflect the views of the candidates themselves. It showed that, as a rule, the incumbent winners were less willing and interested in analyzing their own campaign efforts and consequently were less likely to discuss campaign problems or techniques, particularly with national committee staff members.

The losers—having depended to a far greater extent on their own resources in mounting their campaigns and being bruised, introspective, and disappointed—were more willing to analyze strengths and weaknesses to provide information which might help future candidates and the efforts of the national party committees.

The material gathered through the questionnaire has been supplemented by approximately thirty interviews with losing candidates, with congressmen, and with campaign aides, managers, state chairmen, and national committeemen and women. Officers and staff members of the national committees and the congressional campaign committees were most helpful in supplementing the authors' observations of their respective roles in the campaign.

A note of caution on our intent in this study. We have not presumed to assign causes nor have we set forth general principles on how to avoid being defeated. The former would require a deeper understanding of human motivation and behavior than we possess, and the latter would be foolhardy in view of the circumstances under which candidates become involved in politics. Instead, our interest is in the phenomenon of defeat as it relates to congressional campaigning; in the candidates' self-described overt motives for entering the fray; and finally, in their highly personal analyses of the campaign and its relationship to the political establishment.

In one very real sense this is also the final report to our respective party chairmen on that questionnaire of November 1962. In another sense it is but a beginning and seeks only to open inquiry into a long-neglected area of the political system: the congressional elections and the congressional campaign.

We owe the customary debts of gratitude to friends, colleagues, and families. Cornelius P. Cotter and Bernard C. Hennessy, both of whom were earlier Faculty Fellows, were a constant stimulus to us. Charles O. Jones and Norman Zucker read the manuscript and made many helpful suggestions. To our fellow staff members at the Republican and Democratic National Committees we owe a special word of thanks. We refer particularly to Maureen Drummy, Therese Bruneau, Pat Krause, and Hannah Stokes, who gave us support in full measure when the postelection pace of work should have resulted in a reduction of their efforts. Huckshorn is especially indebted to Albert B. (AB) Herman and William S. Warner, respectively Campaign Manager and Executive Director of the Republican National Committee in 1962, and to Ed Terrar, Executive Director of the Republican Congressional Campaign Committee. Spencer, on the other hand, owes special debts to Sam Brightman, former Deputy Chairman for Public Affairs, and Charles Roche, former Deputy Chairman for Organization, of the Democratic National Committee. Although some of these individuals are no longer with the national political parties, their leaving does not diminish our debt.

It goes without saying that our efforts would not have been possible without the generous cooperation of Chairman Miller and Chairman Bailey. For this we are indeed grateful. We particularly want to thank Mrs. Myrtle Cassel, who typed and retyped the entire manuscript. Last but not least to our respective spouses, Carolyn Huckshorn and Edith Spencer, we owe our personal thanks and gratitude for bearing with us during long weeks on the road in the midst of the campaign and long months of neglect during the preparation of the book.

We, of course, accept total responsibility for errors of commission or omission, since unlike some of the defeated candidates, we have been unable to find anyone in our respective party or academic establishments to whom we might pass the buck.

Boca Raton, Florida—R.J.H.
Springfield, Illinois—R.C.S.

Contents

The Politics
of Defeat

1.
The Politics of Defeat: Campaigning for Congress

Any coward can fight a battle when he is sure of winning; but give me that man who has pluck to fight when he's sure of losing. That's my way, sir; and there are many victories worse than a defeat.—GEORGE ELIOT

THE candidate was destined for defeat the day he announced and filed his petitions for his party's nomination for election to the U.S. House of Representatives. No nominee of his party had received more than 42 percent of the vote in the congressional election in that district for over thirty years. His opponent was an entrenched incumbent, who entertained no thought of retirement and who had taken the measure of six different opponents in the past fourteen years.

The petitions, hastily filed on the day before the legal deadline, bore the names of a few family friends, volunteers, and those party faithful who had perfunctorily lent their signatures to other candidates over the years. These loyalists saw nothing incongruous in signing the nominating petitions of a man they had just met and, in some cases, of whom they had not previously heard. It was, they reasoned, better to have any candidate representing the party than to permit the seat to go unchallenged. The candidate, unencumbered by previous experience, fatally interpreted this party courtesy as genuine support, because at this point the signatures nourished his ego as well as his overconfidence.

The leaders of the party, used to losing this particular contest, provided but perfunctory encouragement. Realizing full well the hopelessness of the effort, barring a miracle, they were reluctant to discourage a candidate who, for whatever reason, was willing to enter the fray. At this point they probably believed that the futility of the venture would be offset by the struggle of the candidate and that little actual harm could be done to the cause of the party in the district. At best, some long-range benefit might result.

The candidate's family, at first perplexed and reluctant to encourage his plunge into politics, responded slowly to his contagious enthusiasm. His wife yielded her domestic and social routines and gave grudging support to the campaign effort. During the late summer and early fall, however, as the family finances were squeezed and the candidate's long absences from home increased, the forbearance of his family was badly strained.

Business and professional associates, unable to dissuade their respected friend from pursuing what appeared an unnecessary sacrifice, dug into their pockets to help pay the first round of printer's bills. Privately they had expressed the hope that the candidate would tackle his political office with the same prudence which had enabled him to build a successful and profitable business enterprise. But their honest caution was misinterpreted, and the candidate felt offended at what seemed to him a lack of faith. He was nonetheless undeterred in his bid for a political career.

From the outset the candidate underestimated the personal, emotional, and financial costs of the campaign. At the same time he unrealistically overestimated the possibility of the district's loyal party voters' splitting their tickets to support his candidacy. Yet committed by birth, tradition, or conviction to the other party and its incumbent congressman, most voters would have to engage in massive ticket splitting for the candidate to win. Since there was little reason to believe that the incumbent, the party, or the nation were in serious danger, few voters saw any grounds for lending active support to the challenger.

The candidate's inexperience cost him dearly at almost every turn. Since the nomination was uncontested, the candidate had no primary-election "rehearsal" for the main event; he even doubted the value of a primary as a proving ground for the general election campaign.

The campaign, though unquestionably energetic, was frequently amateurish. Entrenched party officials offered only token support, forcing the candidate to rely on volunteers, business associates, personal friends, and family members for the actual campaign labor. The precinct list provided by one county committee was hopelessly outdated, not having been revised for several years. Three of the four newspapers in the district simply followed custom and routinely endorsed the opposition; the other ignored him. The candidate's campaign manager, a former business acquaintance, was well-meaning and sincere but unimaginative and inexperienced in fund raising, public relations, and political organization.

For this candidate the election was an anticlimax. On election night he was denied even a moral victory, since his margin was hardly better than had been those of his predecessors. He received no plaudits from party officials and no encouragement to continue a political career. His business was badly shaken by the six-month campaign, and his family relationships were in need of mending. Personal debts of several thousand dollars caused him embarrassment and some personal hardships.

Disillusioned and bitter, he was perplexed by this "ignominious defeat" and resented the well-meant commiserations of his friends. Apparently, despite his effort, the prevailing apathy within his party had only been consolidated. His own chances for renomination in a later election were diminished if not destroyed. The cynics in the party were confirmed in their belief that "this is a one-party district, and nothing is going to change it." The candidate was in no position to challenge that assumption.

A typical experience? Perhaps not, but similar in many respects to scores of congressional contests throughout the nation in any election year. The simple fact is that most congressional elections are not competitive, nor are the major political parties organized in such a way as to offer meaningful assistance to nonincumbent candidates. Congressional district politics, as now manifested, is not a viable part of our established party structure. One purpose of this study is to determine the views of the candidates with regard to the relationship between established party organs and individual congressional campaigns.

The armchair political "expert" tends to think of politics in highly competitive terms. Theoretically all candidates have an equal chance, and "may the best man win"; all elections are decided on some combination of issues, candidate appeal, and party organization; candidates, they believe, are carefully selected by party officials on the basis of some unspecified criterion designed to assure victory. A survey of any newspaper's "letters to the editor" will substantiate these questionable assertions.

Such ideas evolve from stereotyped beliefs about the traditional American two-party system, which for each contest always provides a winner and a loser. They also result from unsophisticated instruction in civics and government—the training, one suspects, given most frequently in elementary and secondary schools in our society. Finally, belief in the competitive nature of American politics derives from our devotion to games and contests in which the "best" man, the "best" team, or the "best" horse normally wins. The belief, however, is not always true of sports any more than it is of politics. Whatever the source and however true, the fact is that congressional races are rarely competitive, are highly individualistic, are often amateurish, are seldom well-supported, and are neglected by the political parties.

Dimensions of Marginality

Any systematic study of congressional elections must take cognizance of the fact that a large majority of the seats are "safe" for one or the other of the parties. Of the "safe" seats, most are held by incumbents; a recent study indicates that from 1952 to 1962 only 22 percent of the congressional districts in the United States had representation from both major political parties. Over one-half were in the hands of a single party, and a large proportion of those were occupied by a succession of only two or three incumbents during the ten-year period. Most incumbents in safe districts were therefore removable only by voluntary retirement or death.

Charles O. Jones' analysis of data from congressional elections leads him to state:

Increasingly, it seems, if the present trends continue, the incumbent will win. Based on the data here, a simple prediction that the incumbent will win five consecutive elections will probably hold true for 70 to 80 percent of all congressional districts.[1]

James MacGregor Burns makes essentially the same point in his comment on congressional elections:

The base of the congressional system is the one-party district, as established and protected by the state legislatures. Though we hear much about congressmen's "safe seats," it is still hard to grasp the extent of noncompetition in congressional elections. Almost half of the House seats never change party hands. Another quarter, roughly, switch only on rare occasions. Aside from great sweeps such as those of 1920 and 1936,

1. "Inter-Party Competition for Congressional Seats," *Western Political Quarterly,* 17, no. 3 (1964), 461–76.

about 150 Republican seats and about the same number of Democratic seats never switch to the other party. Reasonably competitive districts number about 125 out of a total of 435.[2]

To careful observers the noncompetitiveness of congressional elections is obviously no revelation. Indeed, the number of competitive districts is so small a portion of the whole that the idea of marginality now serves as a standard for political leaders in measuring election potential and results. Consequently, the "five-percent rule" of marginality has assumed a place in the glossary of political science.

THE FIVE-PERCENT RULE

In 1962 only 88 seats (20 percent) of the 435 were marginal under the five-percent rule usually applied to congressional contests. This rule treats as marginal any majority outcome of 5 percent or less of the votes in the immediately preceding congressional election. Thus the party winning the seat by a vote of up to 55 percent considers the seat marginal and possibly in jeopardy in the next election. And the party losing the same seat, if it polls 45 percent or more, treats the upcoming contest as especially important—a potential gain.

Between 1960 and 1962 nineteen states redistricted congressional seats in response to the 1960 decennial census. Since the new district lines often did not correspond to the old, adjustments in the five-percent rule were necessary to accommodate the changes. These adjustments were usually made by using the two-party congressional or gubernatorial vote from the counties within a new district in order to arrive at an estimate of its marginality. In those districts which remained unchanged no adjustments were necessary, and the 1960 congressional vote was used.

According to the *Congressional Quarterly* (*CQ*) thirty-eight incumbent Democrats and fifty incumbent Republicans were classified as marginal in 1962. These calculations also showed that in eighteen districts a switch of less than 1 percent of the vote would have altered the outcome in 1960. Of these close districts the Democrats won eleven, while the Republicans captured seven that year.[3]

2. *The Deadlock of Democracy: Four Party Politics in America* (Englewood Cliffs, N.J.: Prentice-Hall, 1963), p. 241.
3. *Congressional Quarterly Almanac, Eighty-seventh Congress, First Session* (Washington, D.C., Congressional Quarterly, Inc., 1961), p. 1026.

THE CONGRESSIONAL QUARTERLY RULE

Periodically during each preelection season the *Congressional Quarterly* has published an evaluation of each district, assigning it a designation as "safe," "leaning," or "doubtful." These appraisals by the editors of *CQ* are based upon reports from the field, their knowledge of opinion polls within the district, previous electoral performance, and a certain amount of subjective judgment. By adding these factors to the five-percent rule, *CQ* suggested in May 1962 that forty-four districts "leaned" to the Republicans while forty "leaned" to the Democrats. Forty others were considered to be "doubtful," while 311 (71 percent) of the 435 seats were listed as "safe." It should be noted, however, that these evaluations were made before primary elections were held in some states.

While this picture of the "safe" incumbency might appear so formidable as to dissuade potential candidates, these data are seldom studied by the candidates or by their managers before they file for election. As candidates get caught up in the excitement of politics and as their contacts narrow to an exclusive circle of friends who nourish their ambitions, many seem convinced that the incumbent can be defeated; that it is just a matter of running a strong opposition candidate; that it is an unusually good year; or that a 5 percent vote deficit can be overcome by hard work, a strong campaign, and "hitting the issues." Even those who are cognizant of the probable futility of the campaign effort are hesitant to admit their doubt. As one Republican respondent put it, "Every newcomer thinks he is God's gift to government. It takes a lot of persuasion to convince a guy that his personality and views do not appeal to most of the people." Another Republican stated, "Half those fellows I met at the candidates' school thought they were on the first leg of a long trip to the White House. Who's going to tell them otherwise?"

Campaign dopesters and political observers must have some method of deciding which candidates are most likely to be elected. Since the measurement of districts is easier than the measurement of men, most listings are based on some version of the five-percent rule. But this method does not guarantee a profit on the political investment for state and congressional campaign leaders. They apply a different standard of marginality than the five-percent rule, one which is more subjective but at the same time has more meaning in the real world of politics. They are fully aware that statistically the vast majority of congressional seats are virtually unchallengeable; the campaign strategist must find some way to determine which are politically vulnerable.

OFFICIAL PARTY DESIGNATION OF MARGINALITY-TARGET DISTRICTS

It soon becomes common knowledge in the candidate group that to be officially, but quietly, designated as "marginal" reaps a valued reward: the magic circle of "marginals" is believed to receive more money and more attention; is favored with more visits from "name" speakers; and is frequently assisted by trained field workers representing the national party organizations. With this support marginal candidates, moreover, are actively encouraged to believe in ultimate victory. It is little wonder that the "marginal" designation of one becomes a source of envy for some and despair for others.

Party officials at the two national committees and the national congressional campaign committees are responsible for disbursing a comparatively modest amount of money and distributing a limited amount of campaign assistance and advice to maximize candidate opportunities. To carry out these functions they must make a determination as to which districts in any given election are most contestable. As guidelines for the distribution of campaign assistance both parties have developed the notion of "target" districts.

Preparation of target lists in the Republican party is the responsibility of the National Congressional Campaign Committee. The Democrats, though less systematic, generally rely on the Research Division of their National Committee. Although there are some similarities between the two, there are also significant differences, to be discussed separately.

In 1962 the Republicans compiled and distributed on a restricted basis three different sets of target lists. The first of these was issued in May 1962 and included three distinctive groups. The first two listed those districts won in 1960 by the traditional five-percent margin—one for the Democrats and one for the Republicans; thirty-seven marginal Democrats and fifty-five Republicans were included on this initial list. The third group designated Democratic target districts—districts which appeared to Republican strategists as possible gains for the party regardless of the 1960 vote margin. The concept of target district adopted by the GOP utilizes a number of political standards: the voting history of the district; an evaluation of the candidates' personal attractiveness and political astuteness; the overall strength of the state ticket; economic, social, and ethnic factors within the district; and unvarnished subjective judgment. Ninety-nine districts were included in the first Republican list. Some were new and had not been tested in an election before. Because of redistricting, some incumbents were forced to run against each other. Still others denoted districts or incumbents thought to be more vulnerable in 1962 than they had been in the past.

For example, one incumbent Democrat was included, although his 1960 opponent had received only 39.6 percent of the vote. Not only did this vote not represent a near-victory, it did not even come close to falling under the five-percent rule. A decision was made to include this district because the Republican governor of that state believed that the 1962 candidate was politically strong and personally popular. Furthermore, reapportionment had caused a slight shift in district lines which resulted in the inclusion of an uncertain number of new GOP voters. Finally, the incumbent Democrat, as chairman of a House subcommittee, had received some unfavorable publicity over certain well-publicized positions on matters affecting the district. Though this district was included on the first two GOP target lists, it was dropped after it became apparent that the Republican contender had not caught the public's fancy.

In September 1962, after the primaries and conventions, the Republican Congressional Committee issued for general distribution a hundred-page book entitled *Marginal Districts—1962*.[4] This compilation was distributed on a confidential basis to campaign leaders in the congressional, national, and state central committees. Fifty-five Republican districts and thirty-eight Democratic ones were listed.

Each district was described on two pages, with a map showing county and district boundaries; a voting analysis of the district (or its predecessors) from 1948 to 1960; a list of all former incumbents; pertinent economic and social facts about the district; voter registration figures for 1960 and 1962; and finally, a list of principal farm and industrial products in the district. This unusually valuable book was prepared after redistricting was completed in the states, thus providing the most up-to-date and informative analysis of these crucial districts.

4. National Republican Congressional Committee, *Marginal Districts—1962* (Washington, D.C., Republican Congressional Campaign Committee, 1962).

These Republican efforts were considerably more systematic than were the Democrats'. The National Democratic Congressional Committee, organizationally a shadow of its GOP counterpart,[5] issued no formal lists of marginal contests in 1962.

In January 1962 the Research Division of the Democratic National Committee circulated a confidential memorandum to top party officials listing fifty-two Republican and forty Democratic old marginal districts outside the South. Using the five-percent rule as well as political hunches, it listed marginal new districts; southern new marginal districts; and districts with "long shot" possibilities. This memorandum was not circulated outside the precincts of Democratic officialdom in Washington.

As the campaign got under way, the Research Division selected those contests of enough significance to justify the preparation of sixty-four individual district "briefing books." These included data on the impact of federal programs collected from federal agencies (a privilege accorded the party controlling the presidency) and material describing the political, social, ethnic, economic, geographic, and political characteristics of each district. Frequently they included fresh results from the Harris Poll or other appropriate polls.[6] The "briefing books" were distributed on a limited basis as a guide to those involved in designing campaign and speech materials for the particular target contests. Other lists, publicly distributed, included those districts falling under the "five-percent rule."[7]

Lists of this type are developed in the Washington headquarters of

5. The differences between the two committees is discussed at length in Chapter 5. For additional information see Hugh A. Bone, *Party Committees and National Politics* (Seattle: The University of Washington Press, 1958), pp. 130–41; Hugh A. Bone, *American Politics and The Party System* (New York: McGraw-Hill, 1965), pp. 195–202; Charles L. Clapp, *The Congressman: His Work As He Sees It* (Washington, D.C.: The Brookings Institution, 1963), pp. 363–66; Neil MacNeil, *Forge of Democracy: The House of Representatives* (New York: McKay, 1963), p. 112; and Cornelius P. Cotter and Bernard C. Hennessy, *Politics Without Power: The National Party Committees* (New York: Atherton, 1964), pp. 8–9.
6. See Chapter 6.
7. In 1966 both party organizations followed essentially the same methods in designating marginal or target districts. There was, however, one significant difference. Both groups treated the fifty-eight freshmen Democrats elected in 1964 in the Johnson landslide as a "target bloc." Most of these fell within the five-percent rule, but even those that did not were included.

the two parties but are not usually made public. They are not available to the candidates themselves and seldom to anyone outside party headquarters. Indeed, they are treated with considerable secrecy within the party leadership.

DIMENSIONS OF MARGINALITY: THE POLITICS OF VICTORY

For our purposes a working designation of marginal districts was difficult but, at the same time, imperative. The standard five-percent rule did not precisely meet the needs of the project because the two parties did not respond in identical fashion to the changes resulting from redistricting. Nor did their judgment coincide with the designations of *Congressional Quarterly* for each district as "safe," "leaning," or "doubtful." There were striking similarities between the three series of lists, but there were also important differences. Therefore, in order to make meaningful comparisons between marginal and nonmarginal districts a definite method of selection had to be constructed.

We classified as "marginal" any district which was included on any two of the final three lists: that of the National Republican Congressional Committee; the Democratic National Committee; and, those rated as "doubtful" or "leaning" by the May 1962 *Congressional Quarterly Weekly Report*. A total of eighty-four contests were found on two of the three lists, and of these sixty-two (or 74 percent) returned questionnaires for this study. Forty-four of these were losers, and eighteen were winners. Twenty of the losers were Democrats, and twenty-four were Republicans. Of the marginal winners who returned questionnaires, twelve were Democrats and six were Republicans. Throughout the remaining chapters we will refer frequently to the response of the marginal candidates as opposed to the losers as a group. Identification of marginal candidates is important in providing a basis for comparative treatment of the data—the only control group used aside from "incumbents."

The fact that so few House contests are marginal simply points up the fact that the nonincumbent congressional candidate occupies a unique place in the American political setting. In addition to the manifold problems which plague him as an amateur, the nonincumbent, depending upon his "marginality," must live with decisions of the national and state party organizations which are almost totally outside his control.

The Hazards of Nonincumbency

Those nonincumbents who failed to receive the "marginal" designations ordinarily had to negotiate certain hazards of their candidacy. One of these is the nonincumbent status itself or, viewed from a different perspective, the need to counter the many advantages of incumbency. Most of these hazards are so important that the nonincumbent is precluded from conquering them before the campaign ends.

Members of congress are nearly always better-known to the voters. Some House members, indeed, spend an inordinate amount of time keeping their names before the public. Charles L. Clapp points out that "it is not uncommon for members of the House to devote a major portion of their time and energy to the non-legislative aspects of their job." Many of them, he reports, expressed surprise that their colleagues could survive without waging a constant and continuous campaign for voter recognition.[8] News releases, news letters, speeches, the postal frank, visits to the district, constituent services, and other methods are constantly used to consolidate or create support for the incumbent congressman. These activities are common all year long and, unless badly mishandled, create an environment of political goodwill that a challenger can overcome only with enormous difficulty in the short time available to him during the campaign. Nonincumbency is a monumental handicap except in highly unusual circumstances.

The congressman also enjoys the support of a paid and trusted staff. The average member is allowed a maximum allotment of $25,-000 to employ a staff of up to ten persons. Some members—those in districts with over one-half million population—are entitled to a maximum allotment of $52,500 annually to employ up to eleven staff assistants.[9] Although few candidates use their entire quota, the availability of fulltime paid staff members provides an advantage not enjoyed by the out-party candidate. The net effect is that the

8. Clapp, p. 53.
9. U.S. House of Representatives, *Salary Tables,* 1965. The allotments of staff and money were raised to these levels in 1965. For a thorough treatment of congressional staffing, see Kenneth Kofmehl, *Professional Staffs of Congress* (Lafayette, Indiana: Purdue University Press, 1962).

member has a dedicated, trained, experienced, permanent paid staff working for his reelection, while his nonincumbent opponent is limited to an unpaid manager and a few loyal volunteers. Most consider themselves lucky to have a volunteer staff put together before the campaign gets under way and hope the staff will remain through to the end.

Most congressmen have now established offices within their districts. Usually staffed by parttime workers, the district offices serve primarily as a source of closer contact with the Washington office. In general they have "case" responsibilities, although occasionally a top staff man is assigned to direct the office as a general arm of the Washington office. The efficacy of the district office depends in part upon the distance of the district from the national capital. It is not as necessary for a congressman to bear the expense of an office in the district if he is able to get home frequently. For those representing distant or urban districts, however, the local office may serve an important constituent function, therefore forming a key element in the incumbent's reelection effort.

As campaign time approaches, many members transfer a portion of the Washington staff to their district office. This change is seldom made ostentatiously, so that charges of campaigning with public money may be avoided. Nevertheless the district office is an important adjunct to an incumbent's campaign. Not only does it provide a nucleus around which to develop the campaign headquarters, but the day-to-day activities of the office throughout the year make the transition into the campaign period far easier.

The challenger candidate, to be sure, has the advantage of permanent residence in the district. Theoretically he is in constant touch with the people, while the congressman impatiently awaits a late adjournment in Washington. The challenger can open his headquarters whenever he wishes, subject only to the financial limitations under which he may operate. But there is a significant difference between the two candidates: the challenger must ask something of the people—he needs their support and endorsement; the congressman, however, has something to offer his constituents. He is their contact with the national government; he asks for their support in recognition of his services to them; he does not need to go to the people of the district, because they come to him. Most congressmen believe that this situation represents a significant advantage. Virtually all nonincumbent candidates would agree.

Organizational problems represent a special hazard to the nonincumbent. He is isolated from the mainstream of the party's campaign, and if he is to be successful, he must develop a highly personalized organization. Consequently, congressional election contests take place in political arenas which do not fit within the established party hierarchy. Chapter 4 is devoted to the problems of personal organization and management inherent in the nonincumbents' congressional campaign. The two subsequent chapters consider the relationship of the national, state, and local parties to the congressional candidate. The first, Chapter 5, explores the uses of research, public relations, and other types of general campaign assistance performed outside the congressional district. Chapter 6 considers the role of the auxiliary units in the national and state party headquarters as they relate to congressional campaigns. The services performed by these units include candidate training programs, field support, special group activities, and public-opinion polls.

Most congressional candidates complain that state party leaders are less interested in them than they are in local contests. Time and again respondents complained that the state organization showed interest only in those races having an impact on the fortunes of the state party. State chairmen and members of the state party committees regularly manifested more interest in contests for governors or other state constitutional officers. With few exceptions, they put their money and energy where their hearts were. Politically, it means much more to a state party official to elect a statewide candidate; one who can dispense favors if not patronage. At the same time, it would be misleading to suggest that all state party leaders share the same priorities.

Exceptionally able party leaders occupied state chairmen's offices in some states in 1962. Examples were the Republican Chairmen in Minnesota and Ohio, and the Democrats' in Pennsylvania, New Jersey, Indiana, and Michigan. These headquarters were reasonably well-financed and staffed, and their campaign efforts were well coordinated. (Examples of the more impressive state headquarters are provided in Chapter 5.) According to the candidates, however, effective organizations existed in woefully few states. In these states the nonincumbent congressional candidate was eclipsed still further by the ineffective state party leadership.

At the same time the local leadership of the parties is often more dedicated to the election of the county sheriff or probate judge than it is to a member of Congress. A county or a ward is usually but a piece of a congressional district, and political credit for a victorious campaign is diffused and must be shared. In countywide or local elections, however, the local party leadership can rightly claim some credit for success. Local leaders are much more likely to receive accolades for the performance of the party in local contests than in larger jurisdictions.

The difficulties experienced by the national party organizations in effectively distributing the limited resources available to them compound the challenger's problems. As noted previously, the national and congressional campaign committees concentrate most of their resources on incumbents and on marginal contests. Regardless of how commendable these efforts are, most nonincumbents are bypassed. All things considered, their isolation is almost complete.

Questions of finance in this era dominated by electronic media consume an inordinate amount of the candidate's time. As noted in Chapter 4, most respondents cited lack of money as a major cause of their defeat. Though it seems unlikely that inadequate financing was a factor of sufficient importance to have changed the outcome of many races, some close losses might well have resulted. Unquestionably, nonincumbents could have used their valuable time to better advantage than in pleading for funds. Incumbents and "target" candidates received maximum, though not lavish, support from the party. They also had an easier time raising money from private donors. Neverthless, the fact is that few unsolicited campaign contributions arrive at the candidate's headquarters. Consequently, financial support is one of the major problems encountered by the nonincumbent candidate for Congress.

A few states retain district committees to assist congressional candidates. Most of these remain dormant, but a few are active in varying degrees during the congressional campaign. There has been a steady deterioration of the district-committee system during the past three decades. Avery Leiserson has noted that "full-time congressional district committees or chairmen are unknown, and such party work as they would do tends to be assumed by the component county, assembly district, ward, town, or parish committeemen."[10] There does not appear to be a reliable estimate of the number of district committees which actually engage in political campaigning today. Of those that exist, Leiserson notes:

10. "National Party Organizations and Congressional Districts," *The Western Political Quarterly,* 16, No. 3 (September 1963), 636–37.

[They] tend to fall into two main types: (1) the county or ward committee type, and (2) the state committee or district delegation type. The former is typical of states in the Northeast and East North Central areas and reflects a structure in which county and ward organization is relatively tight, its representatives occupy a position of autonomous strength in the state committee, and the distribution of influence in the state party structure is relatively decentralized to the county, assembly district, or ward level. The second type is more frequent in the states of the South and West, where local party organizations are weak and either lacking or extremely loose in structure, and the congressional district is used principally as a basis for choosing delegates to the state convention or members of the state committee, so that the *de facto* result is a centralized state party. [P. 637]

Many congressmen minimize party affiliation in their bids for reelection. They view the party chiefly as a vehicle by which to secure the nomination. They prefer to rely on personal supporters and staff after they have transformed the existing district organization into a personal campaign group. Nonincumbents, on the other hand, are unable to generate any party enthusiasm after the inevitable twilight period which follows each election. A viable party organization sustains itself on money, organization, and staff; few of these elements are available to the congressional district committees in those states where they are still operative.

Congressional district lines cut across political jurisdictions with little regard to other electoral boundaries. Counties are separated from their neighbors and wards from their cities. Haphazard congressional district lines slice through the states without apparent reason or purpose. As a result, few state or local party leaders have an abiding interest in or loyalty to a candidate seeking election to the House. It is most difficult to coordinate campaigns between candidates in different jurisdictions; even when the effort is attempted, candidates for offices at different levels find little common ground upon which to base joint efforts.

The importance of congressional races is often further diminished by a bewildering complex of voting machines and ballot designs. In some states the congressional candidates' names are so far down the ballot that they only take precedence over county or local candidates. State constitutional or legislative provisions force voters in some states to choose a multitude of state officials, most of whom outrank the congressional candidate in ballot position. One Democrat in a western state complained that his name followed those of fourteen other candidates. Under such circumstances it is questionable whether a nonincumbent candidate can effectively separate his efforts from those of others occupying a relatively higher position on the ballot. Even a hard-fought and effective campaign may become a mere ripple in a party tide on election day.[11]

The development of issues is also a difficult one for the congressional candidate. His problem in trying to bridge international, national, state, and local issues illustrates anew the separateness of his political system. It is difficult for him to attract voters' attention to his views on international and national questions when he is forced to compete for news space with incumbent congressmen and with candidates for the Senate.

One-fifth of the candidates in this study attempted to disassociate themselves from controversial statewide issues. Yet voter reaction to questions of this sort and to the party position on them almost certainly affects the congressional contender. Local problems, too, are difficult to develop. A Republican noted:

> I often found that the things the people wanted me to talk about were not within the purview of Congress at all. They would ask me what I would do about county taxes or state roads. All I could do was try to explain that these things were not the concern of a congressman. This didn't seem to be satisfactory.

The difficulties encountered in issue development probably accounted for the number of candidates who depended chiefly on a personalized effort at personal image building within the district. In Chapter 7 we discuss the use of issues in the 1962 campaign.

Systematic study of congressional campaigns requires that we include a profile of the defeated candidates who constituted the universe used in the study. It is doubtful if any single aspect of legislative behavior has been so thoroughly explored as the career patterns and social characteristics of lawmakers. To understand the legislative process, one must understand the legislative man. To understand the campaign process as a part of the larger political process, one must undertake to understand the political man. To that end we introduce in Chapter 2 the men of the congressional campaign of 1962. It is

11. This was notably apparent in 1966, when many well-organized and well-financed Democratic candidates were seemingly caught in the Republican sweep and were defeated for reasons which were seemingly unrelated to the campaign or local conditions.

our assumption that the candidate's place in the social milieu and his experience in the political world are directly related to his role in the congressional campaign.

At most levels of politics it is assumed that candidates are recruited by the party and nominated, in one fashion or another, by the people. At this level, however, recruitment is considerably different. More often than not candidates are self-selected or coopted, and this fact accounts in many respects for the difficulties inherent in a congressional campaign. In Chapter 3 the processes of recruitment and nomination are considered—not as separate phenomena, but as they affect the campaign and ultimately the candidate. It might be said that the looseness of candidate selection at the congressional-district level constitutes the first hazard of a successful campaign.

Considering these hazards, is it any wonder that so many non-incumbent candidates appear to be foredoomed? They occupy a niche in politics that does not really fit within the framework of the American party structure and, consequently, must organize do-it-yourself efforts—inadequately staffed and financed and based frequently upon bootlegged issues. Sometimes they must build their campaigns around their own personalities, and, that is not enough in contests which depend on a buyer's market.

If the incumbent congressman feels that he is doomed to perpetual anonymity, how much more must the nonincumbent feel the same. The organizational vacuum in which he must project his candidacy and the low visibility of his efforts are vividly demonstrated by a comment from a Democratic candidate in 1962: "My plight became painfully apparent when state party headquarters informed me that there was no room on the bumper stickers for my name."

2.
Social Characteristics and Career Patterns of the Candidates

Among the constant facts and tendencies that are to be found in all political organisms, one is so obvious that it is apparent to the most casual eye. In all societies—from societies that are very meagerly developed and have barely attained the dawnings of civilization, down to the most advanced and powerful societies—two classes of people appear —a class that rules and a class that is ruled. The first class, always the less numerous, performs all political functions, monopolizes power and enjoys the advantages that power brings, whereas the second, the more numerous class, is directed and controlled by the first, in a manner that is now more or less legal, now more or less arbitrary and violent.—GAETANO MOSCA

THE social characteristics and career patterns of legislators have been of interest to scholars from their earliest efforts to systematically study the politics of decision making. Political scientists and sociologists have recognized the need to measure legislative performance and campaign promise against the background and experience of the performers. Many of these studies have been drawn from "official biographies" based upon information furnished by the legislators themselves. These sources have, at times, reflected the subjects' personal goals rather than their actual attainments. A self-proclaimed farmer, for example, might turn out to be a banker, or a retired business executive "farming his land in the soil bank."

More recent studies of the social characteristics of legislators, and the environmental influences which helped to shape them, have relied extensively upon personal interviews and questionnaires, and the data have been carefully gathered and are more accurate. This accumulation has provided a clearer profile of the men and women who serve as legislative decision makers.

While this collection of material has grown, data on losing political contestants have been nonexistent. Political scientists, as well as party leaders, have expended little time or effort on the also-rans. Nevertheless, losers are important actors in the drama of politics, representing nearly 50 percent of all congressional candidates. There is ample evidence to prove that on occasion they have provided strength and vitality to ailing or defunct party structures—infusing them with new vigor and fresh volunteers. Furthermore, a contest between an entrenched incumbent and a challenger, one-sided though it may be, provides a forum for raising issues and an opportunity for public education on national policy questions at the local level. For some, moreover, an unsuccessful congressional contest may be the inauguration of a budding political career.

For this study candidates were asked to supply information on age, occupation, residence, education, and previous experience in public life.[1] These data were compared and checked against materials in the files of the national and congressional campaign committees in an effort to guarantee a higher degree of accuracy. Even so, methodological problems do exist, and there are important gaps in our knowledge of legislative backgrounds.

These compilations revealed striking differences in personal characteristics between the incumbents and the losers. In some categories there were significant distinctions between Republicans and Democrats. Certain social characteristics of the unsuccessful candidates—such as age, occupation, length of residence, and previous public experience—appear to be related to the decision to run for office, the style of campaign, availability of financing, and degree of public support. Such comparisons may, in some instances, serve as yardsticks of predictability of the viability of congressional contests.

---

1. Data regarding the religious affiliation and income of candidates were omitted because our pilot study convinced us that some respondents would be offended by such questions emanating from the national party committees.

Age

A candidate's age is related to his interest in and availability for candidacy and public office. A candidate's age and vigor are important considerations in estimating the number of years he might serve if elected. Although probably of little concern to the voter, tenure in office will obviously affect seniority, committee appointments, and other factors which can be related to the candidate's age. A number of respondents mentioned age as a consideration in their determination to run for the House. Younger men professed to see advantages for themselves and the people of the district in electing them to office. They related age to their potential for leadership and their future as a representative of the district.

Incumbent congressmen are generally seven to nine years older than their junior colleagues who are freshmen. The average age of incumbents at the beginning of the eighty-sixth, eighty-seventh, and eighty-eighth Congresses was 51.7, 52.2, and 51.7 years respectively. New members in each of these sessions averaged 44.0, 43.1, and 42.3 years. These age differences between seasoned congressmen and newly elected members are not surprising in light of the stability of House seats.

It is interesting to note, therefore, that the average ages of the losing candidates were to a certain extent markedly different from those of the new winners and the incumbents. The losing candidates in 1962 averaged 46.1 years of age, or 3.8 years older than their fellow candidates who won and were seated in 1963. Furthermore, there was a ten-year differential between the Democrats and the Republicans—the former averaging 41.0 years of age and the latter 51.3 years.

Within the universe of nonincumbent challengers, those who ran in marginal districts were younger than those who did not. The marginal candidates averaged 43.1 years of age, compared with 46.1 for all the losers. This average age of marginal candidates is very close to that of new members elected in November 1962. Furthermore, the average age at which *all* incumbent members of the Eighty-eighth Congress were first elected to office was 42.2 years. Youth favors the marginal candidates over the losers—and the average age of the former approximates both the new winners and the age at which incumbents first went to Congress. It might be reasonable to infer from this that the contests in which chances are favorable attract younger candidates.

It is less easy to explain why, among the 1962 crop of losers, Republicans were older by 10.3 years. Indeed, the Democratic losers were younger than the average age of incumbents when they first took office and younger than the freshman Democrats who won seats in 1962. This discrepancy can be partially explained by the modest decline in the average age of freshman congressmen in recent years, from 44.0 years in 1959 to 42.3 years in 1963. During this same period the average age of new GOP members declined from 47.0 years to 41.9 years, while new Democratic winners declined only 0.4 years, from 43.0 to 42.6 years. The trend among Republican winners has been toward youth, while the average age of new Democratic members has remained about the same, although originally it was lower by some years than the Republicans.

No data are available concerning the personal characteristics of losing candidates in earlier congressional elections. Conjectures concerning the youthfulness of the Democrats as opposed to the Republicans in 1962 must therefore be made from the circumstances surrounding the election. Bearing this condition in mind, it might be argued that the emphasis upon youth and vigor which appeared to be so much a part of the Kennedy administration stimulated greater interest in politics among younger people and candidates in the Democratic party.

Occupation

No political candidacy is undertaken without some personal or professional risk. These risks are especially great for those in high-status or elite occupational groups. Professional people and businessmen sacrifice money, time, and in some cases reputation to run for public office. Yet studies of political socialization have demonstrated repeatedly that entrance into American political life is more easily attained by those in high-status occupational groups. These occupations provide the politically motivated professional with leisure time; additional income and financial contacts to meet political obligations; greater access to the channels of public opinion; and an arena in which political skills can be nurtured.

Many have noted that the "high priests" of American politics are members of the legal profession.[2] The man who practices law, more than those engaged in other professional endeavors, is able to combine a vocation with an avocation. Lawyers, more than others, are generalists who deal with the worlds of government, commerce, labor, and business. The men who populate these worlds are important in the shaping of public policy. The lawyer is often their channel, and his daily engagement prepares him for the practice of politics and whets his interest in it as an art.[3]

Forbidden by the ethics of his profession from advertising, the young attorney frequently finds public life the best means to become known to the public and to acquire or build a practice. The skills developed by the lawyer in general practice are frequently useful in his role as politician. The work of the lawyer in advising clients on the technicalities of the law, legislation, and government rules and regulations must quickly bring many to the realization that they might as soon be the players as the coaches. The subject matter of politics is the law. And the lawyer, unlike other professionals, need not altogether sacrifice his legal or technical training and skill to engage in a totally new and different calling. The paths to political activism are more readily open to those in the legal profession.

2. The term was used by Donald R. Matthews, *The Social Background of Political Decision-Makers* (New York: Random House, 1954), p. 30. See also H. Dewey Anderson, "The Educational and Occupational Attainments of Our National Rulers," *Scientific Monthly,* June 1935, 511–18; Donald R. Matthews, *U.S. Senators and Their World* (Chapel Hill: University of North Carolina Press, 1960), pp. 33–36; Joseph A. Schlesinger, "Lawyers and American Politics: A Clarified View," *Midwest Journal of Political Science,* May 1957, 28; Charles S. Hyneman, "Who Makes Our Laws?" in John C. Wahlke and Heinz Eulau, *Legislative Behavior* (New York: Free Press, 1959), p. 255, Table 1; Leon D. Epstein, *Politics in Wisconsin* (Madison: University of Wisconsin Press, 1958), p. 188, Table VI-A; David R. Derge, "The Lawyer in the Indiana General Assembly," *Midwest Journal of Political Science,* 6 (February 1962), 21; William Miller, "American Lawyers in Business and in Politics: Their Social Backgrounds and Early Training," *Yale Law Review,* 60 (January 1951), 73; M. Louise Rutherford, "Lawyers as Legislators," *The Annals of the American Academy of Political and Social Science,* 195 (January 1938), 53; David R. Derge, "The Lawyer as Decision-Maker in the American State Legislature," *Journal of Politics,* 21 (August 1959), 427; John Brown Mason, "Lawyers in the 71st to 75th Congress: Their Legal Education and Experience," *Rocky Mountain Law Review,* 10 (December 1937), 44; and Heinz Eulau and John D. Sprague, *Lawyers in Politics* (Indianapolis: Bobbs-Merrill, 1964).

3. Eulau and Sprague (pp. 3–30) discuss the role of the lawyer in politics, as vocation and avocation, and the professionalism of the politician.

The number of attorneys elected to the House would appear to be quite stable. Donald R. Matthews reported that in 1949–51, lawyers made up 56 percent of the House in the 81st Congress.[4] This was almost the same proportion of lawyers as were in the Eighty-eighth Congress fourteen years later, when 57 percent reported the law as their profession. Indeed, the proportion of lawyers among lawmakers in the House has not dropped below 52 percent during the last five sessions of Congress.[5]

No data are available regarding personal characteristics of challenger candidates in years past. However, if the 1962 nonincumbents are compared to incumbents, there is a striking difference in the percentage of lawyers among them. Only 29 percent of the losing candidates were lawyers—35 percent of the Democrats and 25 percent of the Republicans. When compared to the number of lawyers in the Eighty-eighth Congress, this difference is noticeable indeed (See Table 2.1).

It will also be noted that among the nonincumbents 10 percent more Democrats were lawyers than Republicans. The best explanation for this occupational differentiation between the parties was offered by Matthews in his study of U.S. senators from 1947 to 1957:

> The Republican party is, on the whole, more friendly with, and sensitive to the needs of, the American business community; hence a far larger proportion of its senators are former businessmen. The Democratic party (outside the South) draws a disproportionate share of its support from the lower reaches of the economic hierarchy and from members of minority groups. Leadership selection in such a party is more difficult than in the Republican case. Fewer Democratic voters have the status, education, skills, or opportunity to be active office seekers. By necessity the "underdog" must turn to men and women of relatively high status for political leadership. Yet the upper reaches of American society are mostly Republican. The politically oriented professional man—especially the lawyer—seems to fill this need for "underdog" political leaders.

This statement was offered in explanation for his finding that 63 percent of all Democratic senators during the decade he studied were lawyers, while only 45 percent of the Republicans were.[6] It seems a reasonable explanation for the 10 percent difference between the parties among the nonincumbent losers in 1962.

4. *Social Background,* p. 30.
5. As reported by *Congressional Quarterly* in biannual compilations of personal data concerning the members of newly elected Congresses.
6. Matthews, *U.S. Senators,* p. 36.

Table 2.1

Occupational Distribution of Members of the 88th Congress Compared With 238 Losing Candidates for Congress of 1962

Occupation	All House Members of 88th Congress			1962 Congressional Losers			1962 Marginal Candidates		
	GOP (N = 176)	DEM (N = 258)	ALL (N = 435)	GOP (N = 128)	DEM (N = 110)	ALL (N = 238)	GOP (N = 30)	DEM (N = 32)	ALL (N = 62)
Law	53.0%	60.0%	57.0%	25.0%	34.6%	29.4%	33.0%	47.0%	40.0%
Teaching/Education	6.8	9.3	8.3	6.2	15.5	10.5	6.6	6.2	6.5
Journalism/Media	7.6	7.0	7.1	7.8	10.0	8.8	6.6	3.1	4.8
Medicine	.5	.2	.7	5.5	0.0	2.9	3.3	0.0	1.6
Business/Banking	38.0	26.0	31.0	40.6	20.0	31.5	40.0	28.0	34.0
Agriculture	13.6	8.5	10.4	7.3	4.5	5.9	6.6	0.0	3.2
Other (Govt., Labor, etc.)	5.1	4.3	4.6	7.8	14.5	10.9	3.3	15.6	9.7

Source: First three columns: *Congressional Quarterly Almanac*, 9 (January 1963), p. 34. The last six columns are based upon data compiled from this study.

An examination into the number of lawyers running in marginal congressional districts revealed a significantly higher proportion of lawyers as candidates; 40 percent of all marginal candidates were in this occupation group. Again, however, the number of Democrats far outnumbered the Republicans. Among the marginal Democrats 47 percent were in the profession of law, as contrasted with only 33 percent of the marginal Republicans. When these figures are compared to those representing the total number of lawyers in the non-incumbent universe, it is apparent that the availability of attorney candidates is directly related to the chances for victory. There is, admittedly, a greater chance for election in marginal districts, making the risk to reputation and legal practice less serious. By the same token, the greater prospects for election make the campaign seem more palatable and rewarding to the lawyer.

Education has never been a major source of political decision makers in the United States. Teaching may provide an entry into politics in certain noncompetitive districts, where other professional groups might predominate if the chances for victory were more promising. Traditionally teachers have been hemmed in by school calendars and professional rules which have conspired to make entry into politics difficult and often impossible. Schoolboard directors and college trustees have frowned upon teachers in politics, just as they once frowned on married elementary-school teachers. The tradition of nonpartisan local control of schools and the fear of indoctrination and government control have been contributing factors. The tolerance level of the populace and of school governing bodies has been quite low with regard to active participation in political activity. The effect has been to keep educators relatively inactive and the number of officeholders with education backgrounds has remained quite low.

Among the losing candidates in 1952, 10.5 percent listed teaching or education as their profession—a higher percentage than among those actually serving in the Eighty-eighth Congress. *Congressional Quarterly* listed 8.3 percent of the members of the House in this category, the Democrats having 9.3 percent and the Republicans 6.8 percent.[7] Only 6.5 percent of the marginal candidates were listed as teachers.

Several educator candidates were college faculty members who, after their nominations, took leaves of absence from their institutions

7. *Congressional Quarterly Almanac, 1963,* 9 (1963), p. 34.

to make the race. They were not singularly successful. In fact, academic candidates fared more poorly at the polls than did lawyer candidates or the total candidate group. Republican teacher candidates averaged 35.9 percent of the vote, compared to 37.1 percent for all GOP losers and 36.2 percent for lawyers. Among the Democrats, teacher losers averaged 39.2 percent of the vote, as opposed to 39.7 for all Democratic losers and 40.2 percent for lawyers.

Those who write, persuade, or comment upon public affairs have been grouped in a single category as the "image industry," which includes journalism, advertising, radio-television, and other similar endeavors. To a certain extent individuals engaged in this area are similar to lawyers in that their experience and training include skills characteristic of the political arena. They are, in a very broad sense, engaged in public-relations activities, as are candidates for office. Nevertheless, few individuals in 1962 fell into this category.

Between 7.6 and 8.2 percent of all incumbent congressmen since 1958 have come from the image industry. The proportion of this group among the losers in 1962 was essentially the same—10 percent for the Democrats and 8 percent for the Republicans. Among the marginals only 5 percent were so classed. It should be noted that none of the candidates in this group was a member of the working press. Those "journalists" included were usually publishers of small newspapers. It has been suggested that the working press has firsthand knowledge of the perils of politics and that this awareness, perhaps, deters its members. In any case, the image industry has not, it would seem, become a significant source of candidates for the House of Representatives.

Doctors belong to one of the high-status professions. They have rarely engaged in political activity at any level of government, and relatively few physicians have made their way to Congress. When physicians enter politics, it is with an understandable risk to professional specialties and personal practices. In Chapter 6 we discuss the effects of the administration's proposal for medical care for the aged on members of the medical profession. Fought bitterly by the American Medical Association and conservative groups, Medicare was a powerful issue in the developmental stages of the 1962 campaign. Even where physicians were not personally active in the campaign, their presence was felt through the efforts of national organizations attempting to influence the debate over Medicare.

There were only three physicians among the incumbents in the Eighty-eighth Congress. But in the 1962 campaign there were five doctors, two pharmacists, and a director of a county medical society. All were Republicans, the Democrats failing to field any candidates from the medical profession. In all but one case the respondents gave the Medicare issue as the major reason for their candidacies.

Democratic candidates were under considerable pressure from the White House, the Democratic National Committee, and the National Council for Senior Citizens to feature the medical-care issue in their campaign talks and literature. Indeed, the traditional White House campaign picture of the candidates conferring with the President was focused toward the issue by reproducing such a picture on the cover of a Medicare campaign brochure. This was in response to President Kennedy's call for the election of candidates to the Eighty-eighth Congress who would support the program.

Available occupational data suggest that the number of business-men elected to legislative office varies widely from state to state and according to the governmental level. Businessmen are second only to lawyers in the number of seats they hold in Congress. The types of businessmen elected appear to differ somewhat markedly between the parties.

Matthews found that there were almost twice as many Republican businessmen in the Senate as there were Democrats; he attributed this distribution in part to the close association of the Republican party to the business community. He also maintains that the parties tend to elect distinct types of businessmen.

The Democratic businessmen are mostly merchants, contractors, oil and gas producers, and insurance and real estate men. The Republicans tend to be publishers and manufacturing executives. These industry differences between the businessmen in the Senate seem to reflect, to some extent at least, differences in the party preference of different segments of the business community. Publishing and manufacturing are heavily Republican in their sympathies; finance and insurance less clearly so. Oil and gas producers, perhaps because of their concentration in the Southern states, have been a major source of campaign funds for the Democratic party. Contractors, who normally do a large share of their business with the government, may prefer the Democrats' free-spending policies to Republican "economy." Retail merchants, dependent as they are on mass demand, are also likely to be sympathetic to the party which promises to pump spending power out to the masses of the people. Even if these differences between Democratic and Republican businessmen do not reflect significant party cleavages within the business world, they are big enough and consistent enough to indicate that, in the Senate, Democratic and Republican businessmen tend to be different. [Pp. 40–41.]

Table 2.2

Classes of Business Activity of Losing Candidates by Party: 1962

CLASS	GOP (N = 52)	DEM (N = 25)	BOTH PARTIES (N = 77)
Small or Independent Business (small manufacturing, real estate, insurance, developers, etc.)	49%	72%	56%
Business Employees, Including the Managerial Class (executives, manufacturers, purchasers, sales, etc.)	36%	24%	33%
Bankers, Brokers, and Property Managers (corporate directors, brokers, investment and property management, etc.)	15%	4%	11%

Businessmen have an important place in American legislative bodies. Not only are they important contacts between the business community and the Congress, but they also provide essential experience and personal knowledge about the economic life of the nation. Their number includes representatives from many facets of the business multistructure. But these are not necessarily the primary reasons for their election.

The businessman also represents more direct contact with the major sources of campaign funds—business. This circumstance makes him the prime target for political recruiters and often gives him the wherewithal to become a self-starter. Furthermore, the businessman has a continuing personal interest in the American economy and in government programs which may affect him directly or have an impact upon his business colleagues. In short, he, like the lawyer legislator, has a special stake in congressional deliberations and he brings special talents to them.

Among the businessmen candidates in 1962 three groups were classifiable: the small or independent businessman; the business employee, including the managerial class; and, the banker, broker, or property manager.[8] Table 2.2 shows the percentages of businessmen candidates by party classed according to these groupings.

8. It was necessary to arbitrarily assign some respondents to one or the other of these classes in view of possible multiple listings. In each instance we classed the individual candidate according to that information available to us, although acknowledging the possibility of error.

Small businessmen were a clear majority of all the losers drawn from the world of business. This group included the self-employed, such as insurance agents and real estate brokers, as well as small retail merchants and the owner-operators of service establishments. Democrats outnumbered Republicans in the small business class 72 percent to 49 percent.

One-third of all the businessmen indicated employment by others in larger business establishments. Ten Republicans described themselves as executives in purchasing, sales, or expediting. Four Republicans and a Democrat called themselves consultants.

The field of finance was represented by 11 percent of the losing candidates described as businessmen. Republicans outnumbered Democrats nearly four to one—15 percent of the former and 4 percent of the latter. Some members of the financial world were retired from business, although most of them were still active.

Careful consideration of these data allows certain generalizations. First, the kind of businessman who is free to pursue a congressional campaign is not a mogul from the world of finance or big business. More typically he is a small or independent entrepreneur whose interests, resources, schedule, and community involvement allow his commitment to the campaign. These contests were often undertaken at considerable personal economic risks, and it was not uncommon to have the respondents cite losses of business as a result of political vindictiveness. Nor was it unusual for small businessmen to seek loans to finance the campaign, offering the business itself as collateral.

A second inference that can be drawn from the data about this occupational group deals with the party differences of the business candidates. Republicans were more inclined to be from the fields of finance and banking or were retired from those fields. Nearly three-fourths of the Democrats were engaged in small independent business enterprises, while less than half the Republicans were in that class. It is possible to conclude, therefore, that the two parties produce candidates from distinctly different worlds of business. This is, of course, consistent with Matthews' conclusions regarding United States Senators.

Mechanized agriculture and the decline of the family farm have caused difficulty in defining what is meant by the term *farmer*. Some who merely manage but do not work the land class themselves as farmers. Others who own but do not operate a farm are also so designated. And of course those who actually own, manage, and work the farm are most certainly entitled to claim the farm as their workplace. It is normally impossible through a questionnaire to determine whether those who list farming as their occupation are, in fact, farmers. So few defeated candidates claimed this status, however, that we were able to confirm that farming was their occupation.

Less than 5 percent of the Democrats and 7 percent of the Republicans called themselves farmers—less than the proportion of farmers found among the incumbent congressmen in the Eighty-eighth Congress, where 8.5 percent of the Democrats and 12 percent of the Republicans were so listed.

Effective political opposition may be related to the availability of members of elite occupations. If so, those who ran against the incumbents in 1962 did not measure up to the elitist standards set by the congressmen themselves.

Length of Residence

The United States Constitution does not require a member of the House of Representatives to reside within the boundaries of his district. The exigencies of American politics, however, normally necessitate such proximity, and our evidence would suggest that the period of residence must be quite lengthy. American voters, unlike the British, generally expect congressional candidates to be one of their own; they want to vote for people who live in and understand the district and its problems. The pages of political history are strewn with the remnants of campaigns decided on the "carpetbagger" issue. There have been some notable exceptions, to be sure, but ordinarily candidates for Congress are bound by unwritten rules requiring them to be long-time residents of their constituent communities.

The redistricting which resulted from the census of 1960 made it difficult to gather meaningful data from the candidates as to length of residence within the districts. Shifts in district lines, major changes in the number of districts in a state, and unsettled court challenges of redistricting plans made it unlikely that accurate data regarding length of residence could be gathered. Respondents were therefore asked to indicate their length of residence within the state; these data, plus a careful check of personal histories, suggested that movement from district to district was minimal.

Better than 70 percent of the losing candidates in both parties had lived in the state from which they ran for twenty-one years or longer. The great bulk of these long-time residents had lived in the same state since birth. Some, in fact, traced their political genealogy through several generations.

The winners in 1962 were, if anything, better able to exploit length of residence as a political asset. Tenure of residence within the state was checked from various public sources on each member of the Eighty-eighth Congress, with the exception of thirty for whom no verifiable information could be found. Of the 405 members verified, 83 percent had lived their entire lives in the state from which they were elected. Most of them represented the district in which they were born, although an accurate determination of this point was impossible because of changes in district boundaries. Only nine members lived in the state represented for less than twenty years, while those with more than twenty-one years' residence, when combined with those who had spent their lifetimes in the states, constituted 91 percent of all the members. So few contests in 1962 were between newcomers and older residents of the congressional districts that no meaningful generalization is possible on the effect of long-term as against short-term residence. Nor was there an apparent difference in length of residence between the candidates of different political persuasion. Both Democrats and Republicans were represented in the various categories in approximately equal numbers.[9]

Losing candidates also appeared to be the products of families of long residence: 28 percent of the Republicans and 32 percent of the Democrats lived and ran in the same state in which both parents were born. Only 15 percent of the Republican losers and 25 percent of the Democrats were children of foreign-born parents. Most of their parents originally came from Great Britain or Northern Europe. A few, 8 Democrats and 5 Republicans, were born of parents who immigrated from what are now Iron Curtain countries.

Nor were the candidates of long residence (twenty-one years or more) limited to those states with more stable populations and older traditions. States undergoing rapid growth patterns reflected the same tendency to field candidates who were long-time residents. Those states with the largest percentage growth between 1950 and 1960 were Florida, Nevada, Alaska, Arizona, and California.[10]

9. Inadvertently Republican challengers were not asked to indicate the number of years of residence in the congressional district. The Democrats, however, were asked and averaged 23.5 years in the district represented.
10. U.S. Bureau of the Census, *County and City Data Book, 1962,* A Statistical Abstract Supplement (Washington: Government Printing Office, 1962), p. 2. The rates of percentage growth were: Florida, 78.7; Nevada, 78.2; Alaska, 75.8; Arizona, 73.7; and California, 48.5.

All the Florida congressmen, except one who did not furnish information, were lifelong residents or had lived in the state for forty years or more. Of the losers, three Republicans were native-born and one of the two Democrats was a lifelong Floridian. No information was available concerning the Republican candidate in Nevada, but the Democratic incumbent was a lifelong resident.

Two of the congressmen from Arizona were lifetime residents, and the third had lived in that state for over twenty years. Among the losers one Republican was a lifelong resident, while the other had only arrived in the state four years earlier. The single Democratic loser was a thirteen-year resident of Arizona. The Democratic congressman from Alaska had lived and practiced law in that territory and state since 1931. His Republican opponent, although long interested in Alaska, had only lived there for two years prior to the election.

In California, another rapidly changing state, among the thirty-eight successful candidates eighteen were lifetime residents, and an additional sixteen had lived in the Golden State for twenty or more years. Of the winners, only three had lived in the state for less than twenty years. Among the losers, only four Republicans and one Democrat were native Californians. These data suggest that successful congressional candidacy favors the long-term resident or the native-born in California. And this situation prevails in spite of the rapid growth and constant population change in the state.

It is apparent that there is no "iron law" governing the length of time a candidate should reside in the state in which he seeks election. However, it is worth noting that in the five most rapidly growing states the winning candidates for the House were almost without exception lifelong or long-term residents. At the same time the losers, except in Florida, showed a much greater tendency to be recent arrivals in the state of candidacy. Among the winners, in fact, those in the five rapid-growth states were more likely to be long-term residents (twenty-one years or more) than the national average of incumbents; 90 percent of the winners in those states were in this group, as opposed to only 83 percent of the successful candidates nationwide.

A political fact of life in the United States would seem to be that victory comes more easily and frequently to those politicians with well-established families and long residence in the district. This general rule would appear to be borne out at various levels of political activity and regardless of whether the contest is in a state with a stable population or one that is more fluid. Its outcome is that large numbers of people are barred from successfully seeking legislative office.

Education

Analysis of the educational levels attained by losing candidates would indicate little variance with past observations that, as a group, political leaders are among the most highly educated of all occupational groups in the United States. To be sure, few of the candidates in 1962 were nominated on the basis of their educational achievements, but evidence does exist to suggest that voters turn more readily to those candidates who are college-educated. There is no evidence, however, to suggest that successful candidates were better-educated than were the losers.

Among the losing candidates all but three—two Democrats and a Republican—were graduated from high school, and only one had not completed grade school. Almost exactly the same proportions were high-school graduates among the 411 members of the House who furnished biographical information for the *Congressional Directory* of the Eighty-eighth Congress. Analysis of these data revealed that 21 percent of the members were not graduates of an accredited college or university, although all had completed secondary schooling. A number had attended college or trade school but had not received a degree or diploma.

Of the 324 members who were college graduates, 60 percent held bachelor's degrees, while 74 percent held graduate or professional degrees, including 229 lawyers. Only thirty-four members did not indicate any college work, while fifty-one others reported incomplete college work. A number of this last group attended college for several years before dropping out. It is noteworthy that most of those who dropped explained the reasons for their withdrawal in their biographical material, indicating by these explanations that higher education is believed to have political worth.[11]

Significant differences in educational levels of House members were found between the parties. Of the 324 reporting college degrees, 59 percent were Democrats, while only 41 percent were Republicans.

11. *Congressional Directory, 88th Congress, 1st Session* (U.S. Government Printing Office, 1963), pp. 3–186.

One could generalize that the American voter has come to consider educational achievements as an extralegal requirement for election, since the difference in educational achievement between the parties reflects almost exactly their success at the polls. Furthermore, significant differences in educational levels existed between the successful candidates and the losers in 1962.

Only 67 percent of the losing candidates were college graduates, as opposed to 79 percent of the incumbent congressmen. When the losers are considered by party affiliation, the same imbalance in favor of the Democratic candidates is apparent. Of those who answered the questionnaire, 61 percent of the Republicans and 77 percent of the Democrats held college degrees. The same distinction appeared among those holding graduate or professional degrees; 55 percent of the Democrats and 46 percent of all the losing candidates were holders of professional or graduate degrees, including seventy-two law-school graduates. The number of losers who were lawyers (29 percent) was much smaller than the number among the successful candidates (55 percent). The difference might be explained by the greater political sophistication of lawyers residing in established one-party areas—a sophistication which might lead them to plunge into politics more warily than others. An unsuccessful political campaign can be especially damaging to a budding law practice and is not a step a young lawyer will take lightly. A thirty-year-old Republican running in a rural district reported:

> I think I made as many enemies as I made friends. It is too early to say whether my practice was helped or hurt by my running. It wasn't much to begin with, since I only opened my office a year and a half ago, so I hope the campaign brings in business.

A comparison of the unsuccessful lawyer candidates running in marginal districts with those in nonmarginal ones supports the assertion that a political campaign can be a two-edged sword and is approached warily by attorneys. Using the definition of marginality adopted in Chapter 1, the lawyers who lost were checked as to the contestability of the districts from which they ran. We attempted to ascertain whether the candidate had a chance for success or was predictably doomed because of a politically unequal distribution of voters or because an entrenched incumbent made success improbable.

Table 2.3 shows a distinct propensity of attorneys to carefully evaluate their chances for success before entering into active can-

Table 2.3

Attorney Candidates in 1962 by Type of District

	Winners & Incumbents	Marginal Candidates	Losing Candidates
	(N = 435)	(N = 62)	(N = 238)
All	58%	40%	29%
GOP	52%	33%	25%
Dem	61%	47%	35%

didacy. In each party those who were incumbents and nonincumbent winners tended to be lawyers to a much greater degree than did marginal or losing candidates. In fact, there was a definite progression from successful to losing candidates in terms of the number of attorneys running.

Previous Experience in Public Office

As noted earlier, our findings would place the average age at which congressmen are first elected at 42.2 years, while the age of the unsuccessful candidates in 1962 was even older. These individuals have not vaulted into Congress from the university environment. Very few of them have served as congressional aides prior to their election. Most of them used those extra years prior to their election to Congress in building stepping stones to that high office. Indeed, many of them had undergone their political maturation in a long succession of local and state offices.

The existence of "staging areas" for presidential candidates has long been noted by scholars and journalists. Presidential timber is cultivated in the U.S. Senate and in governors' offices across the land. Some areas of political experience are more adaptable to the launching of presidential campaigns than others. Nominations are planned with all the detail and precision of military engagements— managers and publicists playing the roles of generals and chiefs of staff. Attempts are made to develop images which attract maximum interest and acceptability from the widest possible range of voters. In short, the preparation of a presidential candidate is a long and detailed process, involving hard work, generous financial resources, public salesmanship, and career exploitation. If all of these qualities reach the proper blend in the proper sequence of time, a presidential candidate may be born.

A crucial factor inherent in the image which a candidate presents to his party, his convention, and his nation is the public record he has built in lesser office. This record is a vital ingredient and can be ignored only at the candidate's or the party's peril. His performance in the office which he has held is tested by public opinion. Frequently he must undertake the trial by fire presented by the presidential primary. And if his public record is nonexistent or in certain areas lacks strength, like Dwight Eisenhower's or John Kennedy's, the best path to the presidential nomination may lie in the route of the primaries in key states.

Members of the United States Senate have frequently served terms as governor or congressman. Upon taking office for the first time, they most frequently have a public record and a public. Of the Senators serving in the Eighty-eighth Congress, forty-seven were formerly members of the House and eighteen had previously served as governors of their respective states. These offices served as springboards to the Senate. Members of the House of Representatives usually have found it to be more difficult to develop a statewide following, since the "natural" order of political succession which prevails for the Senate does not prevail for the House.

Charles Clapp states:

Service in the state legislature is often the route by which a seat in Congress is attained; some members "inherit" their seats from a parent or spouse; and others go to Congress on retirement from their life work. A number are successful primarily because fortuitous circumstances projected them into a favorable position unanticipated by themselves or potential opponents when first they sought nomination or election.[12]

None of these routes to Congress represents a "staging area" nearly so identifiable as those for the U.S. Senate or the presidency. The development and selection of candidates and the planning of nominating campaigns at the congressional district level do not fit established patterns of political incubation.

Over 90 percent of the Democratic and 80 percent of the Republican losers made their first bids for congressional seats in 1962. The depth of planning and the degree of previous involvement in public life varied greatly among these men, giving an almost haphazard

12. Charles L. Clapp, *The Congressman: His Work as He Sees It* (Washington, D.C.: The Brookings Institution, 1963), p. 30.

and quixotic quality to the congressional nominating process. Few windmills fell before the onslaught because there were few to attack.

In addition to being new to congressional politics, 60 percent of the Democrats and 45 percent of the Republicans were making their initial debut in public life at any level in 1962. These candidates were nominated and ran for Congress with no previous experience in elected or appointed office.

However personally well qualified or professionally competent these newcomers were, they were forced to learn their politics during their campaigns by intensive on-the-job training, with little supervision. The only staging area for their candidacies was in private life—not in public office. They served no apprenticeship, climbed no political ladders, built no images, had no public record—and, of course, were defeated.

The supposition that previous political experience is important to the political campaigner is reinforced by the share of the total vote received by those candidates who lacked it. As a group, all losing Democrats polled an average 39.7 percent of the two-party vote, while the 45 percent who ran with no prior experience polled an average of only 37.9 percent. Among the Republicans who lost, 59 percent ran with no prior public experience and were penalized somewhat less than the Democrats, polling 36.1 percent in contrast to the 37.1 percent received by all GOP losers. Though these differences between the losing margins received by those with no prior experience and those who had previously held public office are not extremely significant, those who were without prior political experience did not in fact do as well as those who had such experience.

Furthermore, the advantage of some experience in public office is shown more dramatically than is the disadvantage of no experience. Among the losers, 41 percent of the Republicans and 55 percent of the Democrats reported some experience in public office— both elective and appointive. About half the candidates had served in appointive offices, while half had been elected.

Those who had held appointive office had served as local judges, law-enforcement officers, municipal commissioners, and federal attorneys. As a staging area for a congressional campaign, appointive offices yielded no appreciable vote gains for candidates of either party. Republican candidates in this group averaged less than the percentage of the two-party vote won by all GOP losers—36.1 percent contrasted with 37.1 percent. This difference is obviously inconsequential. Democrats with prior experience in appointive offices garnered exactly the same percentage of the two-party vote as did all Democratic losers.

On the other hand, those candidates whose prior experience was in elective office turned it to their advantage in the 1962 contests. Of the losers, 27 percent of the Democrats and 21 percent of the Republicans had held elective office before. The Democrats averaged 42.9 percent of the two-party vote, as compared to the 39.7 percent won by all Democratic losers. The Republicans did even better, receiving 41.9 percent, in contrast to the average 37.1 percent for all GOP losers.

Carried one step further, the analysis shows decided advantages accruing to those candidates whose elective experience was in state legislative bodies. Indeed, the different vote levels for former state legislators and former city councilmen was striking. The Democrats in this category polled an average of 44.3 percent and the Republicans 44.8 percent of the two-party vote. When compared with the margins of all Democratic (39.7 percent) and Republican (37.1 percent) losers, the advantages of prior experience in running and holding legislative office are dramatic.

A less apparent difference in vote totals between those losers who had former experience in a city council as compared to all losers was also noted. Former Democratic mayors, councilmen, or other elected local officials averaged 40.4 percent of the two-party vote, while those on the Republican side received 39.6 percent.

It would probably be unwarranted to argue too close a relationship between the percentage of votes won and the extent of prior experience in public office. Nevertheless, each election year produces a number of studies and forecasts based upon the probability of candidates' success in purely statistical terms. Not enough attention is given by either political scientists or professional political leaders to the men who are making the races. It would seem apparent that any real effort to systematically recruit potentially successful candidates should take into consideration the prior experience of a man in running for or serving in an elective office. Yet every two years large numbers of candidates run for Congress who have no experience at all in politics or public life. Many of them receive the party nomination without a primary contest or with only a perfunctory one. Others have been self-recruited, and party officials have taken no part in trying to develop a winning candidate.

One further question might be posed about the relationship be-

Table 2.4

Percent of Candidates for Congress With Prior Legislative Experience, 1962

	New Winners (N = 67)	Marginals (N = 62)	Losers (N = 238)
All Candidates	54%	42%	24%
GOP	39%	30%	21%
Dem	67%	53%	27%

tween prior experience in public office and the percent of the two-party vote gained by the losing candidates. How can it be determined that candidates with more experience were not attracted to those contests in which they had a better chance of success? Is it not possible that recruitment efforts in the marginal districts were more sophisticated and therefore yielded candidates with a better chance of success? Is it not likely that in those districts where the party stood very little chance of success party leaders simply forfeited the election in advance by allowing anyone who wished to run? It could be argued that experienced candidates were concentrated in close districts and as a consequence only reinforced existing marginal election situations and that any advantage of prior experience was simply an added bonus. This proposition can be tested by examining the degree to which candidates with former legislative experience were concentrated in races falling within the marginal or doubtful group. Using our definition of marginality, we compared the vote percentage of losers having legislative experience with those candidates who ran in marginal districts and who also had prior experience in legislative office (see Table 2.4).

There were sixty-seven nonincumbent winners in 1962. We have avoided using the freshmen as a control group because of a limited response from them to the questionnaire. On the matter of prior experience in public office, however, information was available from a number of sources, and we have undertaken an analysis of the political genealogies of these successful candidates.[13] We were able

13. This information was gleaned from an exhaustive search of the *Congressional Directory*, 88th Congress, 1st Session, as well as descriptive paragraphs in the *Congressional Quarterly Weekly Report* for 1962. Especially helpful was a collection of personal campaign literature gathered during the campaign and in response to a request to the candidates. From these sources we were able to determine the prior experience of all sixty-seven nonincumbent winners.

to determine the number who had previously served in public office or engaged in political campaigns as candidates.

Over one-half (53.7 percent) of the men elected in 1962 had previous experience in state legislatures, city councils, or other elective offices. Three had previously served in the House or the Senate, and two were former state constitutional officers. Three had served as administrative assistants in the offices of congressmen— two in the Senate and one in the House. Another 37 percent had been members of their state legislative bodies before going to Congress. Accepting the fact that some of these districts are also included in the marginal category, it is still apparent that the vast majority of the newly elected members benefited from prior electoral experience.

These figures indicate that, for 1962, candidates with prior legislative experience were not more heavily concentrated in marginal districts than in others. As a group, however, those with this experience polled a higher percentage of the vote than did losing candidates without prior political exposure.

It would appear to be just as important for party leaders and candidate recruiters to concentrate on *who* is running as it is to channel support to *where* the race is being run. The fact of the matter is that, except for prior legislative and elective experience, there is no recognizable launching pad for a congressional campaign.[14] Unlike members of the Senate and candidates for the presidency, the members of the House have not come up through clearly delineated channels of party and public office. Those incumbents with long tenure seldom have serious opposition, and those in

---

14. Prior congressional candidacy does not seem to be a major source of candidates. Respondents were asked: "Do you intend to try again for national office? Yes _____ No _____ Undecided _____." "Do you intend to run for another public office? Yes _____ No _____ Undecided _____." "If so, When? What office?" In all, 35 percent of the Republicans and 41 percent of the Democrats answered the first question in the affirmative, declaring their intention to try again for national office. Of these, 82 percent specified their intention to run for the House of Representatives in 1964.

The 1962 candidate lists have been checked against those for 1964, revealing that the 1962 defeated candidate's ardor for another campaign had cooled considerably by 1964. Forty-five respondents in each party (N-110 Democrats and N-128 Republicans) said they intended to run again. Yet a comparison of the total 1962 and 1964 candidate lists for the House of Representatives showed that only eighteen Republicans and fifteen Democrats ran in both years. Of those who did, only eight were elected—seven Democrats and one Republican.

marginal or doubtful districts are usually self-recruited or are chosen as candidates by party officials who make their choice for reasons entirely divorced from the qualities of the man or his prior experience in public life.

This chapter has shown that in losing contests political parties and their leadership permit the self-recruitment of poorly prepared, inexperienced, and naive candidates. The sophisticated world of a campaign for national office is no place for candidates who are not carefully chosen and adequately prepared. If, as many have always believed, one function of the party apparatus is to aid in the selection of attractive candidates, then it is clear that the party leadership has neglected its duty.

If these contentions are correct, one is immediately led to the next question: what can the parties do to enhance their role in this selection process and how can they assist the chosen candidates in the campaign for high office? If the voters are to be given a better choice, it behooves the political leadership to help make such a choice possible.

The problem is admittedly caused in part by historic imbalances in voter registration and allegiance in many congressional districts. A heavily Democratic district offers little chance for reward to a Republican party leader or candidate. The spoils of an occasional victory are the bread of politics. Changes in district composition must be made through legislative or judicial channels. Party leaders cannot be blamed for failures to update district boundaries.

Too often, however, the party leadership has been just as derelict in its duties in marginal districts as it has in safe ones. There is little excuse for the failure of a political apparatus to develop useful and operative recruitment techniques in these areas of high potential. As it stands, a large number of candidates in the so-called marginal districts are destined for defeat because of poor recruitment compounded by lack of party leadership, campaign assistance, and moral support. Obviously no minority party will be able to seriously increase its proportion of seats in the House of Representatives if it must depend on winning only a few marginal seats. These contests represent only a starting place.

A party that maintains a vital and vigorous organization in most of the congressional districts of the nation would present to the voters a list of congressional candidates who possess the traits and qualifications which have proven successful in winning votes.

Younger men of tested ability should be recruited to conduct the vigorous campaigns made necessary by the complexities of modern government and campaigns, the difficult issues facing the voters, and the revolution in campaign styles. Although age was not significant among incumbents in 1962, among the nonincumbent candidates the younger candidates fared better.

Attorneys have always been proven vote getters. Many of them are interested in public policy and politics; they are frequently more articulate and able to leave their practice for the long hours of campaigning that are necessary. Although relatively few lawyers were among the losing candidates of 1962, the high percentage serving in the Congress is proof enough of the voter appeal of the group.

It is apparent that in recruiting candidates the parties might pay particular attention to the length of residence of the candidates within the district or the state. Among both the winners and losers in 1962 those who were long-time residents were more successful. This outcome is not only a result of name familiarity but also stems from the greater understanding of the people and problems of the district that the longer residents possess.

Although we showed that Democratic candidates were on the whole better educated than their Republican counterparts, the high percentage of well-educated candidates in both parties makes it clear that as the educational level of the general populace goes up, the emergence for more highly educated candidates for Congress keeps pace.

Finally it would seem that previous elective political experience can be an advantage for a candidate for Congress. In 1962 those candidates who fared best on election day, whether newly elected or defeated, were those who had previous campaign experience.

As we pointed out earlier, there appears to be no recognizable single ladder of succession by which men rise to congressional candidacy. They are too frequently launched simply by their own ambitions. Such a system does little to promote selection of good candidates. It would be appropriate at this point in the country's political development for the state party organizations to equip themselves to assist in the recruitment and selection of congressional candidates who can best represent the party. With candidates to carry their standard the party organizations should then provide as much campaign assistance as is reasonably possible. Although the number of losers would not be affected, the voters, the parties, and the nation would benefit.

3.
Recruitment, Nomination, and Defeat

The aim of every political constitution is, or ought to be, first to obtain for rulers men who possess most wisdom to discern, and most virtue to pursue, the common good of society; and in the next place, to take the most effectual precautions for keeping them virtuous whilst they continue to hold their public trust.
—FEDERALIST NO. 57

DOES the man seek the office or does the office seek the man? This ancient conundrum nicely sums up the process of political recruitment and the questions raised by it. The recruitment of candidates and the launching of political careers should be one of the most important functions of the political party.

In this chapter we will treat the major problems and "vectors" associated with recruitment of nonincumbents to candidacy. These include: time of announcement as related to chance of election; consideration of recruitment as a party and non-party function; the significance of incumbency and nonincumbency; the sources of influence on the decision to run; the role of primary elections; and, finally, the candidate's own retrospective evaluation of his position as his party's standard-bearer in the congressional election.

Party Function and Political Recruitment

To some authorities the recruitment of candidates and the launching of political careers is one of the most important functions of political parties. Professor E. E. Schattschneider has stated unequivocally that "whatever else they may or may not do, *the parties must make nominations.*"[1] If this is so, party officials should certainly make every effort to control and operate the recruitment machinery governing the selection of candidates for major office. After stating that the "recruitment of political candidates is a basic function of political parties," Lester G. Seligman concludes: "A party that cannot attract and then nominate candidates surrenders its elemental opportunity for power."[2]

Commenting on the recruitment process at the state level, V. O. Key, Jr., noted:

Perhaps the most important function that party leadership needs to perform is the development, grooming, and promotion of candidates for statewide office. Although striking exceptions may be cited, it is in its inadequacy in this role that the most grave shortcomings of party leadership is to be found. To assert that party leadership of many states develops candidates is more an attribution of a duty stated in the textbooks than a description of real activity.[3]

If Key's observation is true of party organization at the state level, it is even more true of congressional-district politics. Here, where few party structures ordinarily exist, where numerous county and local party units share jurisdiction and where the congressional candidate's name is usually submerged among many others on the ballot, recruitment as a party function is virtually obscured.

Further, for better or for worse, the direct primary system seriously compromises the role of the political party in the nominating process. In most jurisdictions the primary election makes it difficult for the party to play a positive role in the recruitment process, although a determined party chairman can effectively bring his influence to bear. If to the impact of the primaries is added the rudimentary party structure typically found at the congressional district level, recruitment as a party function is drained of meaning altogether.

These observations merely emphasize the situation which faced nonincumbent candidates in 1962 as well as in any other off-year election. What are the differences between the recruitment of in-

1. *Party Government* (New York: Rinehart, 1942), p. 101. Emphasis in the original.
2. "Political Recruitment and Party Structure: A Case Study," *American Political Science Review,* 55 (March 1961), 77.
3. *American State Politics: An Introduction* (New York: Knopf, 1956), p. 271.

cumbent congressmen and of nonincumbent candidates for Congress? Is it ambition, pressure from friends, or a last-minute plea from party leaders that pushed the nonincumbents into candidacy? What roles did party and nonparty groups play in the decision? Are marginal candidates recruited in some different fashion than are the "hopeless" ones? And how clearly did most of these candidates perceive that their fate was doomed beforehand, and what motivated them to run if they were even vaguely aware of the futility of their efforts?

Incumbency, Prior Experience, and Recruitment

It goes without saying that incumbent congressmen seldom have reason to ponder the decision to run again. Incumbency itself constitutes sufficient reason for continuing on the job. Indeed, most congressmen are separated from office only by death or voluntary retirement. Defeat at the polls is therefore highly improbable in the overwhelming majority of cases. The party naturally does not recruit the incumbent, nor does he wait for an invitation. To paraphrase *The Federalist Papers,* the interests of the man are connected with his [vested] rights in his position. The incumbent seldom hesitates except for tactical reasons; he expects to run, and he is expected to run by the party.

Only 10 percent of the Democrats and 19 percent of the Republicans had run prior to 1962. Those who had been candidates before were most frequently veterans of the 1958 or 1960 campaigns, but a few had run more frequently in certain lopsided districts. Nevertheless, the label "prior loser" was attached to only 15 percent of all the nonincumbents at the outset. Their decisions to run were quite clear, as were their motives. They were largely self-recruited perennial candidates, whose services were accepted with relief, gratitude, or sometimes embarrassment by party leaders unable to find strong opponents to pit against entrenched incumbents.

For the rest of the nonincumbents the decision to run was considerably more difficult. The possible consequences of an unsuccessful election are serious enough to deter the better qualified men, for whom the candidacy would be a greater sacrifice, as was shown in Chapter 2. Few people realize that the expenditure of time and money in political campaigns cannot be recovered by those who lose.

Similarly, the inconvenience to personal, professional, and family life cannot be predicted or avoided for the newcomer to politics. While the incumbent's decision to run again is made the day he was last elected and thenceforth occupies much of his official attention and energies, the nonincumbent's decision to run, if it is a rational one, must be calculated.

The Decision to Run and Candidate Recruitment

While staff members of the two national party committees, the authors were the beneficiaries of an unusual degree of access to candidates but, by the same token, were prevented from probing into certain sensitive areas of party influence and particularly those in the preprimary period. Such an inquiry might have compromised the "hands off" policy which both national committees studiously try to observe during primary campaigns. Staff assistance, as a consequence, is committed almost exclusively to endorsed party candidates or primary victors during this period, which is reserved by state law for the encouragement of citizen participation in political recruitment.

Without asking the candidates to specify precisely the timing or the individuals involved, we queried them about the sources of influence on their decision to run for Congress. The results (Table 3.1) show not only the multiple vectors operating on candidate decisions, but also the apparently significant role played by informal party contacts.[4]

At first impression the contacts with and the possible influence of party leaders on the decision of nonincumbents to run for Congress appear pervasive. At this juncture, however, the data do not indicate *which* leaders urged the candidate to run or the relative degree of their influence on the decision itself. More important are the impressions of the candidates as to the forces acting on their decision to run. Party leaders and friends (in some cases the same individuals, to be sure) outranked family and the candidate's own manifest motives at the point of decision. Of course a prospective candidate

4. An excellent review of the recent literature relevant to political recruitment is contained in Thomas M. Watts, "Application of the Attribution Model to the Study of Political Recruitment: County Elective Offices," in *Approaches to the Study of Party Organization,* ed. William J. Crotty (Boston: Allyn and Bacon, 1968), pp. 307–39.

Table 3.1

Major Sources of Influence on the Decision to Run

(multiple responses)

All Losers	GOP	DEM
	(N = 128)	(N = 110)
Party Leaders	65%	68%
Friends, Associates	56	61
Candidates' Own Idea	35	34
Family, Relatives	19	15

Marginal Candidates		
	(N = 29)	(N = 32)
Party Leaders	69%	81%
Friends, Associates	59	75
Candidates' Own Idea	17	28
Family, Relatives	14	16

must permit himself to be "available" before he can be urged by anybody to consider the race for Congress.

Party influence in primary elections is not widespread. In some states intraparty division has been a factor ever since the direct primary was adopted. Candidates representing various party factions organize individual campaigns and sometimes engage in vicious infighting. Especially is this true in those states where party leadership is weak or where the formal channels of command are unclear. The fact that most politicians favor the closed over the open primary can be attributed to their desire to maintain as much party control over the nominating process as possible.

An interesting difference between the losers and the marginal candidates is revealed by Table 3.1. Party leaders and friends played a stronger role in urging marginal candidates to run than they did in the decisions of the losers, while at the same time the proportion of candidates rating themselves as self-starters or influenced by family was also greater among the losers. Friends and relatives ranked almost equally in their influence on losers and on marginal candidates concerning the decision to run. In all, candidate self-motivation appears higher in the losing contests than among the marginals; this is a motivation which the primary nominating system encourages.

Clearly family and the candidate's own motives play a more modest role in the rationalization of the decision to run than do the arguments of party leaders or the candidate's immediate friends and associates. This reminds us that recruitment does not take place in a political vacuum—and that overt party influence at the time of decision is very common for losers and almost the rule for marginal candidates. Further, Table 3.1 suggests that the chief variation between the marginal candidates and the losers as a group lies in the stronger roles of party and friends in the recruitment of the former.

Party effort in the recruitment of Democratic losers was significantly greater than it was among Republicans, but so were the influences of friends and relatives; those candidates who claimed their candidacy to have been their own idea were also preponderant among Democrats. The party differences here can be understood if one is aware of the more pervasive "grid" of local Democratic party organizations across the nation and the far greater task which the Republicans faced in finding ·contestants for the more numerous incumbent Democratic seats. The differences between the parties are less important, therefore, than are the rank importance of the categories themselves.

What is apparent in Table 3.1 is the fact that those candidates whose chances of winning were actually greater—that is, the marginal candidates—were more frequently in touch with party leaders at their point of decision than were the losers. The urging of friends was only a bit more important for marginal candidates at this stage of recruitment than it was for the losers.

Further analysis of individual responses used for compiling Table 3.1 shows no significant differences between influences on candidates who later faced primary or convention contests and those who did not. This suggests not only the pervasiveness of informal party and personal contacts in the recruitment process, but it raises a question as to whether the primary election really stands as a significant barrier to party influence on candidate recruitment. In the section which follows further attention will be given to the primary election and its impact on the recruitment of losing and marginal candidates who sought support as congressional nominees in 1962.

Primary Elections and Congressional Recruitment

We have questioned whether the primary system imposes handicaps upon the party, making it difficult for it to play an effective role in the nominating process, and whether the recruitment of candidates by party leaders is thereby also adversely affected. No study of congressional politics is complete without probing in some detail the impact of primary elections on political recruitment. By law, primaries are intended to open nominations to all comers. The electorate, it was argued by the party reformers, would be saved from nominations dictated by caucus and backstage manipulation. Although designed to break the grip of the "bosses" over the selection of candidates and to cure the ills of democracy with "more democracy," primaries have had an uncertain impact on party recruitment. For example, it was assumed that open nominations would be widely contested by candidates representing an interested public eager to throw the handpicked nominees (i.e. rascals) out. Competitive nominations, it was believed, by attracting better candidates, who were not tied to political machines, would make the parties themselves more competitive. Primary elections were to do to party bosses what the Sherman Antitrust Act of 1890 had been intended to do to the robber barons and monopolists of American industry. By maintaining open competition in candidate selection, the public welfare would be protected and American parties would be kept democratic, it was argued.

That this change has not occurred is strongly suggested by the late V. O. Key, Jr., in his finding that the number of uncontested seats in both parties in the state legislatures of Ohio, Indiana, and Missouri increased significantly over the thirty-year period after the adoption of primary laws in those states.[5] Key surmised that the decline of two-party competition in state legislative districts may be directly related to the decline of political party organizations following the inauguration of primaries and the passing of the party nominating convention. He hypothesized: "The atrophy of local or district party cliques derives not solely from local factors but more significantly from the erosion of the organizational superstructure that once linked local minorities to central points of power within the state" (p. 195). For both majority and minority party structures, but particularly for the latter, Key noted that "institutional decay follows deprivation of function" (p. 195). The presence or absence of primary and convention contests for the losing and marginal

5. *American State Politics*, pp. 171 ff. Key emphasizes that formal rules or procedures of the political game do affect the informal organizations of politics, and he skillfully traces the impact of primary elections on state party organizations.

candidates for Congress in 1962 can therefore be related to the pattern of political recruitment exhibited in these contests.

Of all the losing candidacies in this study, only 54 percent were contested in either primaries or conventions (or both, in a few cases). A closer look at many of these nominating efforts reveals that an appreciable number were one-sided events, with but token opposition. An uncontested Democrat explained why his nomination was unchallenged in the primary:

Several Democrats were talked out of entering the primary on the basis of my having more party support in key counties. We were afraid of giving permanent scars to a newly formed district organization and of adding unnecessary costs to a very limited budget.

Another noted that his primary opponent had been "no threat at all. He ran as a write-in, getting less than a dozen votes in the entire district."

Several candidates reported that their primary contests were competitive in name only. But one ruefully noted that his nomination was contested in convention by "an oddball who has run for office a dozen times. He received no votes at the convention but picked up about 1600 in the primary and definitely hurt me." A more realistic view of the situation was given by another loser who had only token opposition for a place on the ballot which his party might have otherwise ignored altogether. "Certain people in the local GOP," he wrote, "believed the party to be better off without any candidate in view of the strength of the Democrat in office."

How is the process of congressional recruitment clarified by an examination of the incidence of contested nominations among losers and marginal candidates? Table 3.2 demonstrates that losing candidates, whose political situation is nearly devoid of hope for victory, are far less likely to have primary or convention opposition for their nominations than are the marginal candidates on whom the betting odds are more nearly even.

Nearly 80 percent of the marginal candidates underwent primary or convention contests for their nominations. It has already been shown in Table 3.1 that party activity in recruitment of marginal candidates is considerably greater than among the losers as a whole. Since most of these same candidates also had contested nominations, it can be inferred that party officials do overcome the inhibitions imposed upon them by the direct primary. More will be said later about the levels of party officialdom involved in political

Table 3.2

Incidence of Contested Nominations Among Congressional Nonincumbent Candidates in 1962

All Losers	GOP	DEM	Both Parties
	(N = 124)	(N = 110)	(N = 234)
Having Primary Contests	50%	46%	48%
Convention Contests	7	6	6
Uncontested Nominations	43	48	46
Marginal Candidates			
	(N = 30)	(N = 32)	(N = 62)
Having Primary Contests	80%	59%	69%
Convention Contests	10	9	10
Uncontested Nominations	10	32	21

recruitment and the pervasive but low-keyed role played by non-party groups.

The differences between Republican and Democratic candidates in Table 3.2 throw additional light on the role of the party in the recruitment process. It will be recalled that Democratic party leaders were found to be considerably more active than Republicans in urging both losing and marginal candidates to run for Congress (Table 3.1). This recognition is further strengthened by the data which show the lower incidence of contested nominations among both Democratic losers and Democratic marginal candidates. This fact leads to the inference that in those contests in which party leaders are active in preprimary selection and recruitment the probability of openly contested nominations will decrease.

To seasoned local and district party leaders the meaning of this proposition is simple. The reduction or elimination of primary contests means that fewer campaigns must be fought, with obvious savings in time, effort, campaign funds, and the effects of disruptive postprimary factionalism. The tables also show that no matter how costly or disruptive a primary contest might be, in marginal contests, where the chances of winning are greater, activity of party leaders is more prevalent. The fact that the incidence of contested nominations among Democrats is lower than among Republicans may point to differences between the parties at the organization level.

If a major thrust of informal party activity in candidate recruit-

ment is directed toward reducing or even eliminating primary contestants, it should follow that in districts where political parties
regularly contest and win marginal and local offices uncontested
primary nominations will be more frequent. For instance, the ethnic,
demographic, and ideological features of the Democratic party in
America have given it a widespread urban base. This should mean
that the party apparatus, the personnel and the cohesive voting
blocs necessary to discourage at the outset the threat of primary
contests will occur more frequently among Democratic candidates
than among Republicans; and among urban candidates more than
among those running in rural areas.

Table 3.3

*Percent of Losing Candidates with Uncontested Nominations for
Congress in 1962, by Demographic Status of Districts*

	GOP	DEM	Rural-Urban Distribution of All Seats (88th Congress)
	(N = 57)	(N = 54)	(N = 435)
Rural	45%	35%	47%
Suburban	2	26	11
Urban	37	8	24
Mixed	16	31	18

Note: Table is based on a regional division of the states used by Congressional Quarterly Weekly Report.

This proposition can be tested indirectly with the data from this
study by examining the proportion of losing candidates running in
uncontested primaries according to the rural-urban status of their
districts, as in Table 3.3.

It will be seen at once that losers in both parties in predominately
rural districts were frequently solitary, uncontested candidates. Further, it appears that unchallenged nominating efforts were least
frequent among urban Democrats and suburban Republicans, and
that in mixed districts, where any of the three demographic characteristics were balanced with the others, that Democratic candidates
were far more likely than Republicans to be free of contested
nominations.

The question may now be raised as to the validity of our earlier
working hypothesis that informal party efforts work to reduce or

eliminate primary contests. Moreover, in those areas where Republicans and Democrats alike are each strongest and best organized nationally, in the suburbs and cities respectively, the frequency of unchallenged nominating bids among the losers is low indeed. Obviously the party and primary activity set forth in Tables 3.1 and 3.2 do not yield any statements of general application concerning recruitment as a party function.

Instead, this seemingly conflicting data illuminates one well-known aspect of the American party system—its highly fragmented structure and disfunctional behavior as an organization when called upon to operate on more than one level at a time. Party activity in candidate recruitment and the relation between primary contests and activity of party officials hardly provide strong clues to the actual role of the party in political recruitment.

Only in a very general sense, then, can it be said that nonincumbent Republican congressional aspirants are more likely to be unencumbered by established local party organizations with strong interests in winning seats from the opposition. The Republicans, it is true, reported more self-starting candidates and, as a rule, more frequent primary contests for their nominations. But this datum does not provide significant clues to the role of either party in recruitment of nonincumbent candidates. The question can best be studied by identifying further the actual level of party functionaries whom the candidates in this study felt to have been most involved with them prior to or just after their decision to run for Congress.

In this section the incidence of primary contests among nonincumbent congressional candidates of 1962 has been analyzed with particular reference to the role of the party as an agent for political recruitment. We have found that, although party leaders hesitate to dabble openly in preprimary recruitment, they are nonetheless active; their efforts appear to be directed toward candidates in the marginal contests in particular. It should be pointed out that several states provide by law for official party intervention in the primary election period. By means of conventions, endorsing committees, or some other means, a "regular" candidate may be designated, or positioned on the ballot for guidance of the party faithful in the primary election.[6]

6. Ten states provide by law for convention, party committee endorsement, or some other means to designate "regular candidates" in congressional primary elections. See *Factual Campaign Information,* Felton M. Johnson, Secretary of the Senate, and Richard D. Hupman, Librarian (Washington, D.C.: U.S. Government Printing Office, 1962), pp. 5, 6.

The data in this study do not indicate any significant differences between recruitment activity in these states and in those with no such provisions. Only five candidates out of the 238 losers in this study reported having received the prior endorsement of informal party selection or screening committees at the time of their announcement. They came from five different states, and all but one seemed marked for sure defeat at the outset. The fifth, who was contesting a newly created seat in the Far West, received only 43 percent of the vote. The others averaged 35 percent of the vote on election day.

We can conclude that the prevailing overt role of the party during the primary period is one of neutrality, with the exceptions noted above. But this neutrality covers a considerable amount of intense activity by official or unofficial party leaders in recruiting and lining up support for real or would-be candidates for Congress. One Democrat noted his party's ambivalent attitude by stating at the beginning, "I had received very much encouragement outwardly, but little actually, because a congressman has no patronage and my chances of winning were remote."

As a matter of fact, most of the congressional nonincumbent contests in 1962 were, to pragmatic party leaders, exercises in futility. Little would be gained for the party beyond the dubious distinction of filling the ticket or calculating the advancement of personal careers for other political goals for a few candidates. This circumstance made the naive enthusiasm of most of the crop of new candidates in 1962 bear little relation to the realities. Clearly, if most incumbent congressmen are expected to win, their opponents are, with the exception of the marginal candidates, expected to lose.

Time of Announcement as Related to Chance of Election

On the day after the 1962 general election a Republican candidate announced that "even though I lost, I am telling the Democrats right now that I am going to run again in 1964, and I am going to spend the next two years campaigning." Late in the summer of 1962 stories occasionally appeared in newspapers reporting that party leaders had prevailed on some individual to make the race for Congress and that the candidate had filed just before the deadline. Such candidates are exceptions, to be sure but their actions raise an interesting question. Does the time of announcement, whether early or late, bear upon the performance of the candidate when the final vote is tallied? It must be assumed that serving as the nominee of one of the major political parties seeking a congressional seat is a high point in the lives of most of the candidates; that being the case, what dictated the time of their announcement of candidacy?

Some candidates build upon prior defeats. Approximately 10 percent of those running in 1962 had engaged in prior election contests, and a few were former members who had served one or more terms in the House of Representatives. These men were seeking to revive past glories and regain for themselves and their parties a prize they preferred to believe had only been temporarily removed from their custody. Others, having never run before, considered the idea for many years, finally deciding to run in 1962. Sometimes, usually in almost hopeless districts, the candidate had been "honored" with the nomination as a fitting reward for many hours of precinct work, fund raising, or committee activity. These "rewards" were sometimes made simply to fill the ticket but in other districts were the legitimate fruits of hard work. They were, in fact, a throwback to an earlier era of "incentive" politics.

Lester Seligman points out that the process of recruitment has two stages. *Certification* is that stage during which prospective candidates are screened for social and political eligibility, while *selection* includes the actual choice of candidate to represent the party in the election.[7] We have dealt with the problem of certification in Chapter 2, and we shall discuss selection here. Recognizing the great diversity of party structure, direct primary systems, convention arrangements, and party arenas, we have attempted to view the process of selection from a number of perspectives. One of these is the relationship between the timing of the decision to run and its effect on the campaign and the election.

During the month and three-quarters that remained of 1960 after the November election, 6 percent of the losing candidates in both parties announced that they would run for Congress in 1962. A Republican was so upset at the election of John Kennedy that he announced during the depths of his frustration; at the other extreme, a Democrat reported he took the plunge after a lifetime of reflection. These candidates were, almost without exception, self-starters, since even the most dedicated party official does not ordinarily begin recruitment such a short time after an election. Only one candidate was encouraged to run as early as 1960. A Democrat was ap-

7. Lester G. Seligman, "Political Recruitment," p. 77.

proached by his county chairman on the day after the election. Citing the narrow margin by which the district was lost, the chairman urged the respondent to consider running in 1962. After a few weeks of contemplation, he announced his candidacy a week before Christmas.

Almost one-quarter of the losers—21 percent of the Democrats and 25 percent of the Republicans—announced during 1961. Although some of them were self-starters, most announced in order to prepare to campaign in early primaries or conventions. Some hoped that early announcements would preclude others from filing, while some expected others who had announced to become disaffected with the prospect of running against formidable opposition.

As might be expected, political candidates are more likely to be attracted by a boiling political pot, and since the year of the election is the time of highest interest, it is also the time when the largest number of announcements are made. More candidates announced for Congress during 1962 than any other time.

An attempt was made to extrapolate data which might demonstrate a relationship between time of announcement and sources of recruitment efforts. For instance, we questioned whether there was a relationship between those who announced during the months immediately preceding the election and the self-starters. Or, following another tack, was there a relationship between time of announcement and electoral support? Did candidates who announced early and subsequently campaigned longer do better on election day?

During the first quarter of 1962, 44 percent of the Republicans and 37 percent of the Democrats announced for the House. Some presumptions can be offered to explain the greater number of early Republican announcements. A large number of Republican hopefuls were convinced that by election time large-scale popular disenchantment with the Kennedy administration would have set in; it was relatively easy for these individuals to translate this "imagined" disaffection into Republican votes. Furthermore, with only 174 seats in the GOP column, the large number of seats making up the Democratic majority offered Republican candidates a mathematical advantage. And combined with the sixty-year record of out-party gains in the congressional off-year elections, the possibilities appeared reasonably good for the Republican gains.[8]

8. For a concise analysis of the Republican performance in 1962 see Lewis A. Froman, Jr., *Congressmen and Their Constituencies* (Chicago: Rand McNally, 1963), Chapter 5, pp. 60–66.

During the second quarter of the election year, from April through June, 20 percent of the losers announced. During the third quarter, July through September, 6 percent of the Republicans and 7 percent of the Democrats decided to run. Since this quarter included the last possible deadline in any state, all candidates were in the contest by the end of that quarter.

In performance the Democratic candidates who announced in 1961 or earlier fared slightly better than did their GOP counterparts. Democrats averaged 43.1 percent of the vote, and Republicans gained an average of 40.5 percent. There were only minimal differences in the votes received by the three groups of candidates who announced in the first three quarters of 1962, all of them receiving from 38 to 40 percent.

Democratic candidates who announced prior to 1962, however, received a higher percentage of the votes than did their colleagues who announced during the election year. The same was true of the GOP challengers and especially of those who filed during the first quarter of 1962, who did better as a group than any of the others in either party. There was no discernible difference in voter performance among marginal candidates who announced at one time or another.

In general these findings suggest that time of announcement of candidacy has very little to do with electoral performance. There were no noticeable distinctions between the number of votes cast for the early starters and for those who filed nearer the election. There was no particular pattern of announcement times according to source of recruitment pressure. The self-starters were not visibly different from any other candidate in so far as time of announcement was concerned.

Let us now turn to the pattern of party involvement with the nonincumbent candidates in an effort to further delineate the meaning of political recruitment in congressional politics.

Party Leaders and Candidate Recruitment

In early 1962 the efforts of both national committee staffs were directed toward activating the interests of state, district, and county leaders in the upcoming congressional contests. To the Democrats, the elections of November 6, 1962, presented the first opportunity since 1934 to break the historic "midterm rule" with a gain, rather than a loss, for the presidential party in House seats after its win two years previously.[9] An outcome such as this would be considered by many to be an endorsement of President John F. Kennedy's programs and leadership after his narrow margin of victory in 1960.

The Republicans saw the midterm election of 1962 as an opportunity to reinforce this pattern of minority gains in the Congress. The winning of new seats would be for the GOP a first step toward repudiation of the New Frontier and a key to strategy for presidential victory in 1964.

It was for this reason that the Democratic National Committee initiated a program called "Operation Know-How" from March to mid-June 1962. This program involved a team of five national committee officials: the national chairman, the vice-chairman for women's activities, one deputy chairman each for organization and public affairs, and the research director. The group made its first presentation at the fourteen-state Midwest Democratic Conference, held at White Sulfur Springs, Virginia, in late February. Between March and early June four sorties were made to seventeen additional states in the Far West, northern plains, and the cornbelt.

Enjoying the direct sanction of President Kennedy, "Operation Know How" was a traveling political medicine show, peddling information, campaign strategy, and political tactics at one-day conclaves of Democratic county and district leaders. Equipped with motion pictures, film strips, brochures on party history, political organization, and material on the Kennedy legislative achievements, the program was calculated to make an impact on and develop support among the lower echelons of the party. It was also one method of emphasizing the potential aid a candidate might receive if successfully recruited to run.

9. The midterm rule is based on the fact that since 1860 the party in control of the White House has lost seats in one or both houses of Congress in every midterm election except two. Theodore Roosevelt in 1902 gained eleven House and three Senate seats, and F. D. Roosevelt in 1934 won nine House and ten Senate seats. The average number lost by the party in power in the fifteen midterm House elections between 1902 and 1958 was forty-four. This powerful record of midterm losses was held to a two-seat net loss for the Democrats in the House in 1962. In 1964 President Johnson swept thirty-eight new House members to victory, while in the 1966 midterm contest the Democrats lost forty-seven House seats. See "Historic Wins and Losses in Congressional Elections at Mid-Term," Research Division, *Data Sheet,* Democratic National Committee, November 1962, p. 2, processed.

Although "Operation Know-How" was at the time a unique phenomenon in American party history as an effort to link national and local party leaders at midterm, in other respects it served the well-established political functions of fence mending by the visitors and jockeying for favors by the local and regional hosts.

The GOP precampaign organizational effort of 1962, less elaborate than "Operation Know-How," relied chiefly on the liaison and organization skills of a team of five field men who gave particular attention to marginal candidates and the new opportunities for recruitment of congressional candidates in the Deep South.

In light of these national party committee activities, nonincumbent candidates were queried on their awareness of the party recruitment efforts in encouraging them to run for Congress. Because of the covert nature of much personal and party maneuvering, and particularly for those candidates who had had primary contests, it was difficult to phrase this question directly. The question stated:

Most counties in the U.S.A. have active party committees. (In some urban areas the major political committees may represent precincts, wards or districts). To what extent did the announcement of your candidacy receive the encouragement of these committees or of their leaders?

Responses to this question were scaled from "very much" to "none." The respondents were then asked whether they had received encouragement from other party officials; if so, they were asked to designate them by name or position in the party. In a further effort to determine whether these party contacts were of a recruitment nature, all candidates were asked: "At what point in your considerations did you discuss it with [the party leader]?"

Table 3.4 shows the response of county and local party committees and officials to the nonincumbents' announcements of candidacy.

Table 3.4

Responses of Local Party Officials to Candidate's Announcement

	Losers		Marginals	
	GOP (N = 128)	DEM (N = 110)	GOP (N = 30)	DEM (N = 32)
Very much encouragement	42%	51%	47%	50%
Some encouragement	32	26	30	28
Little or no encouragement	26	23	23	22

The results indicate that most candidates were aware of the difference between "encouragement" by local party officials and actual "pledges" of support during a difficult and expensive campaign for office. Nevertheless nearly one-half of the marginals, as well as the losing candidates, reported receiving "very much" encouragement by local party officials in response to their announcements.

To only a slight extent did marginal candidates report more local party encouragement than the losers reported from this quarter. Variations among responses at this point reflect the enormous range in condition of local party organizations which are found across the nation, to say nothing of the differential response and awareness of these organizations and their leaders to the congressional campaign.

Table 3.4 provides clear evidence of systematic party recruitment activity at the local level, however, and this appeared without distinction between candidates who later faced primaries or convention contests and those who did not. One candidate from the upper Midwest stated that he was invited to become a candidate by his county chairman and that prior to his announcement he had already discussed his intentions with the party chairmen of the six counties in his district as well as with the head of the state central Democratic committee. He, however, faced no primary opposition and on election day polled 43 percent of the vote against a four-term incumbent.

A marginal candidate, prior to announcement, was interviewed by the local leadership group of his party, including zone leaders and the city chairmen, and reported "very much" encouragement for his candidacy. Several others responded by noting flatly, "I was selected by the party organization." Informal liaison among officers of the Democratic club movement, several incumbent assemblymen, and a state senator led to the decision of one California candidate to run for Congress. He did face and overcome strong primary opposition and, with the added support provided marginal candidates, polled 47 percent of the vote.

One Democratic loser perceptively noted that "very much encouragement was not meaningful" in his case. What he had received was described as "very much outwardly, little actually, because a congressman has no patronage and furthermore my chances of winning were remote." Another, noting that he had received no encouragement from local party officials or committees, commented realistically, "I know this from Citizens for Kennedy-Johnson. They have never cared about the congressional race. I was expendable."

Only three candidates reported that primary elections inhibit local leaders or committees from providing more forthright support at the time of their announcement. One of the two Democrats in this group commented, "In our area the leaders chose to remain neutral. They saw the primary as the testing place of the candidates," while the Republican wrote: "Local leaders encouraged my announcement but the party took no position until the primary nominations were over."

Of perhaps equal or more interest than the comments of particular candidates on the relative enthusiasm of local response to their candidacies and announcements is the nearly uniform comparative behavior of the marginal candidates and the losers in this area of recruitment activity. Obviously if political parties—leaders or committees at the county and local level—were vigorously engaged in a systematic recruitment effort for congressional candidates, one would expect it to be more strongly manifest with respect to marginal candidates. Our findings, indicating an absence of clear patterns of differential recruitment treatment between marginal candidates and the losing candidates, indicate that the steam for the entry of these candidates into the congressional contests came from other than local party sources.

Another question requested the candidates in this study to specify whether they had received encouragement from "other" party leaders; 70 percent of the losers and 81 percent of the marginals answered "yes" and then designated by name or position the people who had thus encouraged them. Table 3.5 indicates in some detail the extent of activity by leaders in the upper echelons of the two parties at the same time of or before the public announcement of the candidates' bids for Congress.

State party chairmen and executives were most active in candidate recruitment, and frequently candidates were contacted by party officials from several levels of the apparatus. One Democratic loser was flattered by the attentions of his governor, state party chairman, and national committeewoman all on the same day. This was also the day on which the deadline for filing occurred and the day the candidate yielded to pressure and announced. Another reported that prior to announcing he had been contacted by both his state's U.S. Senators and by several incumbent state officeholders and neighboring congressmen. In another state a Democrat whose candidacy had received similar party attention added, "We all agreed I had very little chance of winning. They were glad to have such a respectable

Table 3.5

Party Leadership Activity in Candidate Recruitment

	Losers		Marginals	
	GOP (N = 128)	DEM (N = 110)	GOP (N = 30)	DEM (N = 32)
A. Percent of candidates who received encouragement at or before the time of their announcement from upper echelons of party.	69%	75%	83%	81%
	(N = 89)	(N = 83)	(N = 30)	(N = 32)
B. Percent of candidates having these contacts classified by levels in party hierarchy.				
State party executives and or chairmen	54%	41%	56%	52%
Incumbent officeholders, congressmen, senators, state legislators, or executives	21	23	8	16
National committee members or staff	15	18	16	8

sacrificial lamb." Only fourteen candidates in the entire study, all but two of them Democrats, reported that they had been selected by formal screening or selection committees. Half of these faced and overcame primary opposition after their designation, despite the relatively sophisticated treatment given their recruitment by party agencies.

Losing Republicans received only slightly less attention from party leaders in the upper echelons of their party. Particularly in the far western states, incumbent GOP congressmen appeared to play a strong role in encouraging candidates, as did the officials of the Democratic Clubs of California. In general, Republican state executives were more active in recruitment of both losers and marginals than were Democratic officials of the same rank. In cooperating with his state chairman, one GOP candidate even held off announcement of his intentions at the request of his chairman, in order to wait for the decision of another candidate who was receiving unofficial party endorsement. After ten days of waiting, the candidate received his go ahead, announced, and then encountered primary opposition from other unexpected sources within the party in his district.

In a border state both the incumbent U.S. Senator and state Young Republican leaders discussed matters with one hopeful, who noted that "At first circumstances seemed to dictate that I should not run." But upon appraisal by these same people of the probable impact of redistricting upon the incumbent Democrat, the candidate felt that "this tipped the scales in the direction of my making the race." As might be expected, Table 3.5 also shows that marginal candidates in both parties more frequently received upper echelon party encouragement than did the losers as a group; Table 3.4 indicates that more help came from state or national leaders than from the local leadership.

The steadiest attention to marginals in this phase of recruitment came from state party executives and chairmen, who more than many party officials are aware of the importance of full slates of candidates in building party strength. Ironically, Table 3.5 also reveals that marginal candidates received relatively less attention from both incumbent officeholders and national committee members or headquarters staff personnel than did the losers. The exceptions are notable, however, and in several states coordinated efforts of district, state, and national party officials in the recruitment process were gratefully noted by the candidates.

For example, a Republican candidate who ran against heavy odds in a northeastern urban district was contacted and encouraged to run by both of his party's national committee members, by the top candidates on the state ticket, and by county, district, and state Republican chairmen. This instance illustrates the fact that recruitment as a coordinated party function does have meaning in some instances.

Table 3.5 does not show the time when recruitment efforts occurred. The timing of candidate involvement with party leaders is of considerable importance to any generalizations about the party's role in recruitment. If, for example, the candidates' major contact with the party took place only after nominations, it can be assumed that organized party recruitment efforts were nominal or that party officials maintained a posture of neutrality during the primary election campaigns of these candidates. In the latter case it has already been shown that primary contests do not materially inhibit efforts of local and state party leaders in approaching and persuading the losing and marginal candidates to run for Congress.

Table 3.6, showing the timing of the candidates' discussions with party officials in relation to their public announcements, reveals that well over half of all the candidates and three-fourths of the

Table 3.6

The Timing of Party Recruitment Activity in Relation to Announcement of Candidacy

Time of Discussions of Candidacy with Party Leaders	Losers*		Marginals†	
	GOP (N = 128)	DEM (N = 110)	GOP (N = 30)	DEM (N = 32)
Before announcement	56%	74%	50%	75%
After announcement	9	5	13	3
No response	35	21	37	22

* Of the GOP losers whose contacts with the party occurred at or before their announcement, 57% also had primary or convention contests. Of the Democratic losers whose contacts with the party occurred at or before their announcement, 38% had primary or convention contests.

† All the GOP marginals whose contacts with the party occurred at or before their announcement also had primary or convention contests. Of the Democratic marginals whose contacts with the party occurred at or before their announcement, 58% also had primary or convention contests.

Democratic losers and marginals were involved in party recruitment activity prior to their public announcements. Another cross-check of those in the "before" category shows that a sizable proportion of those approached before their announcements also had primary or convention contests. This finding further corroborates previous statements about the noninhibiting effect of the legal nomination requirements upon party recruitment activity. Republicans were more active as party recruiters among both losing and marginal candidates with primary contests than were Democrats. This activity no doubt reflects the concern of state and national GOP officials with increasing their party's stake in the 1962 midterm elections.

Nonparty Groups and Candidate Recruitment

So far this examination of the agencies of congressional candidate recruitment has touched upon the impact of family, friends, associates, and party officials upon the candidate's decision to run. Two additional factors remain to be treated in some detail: the role of the extra-party groups in recruitment; and the candidate's own manifest personal reasons for seeking congressional office.

Although the literature of political science abounds in studies of interest groups in the legislative and policy-making processes, in bureaucratic and judicial decision making, and in campaigns and voting behavior, little or no attention has been devoted to the activity of nonparty groups in the basic function of political recruitment. This is not surprising, since recruitment is itself perhaps one of the least visible of all actions in the spectrum of political behavior.

The almost minimal power of pressure groups in "delivering" votes in elections is well known. In writing of this phenomenon, V. O. Key makes the following realistic comment:

Instead of the picture of group leaders with the capacity to sandbag officials by their command of blocs of votes, the more realistic conception is one of a standing alliance between party leaders and pressure group leaders. Confederates, if not friends, they tend to stand together for the interests of the party and of the group insofar as the two interests are compatible.[10]

Similarly, in a discussion of the impact of nonpartisan elections and the direct primary on electoral behavior, Professor Hugh Bone notes that primary candidates, like nonpartisan candidates, are very frequently without financial support from either local or national party committees and that therefore:

Hopefuls are likely to find pressure groups ready to assist them in the primaries, providing the latter feel the prospective nominee will be friendly to their cause. It stands to reason that candidates who have some chance of winning the primary will receive more help than those less likely to capture the nomination. Occasionally, however, an interest group will support a candidate even though he has little chance of winning. This is done because the group wishes to use the primary campaign

10. *Public Opinion and American Democracy* (New York: Knopf, 1961), p. 523.

as a forum for criticizing an incumbent or championing certain issues. Labor unions have done this on occasion where anti- or non-union views appear to predominate. In this sense, the primary campaign is run as an "educational program" rather than as a potentially successful electoral venture.[11]

These authors suggest that the alliances between party leaders and interest-group leaders at the local level are manifested in campaign assistance to candidates in primary elections and occasionally in contests in which the nominee might be doomed to defeat anyway. What can be said here of pressure group activity in the recruitment of congressional candidates? Several questions in this survey were directed to this point. Two of them were:

Did any private interest groups or organizations at the state or local level encourage you to run for Congress? If yes, please name the group (ABA, AMA, AFL-CIO, C of C, etc.).

After your nomination did you seek or receive the endorsement of any such group? If yes, list the endorsements sought by you from such groups; and endorsements volunteered by such groups.

Respondents were asked to indicate whether such endorsements were accepted or rejected. These questions were designed to elicit responses which would enable us to distinguish between prenomination activity associated with political recruitment and postnomination activity linked to endorsement of candidates by these same interest groups. Table 3.7 shows the responses of the candidates to each of these questions, paired for comparison.

In studying Table 3.7 it should be noted that nonparty or pressure-group activity in congressional candidate recruitment is of less apparent significance than are the other agencies of candidate recruitment discussed earlier in this chapter: family, friends, associates, and party officials. Second, the table shows clearly that Democratic congressional candidates had far more prenomination contacts with nonparty groups than did Republicans. Third, marginal Democrats were somewhat more involved than were Democratic losers, while marginal Republicans reported no prenomination recruitment contacts whatever with nonparty groups.

One might conclude from this series of tables that private groups played a relatively minor role in identifying and selecting congres-

11. "Political Parties and Pressure Group Politics" in *Unofficial Government Pressure Groups and Lobbies, The Annals,* 319 (September 1958), p. 73.

Table 3.7

Nonparty Groups and Candidate Recruitment

	Losers		Marginals	
	GOP (N = 128)	DEM (N = 108)	GOP (N = 30)	DEM (N = 32)
Percent of candidates receiving prenomination "encouragement" from nonparty groups.	12%	34%	0%	41%
Percent of candidates receiving post-nomination "endorsement" from nonparty groups.	34%	90%	47%	94%

sional candidates for either losing or marginal contests. Of course, widespread public notice of private-group activity at this juncture of a candidate's political career might damage the cause of the special interests as well as the candidate. No candidate can afford public approbation as a "tool" of an interest group.

Identification of the groups involved in prenomination recruitment efforts contains few surprises. For the Republicans, these were about equally divided between business groups, medical or paramedical groups, and a third miscellany of farm, "right wing," trade union, and fraternal or local ethnic groups. For the most part the Republican candidates did not seek the party nomination as a result of recruitment efforts on the part of nonparty groups.

Among the Democrats the story was more familiar. Among the 34 percent of the losers and 41 percent of the marginals who reported prenomination encouragement by representatives of nonparty groups, organized labor was predominant. Specific units designated by respondents included the full range of international unions affiliated with the AFL-CIO, particularly those originating in industrial unions, such as the Auto Workers and the Steel Workers, and including both the Longshoremen and the Teamsters. A scattering of Democratic recruitment approaches were also reported from such groups as the National Farmers' Union and from peace groups.

In noting the generous labor support provided his bid for the congressional nomination, one Democrat added gratefully, "and they were truly helpful—they won the primary for me." Another, whose contacts included both the National Farmers' Union and the

AFL-CIO's Committee on Political Education (COPE) endorsement in his primary campaign, stated proudly that he was "encouraged and endorsed by all groups of organized labor. They all helped financially as well as campaigned on my behalf."

How much is added to understanding of congressional recruitment by this delineation of the role of nonparty agencies in the prenomination campaigns? Certainly the long-standing interests of organized labor in national and state political campaigns is compatible with the objectives of the Democratic party in nearly all northern, midwestern and far-western states. Here the group interests stand as confederates and friends to those aspirants for party nomination who receive their blessing and assistance. The same would be true of far less sophisticated nonparty groups which, without being fully aware or sensitive to the delicacy of prenomination recruitment, would nonetheless seek to assist candidates in reaching their decision to run and in the solicitation of pledges for financial support. Such would be the encouragement provided a group of GOP candidates during the primaries by local medical societies and medical political-action groups.

Nearly indistinguishable for many candidates from prenomination recruitment by nonparty groups is the postnomination endorsement and support provided by these same groups following the primaries. It would be naive to assume that the primary election date effectively seals the candidate off from contacts with nonparty groups prior to the event, only to formally legitimize them afterward. Certainly the timing of party influence on candidate recruitment involves no rigid observation of such a catalog of do's and don'ts. Indeed, the postprimary endorsements publicly received by a candidate may only provide an occasion for him to redeem the pledges received when he was prevailed upon to enter the fray at some earlier time. At any rate, the endorsement support provided both losers and marginal candidates (Table 3.7) show clearly the array of influences in the campaign itself and the heightened response of the nonparty groups to the marginal candidates.

As an example, the following pattern of postprimary endorsements was reported by 34 percent of the Republican losers. This was a group of forty-four individuals, of whom thirty were endorsed by medical or dental political-action groups.

Nineteen were endorsed by Americans for Constitutional Action.
Thirteen were endorsed by labor groups, of which six were AFL-CIO

industrial union affiliates and seven were service or craft union affiliates, such as the Teamsters, hotel and restaurant workers, printers, hospital workers, carpenters, teachers, and a Negro labor council.

Six were backed by other "right-wing" groups, including one each from Young Americans for Freedom, "Pro America," "Civic Searchlite," "United Christians," and a Conservative Democratic Association.

Six were endorsed by business and professional groups, including lawyers, realtors, life underwriters, and retail grocers.

Among the Democrats, 90 percent of the losers reported receiving postnomination endorsements from interest groups. The group consisted of ninety-seven individuals.

Eighty-three were endorsed by organized labor, of which the most frequently cited units were the Auto Workers, the Steelworkers, Central Labor councils, and COPE. Next in frequency were the Railway Brotherhoods, the Teamsters, the machinists, and a sprinkling of other trade unions.

Nine were endorsed by ethnic groups, including NAACP and American Indian, Czech, Spanish, German, Polish, and Italian club endorsements.

Eight were endorsed by liberal party or Americans for Democratic Action units (in Illinois, the Independent Voters of Illinois).

Six were endorsed by peace groups.

Four were endorsed by senior citizens' groups.

One was endorsed by a veterans' group.

This examination of the role and identity of nonparty interest groups in the candidate recruitment process provides another dimension of the personal situation of the nonincumbent candidate who decides to stand for a congressional seat. At this juncture it is not clear whether the term *recruitment* is properly descriptive of the activity which leads him to declare his candidacy, but the decision is not made in a political vacuum. Indeed, most candidates—and more particularly the marginal candidates—are prevailed upon by family, friends, associates, party leaders, and to a considerable extent by the agents and representatives of pressure groups in making their decision. We have pointed out elsewhere the personal nature of the congressional campaign. Incumbent congressmen seldom rely heavily upon state or local party support in seeking to hold their seats every two years. And once elected, a member usually makes over in his own image whatever congressional district party organization may have existed. The district, such as it is, then becomes a personal organization of the incumbent, nourished by his staff, his postal franking privileges, his constituent services, the funds supplied by interest groups and the campaign committees on the Hill.

In those districts where new candidates are challenging party control of a seat once held by a long-term incumbent, it is very likely that little or no district organization will be found.[12] Without an organization it is less likely that formal party recruitment efforts will take place, and it is more likely that a candidate will win nomination outside of regular party channels. The result is to encourage self-starters, independents, and group-sponsored candidates.[13]

Clapp notes the importance of volunteers and nonparty groups in displacing atrophied political organizations in the task of reelecting congressmen. This situation should be even more true of nonincumbent candidates, where recruitment may actually fall to a local or state interest group or to a friend of the candidate to fill the vacuum left by the party and/or the direct primary. Generalizing from our data, however, it appears that rarely do interest groups engage in recruitment efforts at the expense of party. Indeed in most cases they have mutually sympathetic goals. Frequently the extra-party involvement is almost one of chance. A young Republican attorney in a far-western state reported:

I was in my office one day about noon and _____, a fellow attorney and secretary of the county bar association, came in and asked me to lunch. During lunch he said that some of the people in the association had been discussing the possibility of my running for Congress against _____. It took me completely by surprise. I laughed about it then, but the more I considered it the more I was convinced that I should try.

Newspapers played a minor role in the selection of congressional candidates. For the most part these few were Republican papers in Democratic territories. Some GOP losers attributed the earliest suggestion of their candidacy to a local newspaper. One observed, "I had thought about running in 1960, but in 1962 the local newspaper editor suggested me as a candidate in his weekly column and I decided to file." There was no way to determine whether party influence was brought to bear on editors, although intercommunications in downtown leadership and luncheon groups makes such suggestions relatively simple.

12. Clapp, pp. 367 ff.
13. For a good discussion of the effects of the direct primary on candidate recruitment at the state legislative level, see Frank J. Sorauf, *Party and Representation* (New York: Atherton, 1962), pp. 95–96.

As a general rule, political leadership, at whatever level, seeks some control over the selection of congressional candidates whenever there appears to be a reasonable chance of victory. Even the most recumbent organization is embarrassed by vacancies on the ticket at this level. Conversely, when the chance of success appears small, the leadership is more likely to concentrate on local, county, or state races, which have a greater party potential and consequently a "low overhead" in organization and financial resources. In such cases the congressional nomination might go begging and might be captured by self-starters or non-party candidates. Under these circumstances, the more remote the chance of victory, the greater the chance for candidate to be recruited from nonparty arenas.

Considerations of the Candidate in Deciding to Run

Statistically the chances of success for a nonincumbent challenger in an off-year congressional election are not great. From 75 to 80 percent of the House seats are usually adjudged to be "safe" for the incumbent, and a sizable proportion of those which are competitive will not change hands. In view of these prospects, why do so many candidates agree (or decide) to run? In 1962 only forty-eight seats were uncontested in the entire House of Representatives, and almost all of them were in one-party districts of the South.[14] What reasons might be offered by the candidates for undertaking what was admittedly a considerable risk and a poor gamble?

In seeking answers to these questions, we were fully cognizant of the difficulties involved in ascribing motivation to political candidates. We have made no pretense at such an effort. On the other hand, so little is known about the reasons why political candidates run that it seemed worthwhile to explore the answers given by the candidates in this survey. We are keenly aware of the difficulties inherent in the exploration of so complex a subject by mail questionnaire. But, it should be borne in mind, in completing these questionnaires the candidates were responding to a request by personal letter from the respective national chairmen. Though some candidates might attempt to mislead the chairmen, the temptation to duplicity are less

14. An exception was Alabama, where a failure to redistrict forced twelve men, representing three parties, to run at large for eight seats. The eight receiving the most votes were elected, and all were Democrats.

than they would be if the questionnaire had come from some less influential source. Recognizing the difficulties, the candidates were asked to describe in their own words and to the best of their ability their reasons for deciding to run for Congress in 1962.

As shown in Table 3.8, most candidates offered more than one reason for their decision. These reasons may be categorized as organizational, programmatic, altruistic, and personal. Those who cited organizational reasons were particularly concerned with building or (rebuilding) the structure of the party in the state or district. For a variety of reasons they believed that their candidacy for the House would help to reach that goal.

Table 3.8

Reasons for Deciding to Run

	Organiza-tional	Ideological	Altruistic	Personal
Percent of Republican Candidates (N = 54)	44%	30%	39%	19%
Percent of Democratic Candidates (N = 53)	44%	35%	27%	40%
Percent in both parties (N = 109)	44%	32%	33%	29%

NOTE: Percentages total over 100 because of multiple responses.

A substantial number of candidates indicated that a programmatic or ideological reason lay behind their decision. Many of these candidates believed themselves involved in a conservative or liberal crusade. The contest was for a cause—not usually for a party.

Some candidates—particularly southern Republicans and midwestern and New England Democrats—ran, somewhat altruistically, to fill the ticket. The desire of party officials to avoid defaulting on a contest helped to enlist a number of candidates. These were generally hopeless efforts and were recognized as such by the participants. But one measure of effectiveness in party affairs, particularly at the local level, is thought to be a "full ticket," and this motive accounted for much recruitment activity by party leaders. It was also responsible for tapping the dormant feelings of altruism in the hearts of many of the candidates.

Finally, a fourth group cited personal reasons. Some thought in terms of personal advancement; some sought to achieve personal satisfaction from the race; and others wished to test latent abilities. The reasons were varied, but all could be classed in some degree as personal.

ORGANIZATIONAL REASONS

When one Democratic loser was asked why he ran, in view of the odds, he replied, "I ran because we must build our party strength through hard work and by showing the courage of our convictions . . . we can serve without winning." Another, a Republican stated, "I felt it was my duty to chip away the Democratic plurality in the hope that my district might some day be a marginal one." Another Republican argued that "Even though I had no chance, I owed the people the obligation to participate in politics in order to make this a two-party state and keep it so."

Over and over again the losing candidates reflected the same view. Even with the odds strongly against success, it was important to make the race to demonstrate that the party had a spark of life in the district. If there existed no chance at all for victory in 1962, the party organization must be built for future elections. Good organization demands good planning, and a strong organization must be built on a foundation of experience. Taken at face value and placed in the context of the hard work of the campaign, the goals voiced by these candidates displayed a degree of party loyalty surprising in a hopeless district. Among the respondents, 44 percent reported some such reason as a major factor in their decision to run for Congress. That this number included some who were simply seizing upon a self-serving device to rationalize an ignominious defeat is unquestioned; however, the statements of most of the candidates appeared to reflect considerable thought.

The energies expended in behalf of this goal were usually directed toward the party as a vote-making structure more than as the embodiment of programs or principles. Few candidates seemed interested in building the party within the district or state in order to promote party principles. Most of them engaged in the effort in order to build a party organization that could muster votes on election day.

They usually related their campaign to the congressional district —not to the state organization. Many of them indicated that the state organization was remote and distant and of small help in the campaign. They showed little interest in strengthening the state party. One Republican put it succinctly:

Anybody who says the state party committee should receive the most support in our organizing efforts simply doesn't understand the problems of the congressional district. The district is remote and unimportant as far as the state committee people are concerned. If we are ever to have a strong Republican contender in my district, we will have to put all our efforts into a building effort at the district level. Only a fool or a central committee member thinks that if we spend most of our time and money on the state central committee and the state organization that some of it will eventually trickle down to the district. There is no trickle-down theory in politics.

Others, speaking in the candor of anonymity, expressed almost identical views. It was to the district level that the bulk of those calling for stronger organization hoped to direct the most effort. It was to the district level that they hoped "the party leaders" would direct their thoughts and actions. And most of them, in one way or another, indicated their belief that the amount of attention given to the congressional district organization would ultimately determine the strength and well-being of the two-party system.

A number of candidates in both parties tied their desire for a strengthened district organization to long-run personal ambitions. No altruism here: plain old-fashioned nest-feathering was their watchword. One observed:

Because I am sure Democrats will win this district within a few years— and if I am to be a part of this future, I must become known in this broader area.

Another candidate of the same party indicated that he ran in 1962 against an entrenched incumbent so as to have a recognizable claim on the nomination in 1964, "when Kennedy is at the head of the ticket." A number of candidates in both parties indicated they were "getting in line" for a future nomination and that 1962 simply represented a stage in that drive. This view was exemplified by a candidate who noted:

To me this was a party building procedure to enable me to get the party nomination in a graceful way at a later date. If you run when the going is tough, the old pros remember the sacrifice you made and will look favorably on your candidacy when things are better.

The same percentages of candidates in both parties, as shown in Table 3.8, demonstrated a manifest concern with party organization as a reason for their candidacy. Sometimes this feeling was expressed in very personal terms. A number of candidates reported that their own candidacy was beneficial to the party as a whole; it "gave a lift to the whole ticket." One Republican, who apparently viewed his own candidacy with a greater awe than did the voters, believed that he "added an element of quality that had been missing from our ticket for many years." Some of these "ticket lifters" saw wide-ranging effects on the state party as a whole from their experience as candidates. Republicans were more conscious of this role than Democrats; one GOP loser estimated that his efforts gained the party over 20,000 votes in the state as a whole. The prevailing view, however, was one of hope mixed with despair—hope that the campaign and the candidate had made a permanent contribution to the strengthening of the party organization and initial despair over the lack of success as manifested by the defeat.

PROGRAMMATIC OR IDEOLOGICAL REASONS

It has been commonplace to observe that candidates for public office in the United States are not devoted to issues. At most levels this truism may hold, but at the congressional district level an impressive number of candidates indicated that ideology was a factor in their decision to run. Some spoke in generalities, supporting the "New Frontier" or "Taft conservatism." Others espoused particular issues of concern to the district. Many candidates sensed great concern within the district over such issues—Medicare, socialism, farm supports, nuclear war, or corruption in government. Whether viewed in general or specific terms, the prevalence of high-intensity issues was suggested as a major factor in the decision to run of 32 percent of the losing candidates.

Some candidates attempted to engage opponents in debate, but very few incumbents were willing to take part in such exercises. Incumbents were persuaded that the Kennedy-Nixon debates of two years before had done serious damage to the latter, and many of them were chary about lending their personal prestige to the opposition. Most of the constituencies were witness to campaign-long monologues by one or both candidates. Fully one-third of the losing candidates complained that opponents refused to engage in any meaningful discussion of issues. A survey of these campaigns revealed a pattern of nonincumbents desperately attempting to induce the incumbents to discuss issues. One congressman, representative of many, stated:

> I wasn't going to debate my record with him. Almost anything I said would cause me to lose support among some group. Not because my record is bad, but simply because it is not well-known and the less well-known I can keep it the more support I will retain. I spent the entire campaign running against the Kennedys. That was enough in my district.

If such is the view of some congressmen, even more nonincumbent challengers are committed to the opposite tack. It is often extremely important to the latter to try to force issues and voting records into the forefront of the campaign. This tactic serves to gain publicity, helps to raise money, and gives the candidate a topic other than his own qualifications. Presumably those candidates who saw the campaign in these terms considered ideological or programmatic factors in their decision to run.

The percentage difference between the parties concerning the importance of such considerations was slight. It might be noted, however, that there was considerably more indignation and vehemence among the Republican losers than among the Democrats. This datum partly reflected the underdog role of many GOP candidates, who were faced with an overwhelming number of Democratic held seats. But it was also a response to the rising conservatism within some elements of the Republican party. Many conservatives were dissatisfied with most elements in current society and opposed many aspects of the programs being carried out by government agencies. The intensity of their feeling about such matters often led them into vehement ideological campaigns. The pending 1964 conflict in the Republican party was forecast by a candidate who feared distortion of the party's image by a more conservative candidate and who made the race "so that the Republicans should have a candidate who represents the Republican philosophy as whole, not some single extreme segment." The same thought was expressed by another, who noted, "There was need for a good candidate worthy to oppose a liberal incumbent in a responsible way. The other [primary] candidate was a right-wing extremist." This gentleman indicated the above as the sole reason for his entry into the primary and ultimately his unsuccessful campaign for the House.

A subgroup of the *programmatic candidates* might be described as educators. The educators' campaigns were usually designed to convince the voters of the efficacy of the party's program. Several cited the need for voter education as the basis for their decision to run. A Kennedy Democrat stated it well:

I felt the President and the party should have someone in the district willing and able to present arguments on major issues. . . . I don't like sanctimonious monologues by majority party candidates in this district.

A Republican who strongly resented the lack of an articulate GOP candidate in his district in 1960 wrote: "The opportunity to do some basic political education should not be missed." Another maintained that "We need to articulate the Republican philosophy regardless of the odds against us." A deeper motive, one designed to "educate" the incumbent, was expressed by a Democrat:

I felt that I wanted to support the Kennedy Administration and was inspired by the President's progressive legislation. I felt that my candidacy would at least provoke the incumbent into supporting the Administration on such issues as Medicare.

A midwestern Democrat was concerned over the long list of conservatives who had run under his party label in the past and filed in 1962 to "correct the bad habit here of not campaigning as Democrats." Finally, another Democrat looked to the future, announcing his willingness to run again once the district was "Democratized." He noted:

Once the party starts proudly proclaiming the progressive principles we stand for nationally, we shall be able to swing the district into the Democratic column in a few years when our story begins to sink in.

Two groups of candidates, one in each party, might be designated as crusaders. One of these groups, primarily Democratic, was keyed to domestic crises and international tensions. Though they were dubbed "peace candidates" by newspaper reporters, a more accurate 1962 description would seem to be "antiarmaments candidates." The primary concern of this small group was to "give the people of the district an opportunity to read and hear that there are workable alternatives to the arms race as a means of achieving peace." Few of them were able to report significant support from party officials, although one noted that his Democratic state chairman urged the people in the district to listen to his message supporting peace and disarmament because "it was very important." Few of these candidates entered the congressional race with much hope of winning. Most of them were "allowed" to have the nomination in districts not vigorously contested. Virtually all entered the campaign to espouse the cause and without much hope for success.

On the Republican side a similar concern for the fate of the nation was noted—rescue not so much from nuclear destruction but from "the erosions of statism and socialism." These candidates were zealous crusaders, who often spoke of themselves as such and saw parallels to great movements in history. One wrote:

We must replace the liberal-socialist members of Congress because we are about to lose our nation. Time is running out and we must awaken the people. Almighty God put it in my heart.

Others specified the nature of the danger to America by equating their candidacy to saving the nation from a "liberal group with influence in the White House." One conservative Republican noted emphatically:

The 1962 elections were the last chance to protect our free enterprise system from the "Democratic socialism" of the ADA. . . . I ran because Congress is the only hope for saving ourselves from this left-wing fringe group.

The crusaders in both groups did not fare well at the polls. It is difficult to generalize about them, but the results in those districts suggest that they alienated voters with their zealous repetition of the same theme. Furthermore, they usually ran in districts which allowed little chance for victory.

ALTRUISTIC REASONS

If most House seats are safe for the incumbent congressman, then it would appear that most nonincumbents are engaged in relatively hopeless campaigns. Some of those, however, were graced with candidates whose sole purpose on the ballot was to "fill the ticket"; 33 percent ran for this reason, either at the request of a party leader or on their own initiative. Since they could gain little personal advantage from running in such impossible contests, it is difficult to reach any conclusion other than that their motive was basically altruistic.

The desire to fill the ticket, exhibited by many state and local party officials, seems to be grounded in the fear of embarrassment over defaulting on a race. Furthermore, some party officers, intent on building the party organization, consider a blank space on the ballot as a step backward in their efforts. Consequently, as filing deadlines near, there is an energetic effort to get a name—sometimes any name—on the ballot for each office. The belief is ingrained that party leadership will be measured against its ability to provide candidates for such races.

On the other hand, some party leaders make no effort to develop congressional candidates and are perfectly content to see the seat go by forfeit. In some such cases candidates themselves enlisted, to maintain some semblance of party identity in the district. One Republican complained, "My chairman didn't do anything to get a candidate for Congress or anything else. He never has and he never will. The party deserved a candidate in this slot, so I ran."

Most of those who sought to avoid default did so at the request of a party leader. These requests were often couched in desperate terms, as typified by a Democrat who noted, "The ones who thought they could run backed out at the last moment. I was urged to file to fill the ticket." Another, a Republican, filed one hour before the deadline because the unofficial chairman of the ward leaders in his urban district,

came to me barely two days before the deadline and said, "You have to be our candidate against _____. It won't be fair to the party or to me if you don't. I know you can't win, but we have to fill the spot. I'll consider it a personal favor."

Forty-eight hours later he reluctantly agreed after forcing a promise from the ward leaders that the party would pay for the campaign.[15]

Others among the "ticket fillers" were primarily concerned over the future of the party should no candidates be run in 1962. This was especially true of Republicans who, being a minority, had everything to gain from filling every possible space on the ticket. This concern no doubt accounts for the fact that 39 percent of those who listed the desire to avoid default were in the GOP, while only 27 percent were Democrats. Among the southern Republicans there was a noticeable interest in party building. Many expressed interest

15. Interview conducted at the headquarters of the Republican National Committee, Washington, D.C., December 1962. At the time of the interview the party leadership had just turned down the candidate's request for funds to settle some campaign debts.

in participating in the construction of a GOP organization in that region. "I ran because I wanted to make a Republican beginning in this district," noted one. And another stated, "After a hundred years it was about time a conservative Republican ran. We won't be able to get anything going if we don't start."[16]

A Democrat in a Republican district ran . . . "for the good of the party because the leader needed a candidate . . . [there was] a lack of candidates willing to run in such a hopeless district. But we couldn't let it go by default." Some GOP candidates, especially those in the South and those who described themselves as "Gold-water Republicans," ran to avoid failing their responsibilities to conservatism. Interest in the Republican party in these instances was secondary to the development of philosophical conservatism. Thus, one stated, "The liberal record of the incumbent made it mandatory that the Republicans offer a conservative choice or close down altogether." Another with a strong sense of Republican party spirit noted, "I accepted the draft of my best friend, who convinced me that the party would never amount to anything if responsible men were unwilling to help construct it." A Democrat echoed his concern: "My district was written off by the leadership. I ran anyway because I am a loyal party member and we needed someone to oppose this SOB."

The role of the "ticket filler," the candidate who runs to prevent the party from defaulting, is a unique one. It involves elements of altruism and martyrdom. There is little sham among such candidates, since it is difficult (but not impossible) for sham to breed in grounds that are so barren. By and large these candidates, running for altruistic reasons, possessed a strong sense of historic purpose or philosophical dedication. If politicians ever become angels, these individuals, who made personal sacrifices in the name of the party, will be the first to sprout wings.

PERSONAL REASONS

Somewhere in the pages of an obscure manual on the virtues proper to princes must be a reference to the attribute of "magnificence" as cultivated by kings, bishops, lords, and other men of princely

16. Renewed GOP interest in the South was demonstrated by the decrease in unopposed seats from seventy-eight to forty-six between 1958 and 1962. This change represented an increase of 41 percent in contested House seats in that region.

authority. Such a term would describe the manner and bearing to accompany one's public position in church or state. In an affluent democratic society the appearance, if not the fact, of magnificence is available to the ordinary citizen with a taste for it and the credit to buy its trappings and symbols.

With easy access to nominations, aided by the primary election system, candidates may satisfy desires for public recognition, political power, and personal influence. All of these contribute to the cultivation of the spirit, if not the trappings, of magnificence.

Contrasted to the "ticket fillers" are those who for personal reasons sought nomination and ran for election. Since in many cases there was little chance of victory, the reward may have been in the running rather than in the winning. Of all the candidate groups, this one was demonstrably more optimistic even in defeat. It may be that the symbols and the trappings of congressional candidacy satisfied the desire for recognition.

In all, 29 percent of the losing candidates gave personal reasons of one kind or another as a factor in deciding to run. A few expected appointment to office or some similar personal reward. Only one respondent candidly suggested that his own economic welfare was the motivating factor:

> As a lawyer I thought that the publicity could not hurt me, and you always have a chance in politics. Voters are somewhat like a jury; you never know for sure what they are going to do.

In view of his decisive defeat, it may be hoped that jurors will be more moved by his advocacy than were voters by his candidacy.

Several candidates expressed an interest in measuring personal abilities by running for Congress. These people, reflecting on past experience or the challenge of new ones, viewed the campaign experience as a means of satisfying themselves with regard to their own competence. A Democrat running in a heavily Republican district noted, "I wanted to see what impact a total neophyte at politics might make, and to see if the electorate might be persuaded to change its mind." He further noted the therapeutic benefits of his candidacy: "I wanted to encourage others to get involved in politics and to walk into the great experience of campaigning." Another Democrat stated that he ran because he "felt drawn to the decision-making level and thought it worth an aggressive try." A Republican agreed: "This seemed to be as good a way as any to find out if I had the stuff that statesmen are made of." Another Democrat, running in a district which had not elected anyone from that party since the days of Grover Cleveland, tied his desire to test his own political abilities to a wish to use the coattails of the President:

> I thought that Kennedy's popularity coupled with an aggressive campaign might just turn the trick. On the personal level I wanted to see if I was a politician. Thirty-three is a good age to find out, since none expected me to win and I had nothing to lose in trying.

The reasons offered for becoming involved in congressional politics in 1962 were varied. No doubt they differed from motives in past contests because of such factors as the rise of Republicanism in the South and increased Democratic activity in areas of traditional Republican strength. In recent years a trend toward greater emphasis on ideology has developed, attested to by the increased solidity of Southern members of both parties.

Whatever their reasons, most candidates enlisted in campaigns the results of which were foregone conclusions. Few of them had even a mathematical chance for success. Many of them were fully cognizant of their hopeless situation. How, then, did they estimate the chances for winning in these unlikely matches?

Estimates of Success

A powerful motivation of candidates is usually the hope for victory. The probability of success must draw candidates into political forays just as the chance of the long shot attracts bettors to the horse race. In a nation in which batting averages and league standings are in the intellectual baggage of many adults, one should expect to find an interest in election statistics and probabilities among political activists. If such existed, however, one would be hard pressed to find many knowledgeable persons willing to bet on challenger candidates in congressional elections. To any close observer the outlook for an exchange of many seats in 1962 must have appeared very slim indeed.

In view of this generally bleak outlook for the challenger candidates, we sought to determine the respondent's own estimation of his chances for victory. The candidates were asked: "At the time of your decision to run for Congress, what chances of winning did you feel that you had?"

No candidate suggested that he evaluated his chances as "certain." But 15 percent indicated that their chances were "good," while almost 40 percent thought theirs were "fair." Obviously well over 50 percent of the nonincumbents viewed their chances as considerably better than mathematical probabilities would allow. Just how unrealistic these judgments were is indicated by the fact that these candidates averaged only 42 percent of the vote on election day. There was a 2 percent difference between those who viewed their chances as "good" and those who estimated them as "fair," the former receiving the higher average vote. The remaining candidates more realistically evaluated their chances as "remote or nil." They averaged 34 percent of the vote, the Democrats outperforming the GOP losers by an average vote of 37 to 31 percent.

Republicans tended to be more hopeful and less realistic than the Democrats; 42 percent of the GOP candidates and 52 percent of the Democrats thought their chances were "remote." Among those losers who saw their chances as "fair" the same distinction was noted, the optimistic Republicans outnumbering the Democrats by a full 10 percent. Nearly equal numbers from both parties believed their chances of victory were "good," but not one of them won. Among those candidates who commented on this question were a number of Democrats who based their hopes on the effect of presidential coattails, although the election was in an off year. A few Republicans were optimistic because of the alleged coattail effect of a popular U.S. Senatorial or gubernatorial candidate on the ticket. This belief in coattails was particularly interesting in view of the reverse coattail effect in the 1960 election, when Democratic House candidates received 863,535 votes more than did President Kennedy.

Malcolm Moos, in his 1952 study of presidential coattails, found that rigorous examination of his data indicated far less evidence of this phenomenon than many scholars had previously assumed. Moos attributed this discrepancy to the mistaken assumption that the average 7 percent more votes cast for the presidential candidate than for congressional candidates in his party represented a pulling force —which, in fact, does not exist. He maintains that the additional presidential votes are cast by people voting for the highest office but not voting for congressional candidates. His conclusions suggest that while there may have been a coattail influence in some districts at some times, there is impressive evidence that none at all exists in others and that in some the congressional candidate eases the election of the presidential candidate.[17]

Obviously this analysis does not explain why some candidates—

17. Malcolm Moos, *Politics, Presidents and Coattails* (Baltimore: The Johns Hopkins Press, 1952).

relatively few, to be sure—would involve themselves in a congressional campaign in a nonpresidential year. Observation suggests that the House candidates misunderstood the coattail influence and confused it with the effects of a president's personal popularity. At the time of the 1962 campaign the popularity of President Kennedy, as reflected in public opinion polls, was at an all-time high, sometimes topping the comparable ratings of former President Eisenhower. While such popular presidential appeal might be of help to some candidates, it could not be considered as a coattail effect under the established meaning of the term, since the President was not on the ballot.

An explanation for this misplaced optimism might be that these candidates hoped to capitalize on sharing the ballot with strong senatorial or gubernatorial candidates. It is difficult to accept even that explanation in view of some of the candidates who headed those tickets. Some of the state tickets were led by completely undistinguished and unknown men who could not possibly furnish coattails for any lesser candidates.

Marginal candidates tended to rate their chances considerably higher than did the nonmarginal ones. Even though most of them were unaware of that special status, they were certainly aware of the factors which were taken into consideration in awarding them the nomination. They knew that an incumbent opponent had formerly won by a small margin or that a special circumstance within the district increased the chances of upset. These views were reflected in their responses to our efforts to get an evaluation of chances for success.

Among the Republican marginals 71 percent stated that they believed chances for victory were "fair," and an additional 25 percent felt that they were "good." Democratic marginals were even more optimistic, with 50 percent evaluating their chances as "good," while 35 percent noted that they had a "fair" chance of winning. Only 15 percent of the Democrats and 4 percent of the Republicans assayed their chances as "remote."

Odds On Favorites—To Lose

We began this chapter with a conundrum: Does the man seek the office or does the office seek the man? Clearly the seeking is from

both directions. Contacts are made, liaisons are arranged, drafts occur, and vacuums are filled. The ticket is graced by a name—sometimes after a hard-fought primary or a backroom convention maneu-
ver. At other times a candidate is secured only by promises, cajolery,
or outright intimidation. Some of these arrangements originate with
the candidate, while others are a product of party or interest-group
counsel. Some recruitment efforts are straightforward, while others
are oblique.

The problem of recruitment stands stark against the background
of the congressional district. The recruitment equation includes a
recruiter and a recruitee, but at this level the first of these factors is
often nonexistent or uncertain. As a result, congressional elections
are often waged by neophytes who have started themselves on the
road to high public office. More often than not the entire party is
damaged by the ensuing confusion and by a directionless campaign
at this important middle level.

Some cynics have argued that these candidates run in hopeless
contests because of some self-serving personal interest. According
to this view, personal interest supplants party interest in the motiva-
tional considerations which go into their decisions. There were a
number of instances cited by candidates in 1962 suggesting that such
factors may have entered into the decision of these candidates. A
few candidates were open enough to state that they were running to
improve their business, build a law practice, control local patronage,
or get in line for a future nomination. These were self-service interests, to be sure. But of far more importance was the overwhelming
number of candidates who ran for unselfish reasons. Most of these
candidates ran hopeless, badly financed campaigns at great personal
sacrifice and with little prospect of reward. Relatively few indicated
that their personal interests were of prime importance; indeed, there
are far easier, cheaper and more effective ways to accomplish personal advancement.

The 1962 congressional candidates were not unique but were
replicas of candidates in former elections and prototypes of those to
come. They often ran for Congress under some degree of delusion,
but just as often they had other, more rational, reasons. A number
of them complained after the campaign that "You fellows in Washington don't understand our problems. You don't know our needs."
But it seems likely that the party officials were more realistic in their
appraisal of election potential than were the candidates. They worked
hard, were well received, and gradually accumulated self-confidence.

Their crushing defeat was especially galling to many of them in view of these pretensions. When it came, it was often temporarily destructive of their self-esteem, but it gave them a more realistic picture of the American political process than they had held when they began. And, as a number of them pointed out, the experience was good preparation for the next time.

4.
Campaign Organization and Management

*The whole state must be so well organized
that every Whig can be brought to the
polls. So divide the county into small districts and in each appoint a committee.
Make a perfect list of the voters and
ascertain with certainty for whom they
will vote. . . . Keep a constant watch on
the doubtful voters and have them talked
to by those in whom they have the most
confidence. . . . On election days see
that every Whig is brought to the polls.*
—ABRAHAM LINCOLN

AN election campaign presents formidable administrative problems to those responsible for its management. Few, if any, of the canons of the art or science of public or business administration apply to the management of political campaigns. Due in part to the casual recruitment and general inexperience of those who manage and work in campaigns, these problems are the offspring of the chaotic atmosphere in which congressional campaigns take place. They are launched with frenzied impatience; money is spent before it is raised; there are almost no orderly procedures of budgetary control, planning, or accountability; and scientific administrative management is a rare virtue. Only when the campaign is over and the final bills have been received are the total costs computed and the errors in judgment assayed. Indeed, political campaigning constitutes an unusual, a unique kind of management problem.

If campaign management, particularly at the congressional district level, were to be classified as an administrative science, it would fall somewhere between the nebulous practices associated with modern-day carnivals and old-fashioned circuses. The nostalgia associated with these enterprises calls forth visions of barkers, parades, advance men, and occasionally confidence men. There are, to be sure, many resemblances between the sawdust trail and the campaign trail. In all probability, however, the manager of the circus has long since introduced order and reason into the administration of his at once seasonal and nomadic entourage. The same cannot be said of the management of political campaigns, at least at the congressional level.

Yet professional campaign managers, successful candidates, and knowledgeable amateurs will insist that "good" organization is one key to victory. Losers and political novices often lament their failure to construct a "tight" or "efficient" organization. They attribute defeat to organizational problems, even though they may have been on the nether end of a landslide. Good campaign organization is recognized by those most closely affected as an essential element for victory, although it does not guarantee it.

Most citizens are acquainted with the maze of local, county, and state party organizations stretching between neighborhood precincts and Washington. Some of these groups are sanctioned by law, while others have unknown antecedents in regional and party history. Some function the year around while others, with the help of amateurs, materialize a few months before election day, only to evaporate when the votes are counted. Yet, as pervasive as this party machinery is, congressional candidates have little connection with it. At times, to be sure, an established party group may involve itself just long enough to designate a sacrificial candidate, while other, more active groups guide the congressional campaign and offer services which the candidate cannot provide for himself.

Veteran political observer Raymond Moley has noted what generations of losing political candidates have experienced:

> Organization, more often than not, means success or failure in party operations. Issues may be solid. Candidates may be attractive. But when organization operates only periodically before elections, when it falls down in its recruiting and training of workers, when it falters in taking the offensive against its political opponents, when it does not sustain even the interest of its own workers, it must suffer the inevitable, though unnecessary losses. It is an army of irregular "summer soldiers."[1]

A better description of the organizational dilemma of the average congressional nonincumbent would be hard to find. Except in those few states with active congressional-district party committees, the

---

1. Raymond Moley, *The Republican Opportunity* (New York: Duell, Sloan & Pearce, 1962), p. 184.

average candidate for Congress must build his organization across municipal and county party lines and must seek to weld together a highly personal campaign team. He must compete for public attention with issues and events which are far removed from electoral questions and which are frequently capable of enlargement or distortion by the convex lens of the news media. Factors such as these force the incumbent—and to a far greater extent the nonincumbent—congressional candidate to construct a personal organization, using the party structure where possible but departing from it where necessary.

The incumbent congressman facing reelection has fewer and less drastic organizational problems than does his nonincumbent challenger. Aside from enjoying the magnificent tactical advantage of being "inside Washington," he is, first and most important, already known to the public and can rely on a wide range of acquaintances to provide a basic, informal, personal organization. His congressional office staff, some of whom may be highly qualified political organizers, can be distributed between the Washington and home-district offices. As a Member of Congress the incumbent further qualifies for special assistance from his campaign committee on Capitol Hill. Moreover, being a proven winner, he is very likely to be viewed with some favor by his state central committee and to be treated as an asset to the state and local party tickets. Finally, the incumbent will have easy access to volunteers, since even the briefest congressional tenure generates a personal following. All these factors contribute to the advantages enjoyed by the incumbent and enhance his chances of reelection.

If these advantages are true for incumbents, the nonincumbent challenger by the same token faces formidable obstacles. Indeed, only occasionally does a nonincumbent succeed in unseating his opponent. In 1962 only six Republican and sixteen Democratic incumbents failed in their reelection attempts. Of the latter, six lost to GOP incumbents who had been thrown into their districts by reapportionment. Gerrymandering adversely affected others of the defeated group of incumbents.[2] The problems of organization and management, how-

2. Best-known examples of 1962 losses by gerrymander were the six incumbent Democrats who were forced to contend with Republican incumbents. Two of the latter were known members of the John Birch Society, although careful observers have noted that redistricting was probably more directly responsible for their defeat than was their political coloration. The most notable example was the defeat of Congressman Walter Judd of Minnesota, who lost to a relatively unknown state senator due largely to change of district boundaries.

ever, provided headaches and challenges for all. No challenger could afford to risk a badly organized campaign, and few incumbent congressmen could afford organizational complacency because of past victories.

At some party levels campaign organization and management have developed an aura of professionalism, using the most sophisticated techniques of the printed, audio, and visual media. There is no need to dwell here on the advances which modern communications and transportation have brought to political campaigning; these have been thoroughly explored elsewhere.[3] Nor is there much to be gained by evaluating purely local campaigns for office. The problems in these smaller bailiwicks are generally less complicated by comparison, and with the possible exception of urban "reform" candidates, the relationships between local candidates and the voters are frequently long-established and personal ones. The typical congressional district, occupying a political middleground, represents a stratum of campaign effort which should make use of the professional campaign techniques of the presidential contest, but too often it has to make do with the personalized style of small-town politics. The shortcomings in congressional campaign styles were repeatedly noted by the respondents in this study.

While the conditions under which challenger candidates oppose incumbents vary greatly, a number of common elements appear which permit a clearer understanding of the problems besetting candidates and their managers. Five distinct areas of campaign administration will be discussed: overall direction and management; headquarters

3. For treatment of the impact of communications and transportation technology upon presidential campaigns, see Cornelius P. Cotter and Bernard C. Hennessy, *Politics Without Power: The National Party Committees* (New York: Atherton, 1964), Ch. 6; Theodore H. White, *The Making of the President 1960* (New York: Atheneum, 1961), and *The Making of the President 1964* (New York: Atheneum, 1964); Stanley Kelley, Jr., *Professional Public Relations and Political Power* (Baltimore: The Johns Hopkins Press, 1956), Chs. 6 and 7, and *Political Campaigning* (Washington, D.C.: The Brookings Institution, 1960); Paul Tillett, *Inside Politics: The National Conventions, 1960* (Dobbs Ferry, N.Y.: Oceana, 1962); Nelson W. Polsby and Aaron B. Wildavsky, *Presidential Elections: Strategies of American Electoral Politics* (New York: Scribner, 1964); Daniel M. Ogden, Jr., and Arthur L. Peterson, *Electing the President: 1964* (San Francisco: Chandler, 1964); Hugh A. Bone, *American Politics and the Party System* (New York: McGraw-Hill, 1965), Ch. 14; Charles A. H. Thompson, *Television and Presidential Politics* (Washington, D.C.: The Brookings Institution, 1956). This list is not exhaustive but includes most of the better-known works in this area.

staffing; auxiliary nonparty groups; the volunteer worker; and finally, problems of campaign finance.

Campaign Management

Once nomination for Congress has been gained, a candidate is immediately confronted with pressing problems of campaign planning and administration. Indeed, if the candidate encountered substantial opposition in convention or primary election in securing his nomination, he will have already met the question. Campaign management here includes responsibility for general administration of the entire campaign, including recruitment of, workers, organization of volunteers, coordination of publicity, purchasing, finance, accounting, and general strategy for public scheduling of the candidate's time. If money is the lifeblood of campaigns, the manager is the person whose skill and judgment properly feeds it into the organizational blood stream to maximize its effects. The ultimate success of a campaign, in many close districts in particular, may very well hinge upon the caliber of the manager and headquarters staff. It is necessary, therefore, for any candidate to exercise extraordinary caution in selecting his manager, who is for practical purposes his field marshall for the campaign effort.

V. O. Key, Jr., has suggested that "it is probable that not so much cool calculation or cold cunning enters into the [campaign management] process as might be supposed."[4] Key recognized the frenetic, haphazard quality of most campaigns, but at the same time there is some evidence to show careful planning and deliberate choice on the part of candidates in selecting their managers. Others act on impulse and dismiss the judgment of seasoned advisers, substituting their own talents for that of a manager. Most party professionals believe that serious candidates for even "low" office should never attempt to serve as their own managers. As in this study, those who do manage their own campaigns are often found to be those with a small chance of success, and their carelessness is a reflection both of their inexperience and their political and financial desperation.

A seasoned campaigner would consider the role of the manager in

4. *Politics, Parties and Pressure Groups,* 3rd ed. (New York: Crowell, 1952), pp. 491–92.

his campaign to be second only to the choice of the candidate himself, and this value is particularly applicable to a manager with a string of successful elections behind him. At the same time some managers may serve merely as a campaign "front" for a candidate who manages his own campaign. A number of managers are simply fund raisers operating under the guise of managers. Regardless of his role, once the nomination is at hand and the campaign begins, the need for a manager increases with every passing day.

In this study candidates responded to the question of manager selection in four distinguishable ways: (1) the candidate relies upon trusted (and available) friends or business associates; (2) the candidate serves as his own manager or relies upon his wife, family members, or other close relatives; (3) the political party provides a full- or part-time man to serve as campaign coordinator and manager; or (4) the candidate engages and pays for the services of a professional manager. Obviously these are not mutually exclusive alternatives, and in practice campaign operations and duties of individuals often fall into more than one category. For example, a business associate of a candidate who is also an advertising executive may simultaneously serve the dual role of part-time manager and local party official.

It is also apparent that campaign managers can be further classified into professional or semiprofessional (3 and 4) and amateur (1 and 2). It does not necessarily follow that a paid manager is a political professional in the strict sense of that term.[5] Our data suggest that the professional is one having the political experience and campaign-management skills necessary to serve a candidate. The professional tended to be drawn from advertising and public-relations firms, from the working press, and occasionally from business. Neither is it completely accurate to designate a candidate or his wife as amateurs when they may well have been active and gained experience in previous campaigns. In general these categories and subcategories of management types were accepted as described by the respondents.

5. A professional manager is here defined as one who, for hire, undertakes the administration of time and money devoted to major political campaign activities, such as radio and TV and other advertising placement, scheduling of publicity, direct mail, and special printing efforts; scheduling of the candidate's time in public appearances, "shoe leather" expeditions, and staff coordination; and the overall direction of office operations. Campaign management as here defined obviously cannot be delegated to the representative of the usual advertising or public-relations firm, although these groups played a significant role for many candidates in this study.

As noted in Table 4.1, campaign management for over 80 percent of the candidates fell within the nonprofessional or amateur classes; 60 percent selected friends or business associates (often law or business partners), and 22 percent managed their own campaigns or relied on close relatives (frequently wives or husbands). The remainder, 18 percent, were chosen from within the professional or semiprofessional categories. Some of these "pros" were, in fact, drawn from the ranks of paid party employees or staff members, transferred to the candidate by the party for the duration of the campaign.

Among the losing candidates 60 percent had managers who were business associates or friends—individuals who often found it impossible to serve full time and some of whom were forced to relinquish

Table 4.1

Sources of Campaign Management Personnel

Source	All Losers (N = 229)	Marginals (N = 58)
Friends or Business Associates	60%	57%
Self or Relatives	22	6
Party Officials or Staff	14	15
Professionals	4	22

the manager's role in midcampaign. A California candidate who had employed a politically inexperienced college student to manage his campaign was unable to replace him when he returned to law school in mid-September. A Republican challenger lost a talented, although relatively inexperienced, manager whose business began to have difficulties in midcampaign largely due to his absence. And in late September one candidate was forced to appoint a new manager who was not familiar with the strategy and details of the campaign and who had had no previous role in it. Two managers died in midcampaign, only one of whom, according to the respondents, was replaced by a person of approximately equal skill. There was, it appeared, little to recommend management of these campaigns to experienced people or firms unless the congressional contest was a marginal one. Some of the candidates, after losing managers, tried to push on alone; in retrospect they felt this course to have been vastly more of a personal burden than they should have undertaken, regardless of the cost.

The difficulties encountered by candidates in this study indicate that congressional campaign management should be a full-time job. It should, moreover, be one to which the manager devotes his energies over a considerable period. One candidate, having made do with a part-time paid manager, noted in retrospect, "I must have a full-time, competent manager, must begin earlier and have adequate finances." Echoing this statement, another stated, "I would start a year earlier and try to build a larger and better organization. In our state a congressional candidate is a stepchild and must act for himself."

Most candidates came to realize that the job of the manager does not begin on Labor Day and end with election day. He must be prepared to devote himself to his candidate and the campaign from well before the primary, before the announcement or convention contest, through the mopping-up period following the election. Obviously there are plans to be laid at the beginning and bills to be paid at the end. In the interim campaign management requires constant planning, pleading, publicizing, and protecting of the candidate. A candidate who does not, or is unable to, select a manager able to participate fully in these activities begins his campaign with one strike against him, and regardless of his initial popularity, he stands a remarkably good chance of ending it with three strikes against him.

Among the losers 22 percent either served as their own manager or, for various reasons, chose to rely on close relatives. In this latter case the candidate usually ended up taking a major part in the management chores. Repeated but unsuccessful efforts to attract competent management left some candidates with little choice but personally to assume this burden, and some who importuned relatives found them unable to sacrifice the necessary time and energy.

A few candidates consciously chose to manage their own campaigns. They theorized that "central control" was essential to "good management." A Republican noted that he was relieved of scruples of conscience by not managing his own campaign: "The biggest problem in doing it yourself is that you come to know where this money comes from and goes." He implied that it was safer and more discreet for someone else, a manager or finance chairman, to channel funds, relieving the candidate of the care and worry of staying within the expenditure limitations of the law.

With rare exceptions those candidates who appointed wives or close relatives to managerial posts did so out of desperation. Again, the familiar pattern was displayed. Repeated pleas to associates outside the family to assume the management job had been unproductive.

The candidate, realizing the limitations of his own time, money, and energy during the campaign, then designated one of those closest to him to assume most of the routine burdens. One of the authors, after speaking at a congressional campaign school, was approached by a candidate from a western state and asked, "What would the national committee think if I appointed my wife to be my campaign manager?" The query, made in the presence of his wife, told a great deal about the candidate's background and political sophistication in addition to his chances of success in the contest in which he was engaged. The point of this example is that managers serve a special function in relation to candidates. It is necessary to have a manager who not only knows what to do about the job of running a campaign, but who can also complement the candidate's judgment and bring pressure to bear in various quarters when necessary.

Administrative and political know-how are essential to the campaign manager's job, but political muscle is also a necessity. Few wives or close relatives meet these qualifications or possess the needed detachment to assume this role. If, however, a candidate for Congress has a relative competent enough to carry out these activities, there is no practical barrier to such an arrangement.

An obvious source of management skills is the political party; 14 percent of the respondents relied upon full- or part-time party officials, former candidates, or staff men from the state central committee for assistance in campaign management. A few county chairmen were recruited as managers. Two campaigns were managed by the executive secretaries of state committees, who in each case also coordinated the candidates' efforts with the state campaigns. Management responsibilities were simplified and the chances for election apparently enhanced in those few states where congressional campaigns were coordinated with, and in one instance directed from, state party headquarters. The Republicans in Minnesota with few exceptions operated in this fashion, and campaign activities such as radio tapes, advertising, speaker assignments, campaign caravans, strategy, and advice were centralized through the office of State Chairman Robert Forsythe. Similar support was provided Indiana's Democratic congressional aspirants in 1962 under the energetic leadership of then Chairman Manfred Core.

Only 4 percent of the defeated candidates reported buttressing their campaigns with full-time paid professional managers. Obviously this outlay represented a luxury beyond the fiscal capabilities of most candidates. Although it is vain to speculate on what might have been, it is still highly probable that greater use of professional management would have changed the outcomes in several districts, particularly marginal ones.

Without emphasizing the contrast too greatly, the direction of the marginal campaigns displayed more skill and less do-it-yourself management than was true of the losers as a whole. Among the marginal candidates, 22 percent employed professional managers—over five times the number used by the losers. Without question these candidates, their party leaders, and their supporters recognized the greater probability of victory in their marginal districts and stronger management was attempted to enhance their situation. These were, as a group, far better financed and received considerably more support from national and state party organizations than did the losers. Only 6 percent of the marginals managed do-it-yourself campaigns, a sharp contrast with the losers.

Most respondents clearly recognized their problems of campaign management but just as often appeared to recognize them as agonizingly beyond solution. Most blamed insufficient funds, while others named the lack of experienced personnel as the major problem. One Democrat moaned that if he ever were to run again, he would hope to have a "full-time manager (competent) . . . begin earlier . . . and have adequate finances to pay my assistants." Even some few candidates with no major financial problems were unable to recruit managers with the requisite experience and political acumen. A former state legislator, who made his first bid for high office in this contest, set forth his ideal:

A successful campaign would require a well-organized and coordinated organization in all eight counties. It is necessary for a candidate to have a manager, finance chairman, publicity and public relations people to handle these matters, freeing the candidate completely for campaign activity.

Some candidates were forced to make desperate last-minute choices. One Republican persuaded his ex-primary opponent to serve as his manager, while another, representing the new look among Southern GOP leaders, bravely noted that his manager was "the only other man I knew who was a Republican." In several campaigns the manager was an enthusiastic and loyal student. In one the candidate himself was a college professor whose campaign was "managed" by a committee of his students. Finally, one loser reported with either false piety or sardonic humor that "Jesus Christ" had been his campaign manager. He added that his manager had "abandoned me on election day."

Table 4.2

Sources of Campaign Management by Party

Source	All Losers		Marginals	
	GOP (N = 123)	DEM (N = 106)	GOP (N = 28)	DEM (N = 30)
Friends or Business Associates	61%	59%	43%	70%
Self or Relatives	19	25	14	0
Party Officials or Staff	15	13	18	13
Professionals	5	3	25	17

Because of the inherent limitations of the losing campaign and the personal loyalties created by the close associations of any hard-fought campaign battle, few candidates expressed strong dissatisfaction with their managers. Instead they appeared grateful for what help they had received, and most reserved their resentment for the party officials who did not "come through" as expected and/or promised.[6]

Surprisingly in the matter of campaign management, differences between the candidates by party affiliation were not great. According to the candidates' responses, both parties were equal in their failure to provide professional and financial support for congressional candidates. Table 4.2 indicates that there were no great differences between the parties on sources of management skill for the losers. The marginal candidates, however, differed sharply according to party. Republicans

6. Clapp has noted the resentment against state and national party organizations expressed by incumbent congressmen. He found that state party organizations were relatively unimportant in the campaigns of incumbents and that local party groups were, at times, hostile. While many of Clapp's incumbents argued that national party organizations should not and could not effectively recruit candidates for congressional office, they did insist that these groups provide more and better campaign assistance. This attitude tends to distress both national and congressional campaign committee leaders, whose major efforts at midterm are directed toward helping these incumbents. Some observers familiar with Washington party organizations believe that this kind of disagreement results largely from poor communications between the incumbent congressmen and the party committees. In the judgment of the authors of this study, the separation described by Clapp is in great measure due to the built-in discrepancies between the political and financial foundations of the presidentially oriented national party headquarters organizations and the constituent-service oriented base of the long-term incumbents on Capitol Hill. Whatever the cause, there is resentment among candidates, both incumbent and non-incumbent, against those units of the party. See Charles L. Clapp, *The Congressman: His Work as He Sees It* (Washington, D.C.: The Brookings Institution, 1963), pp. 354–61.

utilized professionals or party staff members in 43 percent of the marginal contests, while Democrats did so in only 30 percent. At the same time Democratic marginals did not depend so heavily upon themselves or their relatives for management skills but relied upon friends and business associates to a greater extent than did the Republicans.

Plainly it is harder to locate experienced managers than it is to write about them. As stated by one candidate:

> Let me say here that I found it extremely difficult to locate anyone who could give time out of his regular employment for this very temporary assignment covering only three or four months of activity. We tried but never came up with anyone.

This shortage of experienced short-term managerial personnel applies to both parties equally and generally to all sections of the country. For the candidates it is a problem not easily overcome. It is not that men are not knowledgeable about campaign work—it is more likely that the most knowledgeable ones are the least able to break away from their professional and business responsibilities to undertake a campaign, even if they happen to be in a district where their skills are needed and their sympathies happen to be with the needy candidates. This situation holds particularly for a "loser," whose situation rarely attracts major support in the first place. Then, too often when capable campaign management can be borrowed, the manager's leave of absence must begin too late and end too soon to allow time for effective campaign organization and administration. The net effect is to leave most campaign operations in the hands of the candidate and whatever headquarters staff he is fortunate enough to recruit from among his volunteers. It is important in the light of this to consider the relationships between the national and district campaign organizations.

The Problem of the District Organization

As we have noted, the incumbent has an established organization—one which is loyal and has been tested in past campaigns. The challenger, however, must make a fresh start and build an ad hoc campaign organization to serve a special short-term need. While the incumbent always appears to "run scared," he has no little faith in his own ability to construct an efficient campaign organization. The newcomer, however, is tempted to rely upon advice of others or the formulas suggested by the official manuals of the party organization. Or he may revert altogether to the campaign style appropriate to local election contests he has experienced before.

The Democrats in 1962 left no room for equivocation for the nonincumbent candidate in attacking his problem of campaign management. The national committee staff, prodded by the veterans of John F. Kennedy's campaigns of 1960 and conscious of the implications of the midterm congressional battle for the presidential contest of 1964, advised all candidates to establish

District Committees, which in turn will consult with the Senate and House Campaign Committees. The Congressional District Chairman will be appointed *only* after consultation with the Democratic National Committee.[7]

Whether all Democratic candidates studied this manual and noted this statement is hard to tell, but very few were aware of the concern manifested by the National Committee for the identity of their campaign chairmen. Most candidates were frantically seeking money, manpower, political know-how, and managerial talent, to combine it all into a working organization. This directive, therefore, reflected DNC intentions rather than actuality for all but a favored few Democratic marginal candidates.

A long-standing thrust for both national party committees has been to centralize and integrate the campaign operations of nonincumbent congressional contenders with their own. The 1962 campaign directives of the Democrats, as reflected in the O'Brien manual illustrate the case nicely. Repeatedly the candidate or his aides were instructed to coordinate their activities with the national office:

It is recognized that you are probably familiar with the most effective campaign techniques in your state. You are urged to utilize them fully—

7. *Democratic Congressional Campaign Manual–1962* (Washington, D.C., Democratic National Committee, 1962), p. 3 (emphasis supplied). This 1962 DNC *Manual* was a rewrite of the famous "O'Brien" manual written by Lawrence F. O'Brien for the 1960 Kennedy campaign. According to the manual, congressional candidates were placed under the direct supervision of the National Committee. Republican candidates, in contrast, worked with both their National Committee and their Congressional Campaign Committee, primary responsibility resting with the latter organization. In recent years GOP national leadership has encouraged the Congressional Committee to assume an increasingly greater role, so that its activities and services now rival and in some areas surpass those of the Republican National Committee staff. This development is more thoroughly explored in Chapter 5.

but it is requested that all of your activity be conducted within the frame-work set forth in this manual to insure a coordinated national congres-sional campaign. Through each step of this procedure, particularly in the selection of campaign leaders, cooperating with existing Democratic Party leadership is mandatory.

CONGRESSIONAL COMMITTEES ON ALL LEVELS AND AT ALL TIMES MUST CONSULT AND COOPERATE WITH THE EXISTING OFFICIAL DEMOCRATIC STATE AND NATIONAL ORGANIZATIONS. [P. 2]

Detailed directions were replete with imperatives—"should," "will," or "must." In spite of the Democratic effort to establish a national congressional campaign, there was little evidence that many candidates actually subscribed to it. This repeated emphasis of the Democratic campaign manual really provides more insight into the White House–National Committee struggle to take over the leadership of the Democratic Congressional Campaign Committee from the Hill committees than it provided the candidates with a practical working relationship with either "Hill" or "Downtown" Democrats.

In any event, there is considerable evidence to show that in 1962 a major shift in congressional campaign leadership was brought about by the Democrats. This shift was of particular benefit to the candidates for marginal seats for whom "all-out" support was provided. On the other hand, candidates for the "hopeless" seats enjoyed the same distant relationships with their own state committees as they did with national committees, despite the major programs provided them in candidate conferences, the flood of published material, and the like.

For those candidates lucky enough to have a choice, prior to ap-pointing their managers and assembling their staffs, some consulta-tion should be undertaken with both state and national party officials. Less than one-fourth of the respondents in this study indicated that such consultations or contacts actually took place. Some marginal candidates (and a few nonmarginals) did receive organized assistance from field men representing the national parties; these were spread far too thinly, however, since neither party was able to field nearly enough men. The Republican National Congressional Committee, for example, was able to use only nine field men to cover the entire nation for no more than ten weeks of the campaign. They were con-centrated in marginal districts, but even if all marginal candidates had been covered, each GOP field man would have been assigned to an average of seven or eight districts each, incumbents and nonincum-bents included. It is quite obvious that it is physically impossible to accomplish such an assignment at a level commensurate with need.

Raymond Moley has estimated the number of field men needed by each party for a fully manned congressional campaign to range as high as 200.[8] Restrictions on the use of field men were imposed by shortages of money and trained or experienced personnel. Other observers were of the opinion that Moley's estimate was far too high. They noted that far fewer field men than that would have enabled the parties to perform more effectively in the 1962 congressional campaigns. One staff member of the Republican National Congressional Committee voiced the opinion that twenty-five trained full-time field men would have had a major impact upon the outcome of the House contests (particularly the marginals) for the GOP. The Democrats in 1962 had the great advantage of occupying the White House and consequently were able to borrow "advance men" from the political cadres of certain executive agencies for the purpose of assisting candidates with campaign management and strategy.

Candidates, of course, differ in many respects—both in what they offer to the voters and in their needs as candidates. Some are more knowledgeable and vastly more experienced than others; some are articulate and project an effective "image," while others do not; some are well financed, but the great majority are hard-pressed for funds. But each candidate, incumbent or nonincumbent, needs a capable and effective campaign organization. It is to this end that campaign manuals, handbooks, schools for candidates, and the efforts of field men are directed. According to the ideal model, a congressional district campaign chairman (manager) should be responsible for the entire campaign effort. He should supervise the staff, serve as chief of operations, direct chairmen for other campaign activities, and coordinate the strategy and planning for the campaign. He should be responsible for establishing the speaker's bureau, schedule public appearances for the candidate, and serve as liaison between the candidate, his staff, and state and national party organization and officials.

Headquarters Staffing

If experienced general campaign management is a luxury known to few of the losing candidates and to well under half of the marginals, the candidate faces yet another formidable problem in staffing his

8. Moley, p. 192.

headquarters and providing for the multitude of routine and special tasks of a campaign office. This section will review briefly the manner in which the nonincumbent candidates provided for headquarters office staff and, in addition, for other major campaign functions which a "model" organization manual might require.

At this lower echelon of campaign administration the candidate can be easily damaged if the routines of scheduling, materials distribution, press relations, management of volunteers, and transportation are not handled in an efficient manner. Again, no general pool of skilled manpower is available. Friends and associates of the candidate, his own employees, or an occasional party stalwart fill these roles under the direction of the candidate or his manager, if one exists. Most candidates must therefore recruit and train their staffs for the complex duties of headquarters operations.

There is little need to reemphasize at this juncture the advantages of incumbency. As an index, candidates were asked to indicate whether they had engaged paid staff, and how many were employed for the bulk of the campaign in headquarters operations. It was also assumed that every incumbent congressman provided himself with at least some paid office staff, just as they did with general campaign management.

Only 57 percent of the losers in this study had *at least one* paid office staff member during their campaigns. The average number of paid office staff for all losers was 2.4 persons—2.3 for the Democrats and 2.5 for the Republican candidates. The marginal candidates fared better with 86 percent (90 percent of GOP and 81 percent of the Democrats) reporting hiring one or more staff. The number of paid workers per candidate averaged 2.9, 16 percent more than the losers. Republicans averaged 3.1 and Democrats 2.8 paid staff members per candidate. While these figures do not offer startling insight into headquarters operations of the nonincumbent candidates, they do throw additional light upon the problems of campaign organization and management.

Since the employer-candidate typically works without benefit of seasoned political managers, his work with his own staff involves on-the-job training for both boss and helpers alike. A Democratic loser from a western state expressed his position graphically:

I had employed one young man who left for California in August. After that, one young woman. She kept my headquarters open downtown, kept card files, received contributions, wrote receipts, answered mail, gave out or mailed requested literature, supervised volunteer workers in mailings and door-to-door distributions, answered the phone, kept the windows clean, and made timely posters.

This candidate, with no professional campaign manager and with one paid office worker, challenged a Republican incumbent in an urban district containing over 400,000 people and nearly 200,000 voters. The candidate ultimately polled less than 30 percent of the vote.

An impression of the level of skill provided by some headquarters staffers is suggested by the candidate who had not only a paid manager, but also two paid assistants. Of the latter he wrote: "Besides the manager, I had my nephew out of college. He was my leg man and driver. I also had a campaign 'aide' and promotion man whom I had to sack for dishonesty." Obviously the fact that money was spent for headquarters staff does not mean it was spent wisely or that the investment yielded the anticipated results. Without a doubt the quality of headquarters operations for the nonincumbent candidate was lower than it was for the incumbent. And there was little he could do about the situation, since the incumbent's advantage was a result of his incumbency.

Most candidates also operated with "chairmen" for publicity, finance, and other operations on a volunteer, part-time basis. How did the candidates in this study fare in these areas of headquarters operations? First of all, many candidates of necessity secured their finance chairman before seeking a campaign manager. Indeed, the availability of a finance chairman made the decision to run possible for a few. This fact only highlights both the importance and the scarcity of money for the challenger contestant, for the lot of a finance chairman in a one-sided contest is not a happy one. He must somehow persuade the party's known supporters to contribute to the candidacy of a man who may be relatively unknown in a district where there has been in the past little chance of success; moreover, he must raise money in direct competition with better-known standard bearers on his own ticket who do stand a chance for either election or reelection. As a consequence, the congressional candidates in this study repeatedly complained that bills arrived at a faster rate than did the money to pay for them, and for many, sizable obligations remained after the election. Such bills are always the candidate's responsibility.

The postwar period has been accurately described as the era of mass communications. There are strong indications that television, in particular, is altering the electoral process by providing intense audience participation in all current events, giving these events and their actors a political dimension and power which, on reflection, is highly important for traditional democratic theory. The quixotic new jargon of Marshall McLuhan describes the impact upon popular culture and sensibilities of the mass electronic media. Nowhere has this change been more dramatic than in the merciless screening it imposes upon candidates for high public office. Indeed the "cool" candidates (e.g. JFK) have been best suited for and best able to exploit the "cool" medium (TV) in all those campaigns wherein a mass appeal requires a candidate to "come across" with a strong image to the voter whose living room, in McLuhan's phrase, has become his voting booth.[9] It is not our purpose to dwell here on the McLuhanesque paradoxes which the electronic media thrust upon campaigning for public office. Our purpose is simply to point out the powerful need for the unknown, nonincumbent candidate to seek publicity and therefore to utilize this medium in his campaign.

Not realizing fully the high cost of access to radio, TV, and even display newspaper advertising, the nonincumbent finds, to his dismay, what the incumbent already knows—that he must "make his news" by buying time and space rather than through official announcements, dedications, luncheon speeches, and the hundred other ways by which incumbents make their presence officially known and felt.

Under these circumstances the publicity chairman assumes a highly significant role in the congressional campaign. For it will be to this area that the candidate will allot the greatest portion of his dollar outlay. To compound the problem, it is one activity of his staff operations, which requires the greatest professional skill; it is becoming a truism that a realistic candidate cannot operate his own publicity, public relations, and advertising programs. To offset the advantages of incumbency, he must have professional help.

Our data nevertheless shows that not more than one-fourth of the candidates appointed separate chairmen for publicity. Those who did not usually assigned the public relations and advertising burden to their campaign managers; 47 percent of the losers and 61 percent of the marginals hired advertising or PR firms or had them available to assist in all or part of their campaigns (see Chapter 5).

The function of the publicity chairman in headquarters staffing does

9. H. Marshall McLuhan, *Understanding Media: The Extensions of Man* (New York: McGraw-Hill, 1964) and *The Medium is the Massage,* with Quentin Fiore, coordinated by Jerome Agel (New York: Bantam, 1967).

not consist merely of the purchase of time and space in the media. He must see that these matters are attended to, true, but his task is also to nurture relationships with the working press; assist with speeches, interviews, and debates; and prepare routine press releases. Some headquarters operations will also provide basic "research" services by accumulating a file of press clipping on the opposition and by monitoring the candidate's own activities and public utterances.

In addition to filling these headquarters staff positions, the non-incumbent candidate for Congress, depending upon the complexion of his district, may designate a chairman for special groups. This post is a particularly necessary one when the incumbent's political base and organization do not adequately reflect the coalition of voters necessary to win. Republican challengers, particularly in urban districts, were faced with support-building efforts by establishing special campaign groups with ethnic and racial accents. The Democratic campaign manual minced no words about the necessity for candidates to create special campaign groups to reflect the diverse elements of their constituencies more accurately. Such groups also provide the means from which candidates can draw strength. The Democrats were able to drive home the achievements of the Kennedy legislative program: youth, senior citizens, businessmen, labor, and the usual ethnic groups.

When all these duties are assessed and compared to those available to incumbent congressmen, the disadvantages of nonincumbency once more become glaringly apparent. Incumbents, as noted elsewhere, are in a strong position regarding management skills, headquarters staff, and access to the media. Clapp reports that a majority of congressmen maintain permanent district offices and that the rest establish them during election season in one or more district locations.[10] Avery Leiserson has noted regional variations in the pattern of congressional district offices, those in the West and South being manned by a political subordinate to the congressman who manages all his political affairs in the district. More rarely the head of the district-office works closely with group and party organizations. By and large, however, the congressman establishes his own personal organization and uses his own staff to keep it alive between elections.[11]

The day-by-day duties of campaign-staff workers defy description. They range from licking stamps to making impromptu speeches. Some distribute bumper stickers, while others work the county fairs. Volun-

10. Clapp, pp. 66–67.
11. "National Party Organizations and Congressional Districts," *Western Political Quarterly*, 16, 3 (September 1963), 645.

teers must be supervised to see that their energy is not wasted and their talents are properly used.

The 43 percent of the non incumbents who had no paid office staff found it necessary to organize their campaign headquarters using relatives, friends, and volunteers as staff. A real source of strength for many of these candidates was the auxiliary nonparty organization, closely related to, but many times distinct from, the special-group activities already described. Such groups often made up organizational deficits and thereby made major contributions to the candidates' efforts.

The Auxiliary Nonparty Organization

Auxiliary nonparty organizations are agencies set up under nonparty names to accomplish partisan ends. Their purpose is to lure supporters across party lines and to mobilize the support of voters not directly attracted to either party. Such groups have long been standard fixtures of presidential campaigns, and few people question the ring of "Citizens for Eisenhower" or "Volunteers for Stevenson"; they are treated as gatherings of public-spirited citizens. These groups provide avenues of useful political participation for those individuals who wish to work on behalf of a candidate but who do not wish to be aligned with his party. They serve other useful purposes as well: they allow any candidate to attempt to identify his name and his cause with the commonweal, so broad is the American political orthodoxy. By so doing, the candidate tacitly acknowledges that there is a public welfare superior to that espoused by this party. In any event, by using them he gains access to unaffiliated voters, community leaders, and dissidents from the opposition.

Auxiliary nonparty organizations occur in infinite variety, but the typical titles run: "Buncombe for Congress," "Friends of Buncombe," "Independents [or Volunteers or Citizens] for Buncombe." Special group appeal is added by enlisting doctors, Polish or Spanish Americans, senior citizens, and the like. These groups provide a further convenience in permitting outside control of some campaign expenditures, preventing official party organizations from falling into the snare of laws regulating or limiting campaign expenditures and reporting. Ostensibly set up as independent or quasi-independent organizations, the auxiliary nonparty group can free the candidate of some financial worry, draw upon fresh sources of funds, and accomplish these ends without imposing new burdens upon his office staff.

But it is in the area of campaign manpower in which auxiliary nonparty groups make their most important contribution to the congressional campaigns. They often reach people by asking for their help while at the same time asking for their votes.

Auxiliary nonparty groups were established by 73 percent of the losing candidates in this study and by 88 percent of the marginals. Republicans relied on them to a greater degree than did Democrats —a reflection of GOP efforts to overcome major problems of organizational weakness in urban areas and in the South. They also provided a means by which the GOP could broaden its appeal to those who were not identified Republicans.

Councils of Senior Citizens were established by the Democrats to focus attention on the program of medical care for the aging urged on the Congress by the Kennedy administration. Senior Citizens' groups pointed out the "obstructionism" of the Republican incumbents on the Medicare question and were closely tied to the Democratic National Committee campaign programs. Republicans, for their part, sought to defend their position on the question by forming "Doctors for Smith" and "Healing Arts Committee for Jones"; they were aided in these efforts by a nationwide mobilization sponsored by a unit of the American Medical Association, the American Medical Political Action Committee (AMPAC).

An older form of the auxiliary nonparty group, one particularly useful in one-party areas, is the party-switch group. Used frequently by Republicans in the South, these organizations took the form of "Democrats for (Republican)" or "Rebels for (Republican)." The elemental nature of this strategy was pointed out by one Republican, who observed: "Because of the overwhelming Democratic strength we had to rely upon dissident and conservative Democrats. So we first attempted to form these nonpartisan groups." Another Southern candidate noted, "Our major effort in setting up a group was getting support from the conservative elements of the Democratic party."

What of the role of regular and district party organizations in establishing auxiliary nonparty campaign groups for congressional candidates? Most of them (75 percent) were set up with the direct help of the candidate's own organization, while others were established in a collaboration of the party and the candidate. Such was the method used in setting up the Senior Citizens and American Medical Political Action Committee groups. The Republicans were particularly vigorous in forming nonparty groups. One candidate reported that his entire campaign was focused in this area: "We let the party worry about getting out the Republican vote. We organized extensively outside the party for all other activities." Another reported that his non-party efforts had "brought 2500–3000 new workers into the campaign. . . . Citizens for _____, Doctors for _____, Fair Play for _____ (to offset ethnic pressures)." A border-state Republican candidate wrote:

> Considerable effort was made. . . . There was virtually no party structure and absolutely no party campaign structure. Ninety percent of my workers were Democrats and Independents, using _____ for Congress Committee.

While these candidates, like most underdog Republicans, relied heavily on the nonparty groups, one candidate from a state with a newly rebuilt GOP organization stated:

> We decided to run a Republican campaign. Of course, volunteers helped all over the state who were not part of the regular party organization, but they were primarily Republicans and worked closely with the Republican official family.

Democrats relied somewhat less on the auxiliary nonparty group as an organizational device. While several noted that "volunteers were organized and proved our most effective force," others felt that "some attempts were made. . . . A real independent group might have offended the party organization," and "We tried to organize _____ for Congress Committees in each county. This was either directly opposed or reluctantly accepted by county organizations." But again and again, for both parties, it appeared that the auxiliary nonparty group provided organization where the party's was lacking or moribund. A number of candidates in both parties depended on these groups for sponsorship of their radio and TV spots and for display advertising bylines.

Republicans more than Democrats reported these groups as "effective" in aiding their campaigns. In contrast with 42 percent of the Democratic losers, 68 percent of the GOP losers indicated that nonparty auxiliary efforts were effective, and comparable percentages were shown in response to the matter of evaluating the relation of these groups to the candidate's campaign staff. By and large the Republicans reported more extensive use, more direct sponsorship, and better working relationships between the regulars and the auxiliaries than did the Democrats.

The traditional partisan notion of "regularity" and its scientific counterpart, "party responsibility," do not easily tolerate the auxiliary nonparty organization. Like dual unionism in the labor movement, they were considered schismatic affronts to the "regulars" by many, and most frequently by Democrats. But in the absence of adequate district party apparatus, the candidates in most cases had little choice but to form auxiliary groups. Too often the legitimate party structure in the district had gone unused for years and lacked the will or the means to sponsor a vigorous congressional contest, let alone work to win. In still other districts no party organization existed at all. To mount a campaign under either circumstance meant that the candidate had to revamp an old party, build a parallel auxiliary group, or build a new party structure.

More frequently, however, the auxiliary nonparty organization occupied a "mixed" relationship to the regular party. Activities were coordinated with party units, but at the same time the auxiliary groups supplied money, sponsorship, and manpower which the party regulars were unable or unwilling to do. Because of the historic thinness of Republican party structure in certain areas, anything which contributed to a strengthened party apparatus was welcomed by Republican leaders.

No candidate in either party reported that any encouragement or initiative in establishing the nonparty groups was provided by the "regulars"; 68 percent were set up by the candidates themselves, and the remaining 32 percent were set up by friends and associates of the candidates. Occasionally the candidate was assisted by an advance man from the national committees.

What, in retrospect, can be said of these auxiliary units? They were, for the most part, developed on a short-term basis to provide and generate extraparty support. Further, we find that these groups do not fit within the normal party apparatus, nor are their existence and activities always sanctioned, particularly by Democrats. In 1962 the auxiliary nonparty organization was, for the losing candidates, a means of "depolarizing" and reducing the ideological gap between the parties and the candidates. Many of these districts were extremely one-sided, and most of the candidates found it essential to reduce and mitigate polarization between the parties, not increase it. Groups based upon professional, social, and ethnic criteria were designed to do just that. They were established to appeal to dissidents and the unaffiliated, persons out of reach of partisan commitment with the old labels but who might be attracted to a candidate for other reasons.

So long as the American party structures and political behavior remain local in focus and decentralized in operation, it would seem that party officials might lend more overt support to the establishment of nonparty auxiliary groups, particularly in the effort to establish competition between the parties in a great number of areas and congressional districts. Certainly the traditional advocates of party reform omit mention of the special significance of the nonparty group. Few candidates actually sought to undercut the official party; instead, they sought votes and support as best they could in a direct pragmatic spirit. They created auxiliary groups in response to that need.

Campaign Manpower: Volunteers and Workers

Aside from the basic tasks of headquarters staffing, establishing management direction, and nonparty auxiliary groups, every congressional candidate must mobilize workers in sufficient numbers to get his campaign under way and sustain it through election day. In addition, he must constantly increase the tempo of the campaign and maintain its momentum as election day approaches. Most candidates necessarily rely upon volunteers, who with a minimum of supervision and coordination can add much-needed "muscle" to the effort. Volunteers are differentiated from regular party workers in that their role is to assist individual candidates rather than the party as a whole. Without them many congressional campaigns, especially those of the nonincumbents, might take off but never become airborne. Indeed, they often formed the backbone of the campaign effort.[12] In marginal districts literally hundreds of volunteers assumed a wide range of tasks, and many became proficient in campaign skills. Other candidates were lucky to find a few volunteers to man the headquarters phones during the working day. For the most part the volunteer makes up in enthusiasm what he lacks in sophistication, and he undertakes the menial work of the campaign. Several candidates noted that even an ineffective worker can lick stamps and stuff envelopes.

12. For an excellent analysis of the role of campaign workers and volunteers, see Dwaine Marvick, "The Middleman in Politics," in *Approaches to the Study of Party Organization,* ed. William J. Crotty (Boston: Allyn and Bacon, 1968), pp. 341–74.

Although many workers actually volunteered, most were recruited directly through nonparty groups. *The Democratic Congressional Campaign Manual, 1962* assigns this as a duty of the local campaign manager, under the aegis of the party.

Volunteer workers are the backbone of every political organization. It would be difficult and impractical—if not impossible—to conduct a successful campaign without adequate numbers of dedicated volunteer workers. . . .

Volunteers should be recruited from all possible sources, including, where practical, these:

1. persons who have spontaneously offered their services in the Kennedy campaign or in other Democratic campaigns.
2. political action and education committees of labor unions.
3. colleges and high schools.
4. churches, civic and social clubs.
5. persons who express a desire for political experience.
6. mass mailing.
7. the wives, husbands, sons, daughters, sisters, brothers, fathers, mothers, aunts, uncles, cousins and friends of everyone in the first five categories. [Pp. 13–14]

Speakers at the sessions of the campaign schools and candidate conferences conducted by each party during the spring and summer of 1962 exhorted the participants to develop a reservoir of volunteer talent to overcome the natural attrition and to swell the ranks at the peak of the campaign.

Each candidate in this study was asked: "How many volunteers contributed a substantial amount of time to your campaign head-quarters?" To respond to this question the respondent typically had to rely upon educated guesses, but a spot check suggested that the results were reasonably accurate estimates of the actual number of volunteers who actively took part in each campaign.

Over 80 percent of the respondents were assisted in their campaign efforts by volunteers. A total of fifteen thousand workers took part, ranging from as few as two to as many as a thousand per candidate. Although the average number of workers per candidate was seventy-seven, the Republicans were more successful than the Democrats in attracting volunteers, averaging ninety-nine volunteers to the Democrats' forty-nine per candidate. The differences are not difficult to explain when it is seen that the GOP candidates with unusually large numbers of volunteers were concentrated in suburban districts, where the demographic characteristics of the voter and political ethos lends itself to volunteer activity. It is vastly more difficult to recruit volunteers in the cities, where the problem of access to voters is serious unless the party in question is rooted in older neighborhoods with traditional political structures and ties. In the South the GOP candidates found volunteer help their chief support, and in many areas volunteers turned out in substantial numbers.

The marginals were more successful in developing volunteer manpower resources than were the losers. Marginal candidates reported an average of 119 volunteers each: 135 per candidate for the Republicans, and 113 for the Democrats (see Table 4.3). As in so many other respects, the marginal candidates were better able to recruit and sustain cadres of volunteer workers for the work of routine campaign operations. Republican strength in recruitment of volunteers for the marginals can be explained in part by their national

Table 4.3

Average Number of Volunteer Workers Per Candidate By Party

Class of Candidates	Republicans	Democrats	Both Parties
All Losing Candidates	99 (N = 108)	49 (N = 85)	77 (N = 193)
All Marginal Candidates	135 (N = 26)	113 (N = 27)	119 (N = 53)
Marginal Winners	301 (N = 5)	132 (N = 10)	189 (N = 15)
Marginal Losers	96 (N = 21)	86 (N = 17)	91 (N = 38)

effort to whittle down the Democratic margins in the Congress at mid-term, in addition to the reasons previously noted.

Although few in number, the marginal winners in this study utilized over three times as many volunteer workers per candidate as did the losers as a group. The comparisons between the Democratic marginal winners, marginal losers, and all losers, is similar to the Republican figures and points to the obvious conclusion: that those who had a greater chance of winning in 1962 were better able to recruit volunteer manpower to sustain their campaign efforts.

In Table 4.4 we have grouped the congressional losers and marginals according to size of volunteer cadres. The modal group for both the losers and the marginals is twenty-one to one hundred volunteers. When analyzed by party, Democrats in greater numbers were found to develop small cadres of one to twenty volunteers.

While 25 percent of the Republican losers reported using a hundred or more volunteers, only 7 percent of the Democrats reported using that many. The findings in Tables 4.3 and 4.4 demonstrate once

Table 4.4
Percent of Candidates by Number of Volunteers: All Losers and Marginals Compared

Percent of Candidates	All Losers			Marginals		
	GOP (N = 128)	DEM (N = 110)	BOTH (N = 238)	GOP (N = 30)	DEM (N = 32)	BOTH (N = 62)
1 to 20 Volunteers	30%	46%	37%	23%	37%	31%
21 to 100 Volunteers	32	30	31	33	31	32
Over 100 Volunteers	25	7	17	30	16	22
Not Known	13	17	15	14	16	15

again the greater ability of the marginal candidates, particularly the Republicans, to recruit volunteer manpower.

In this section we have considered the volunteer workers from the perspective of the candidate, with special emphasis on his ability to attract them as his party's condition and the marginality of the contest varied. The structure of this study did not permit—indeed, did not warrant—a study of volunteers per se. As a consequence we are unable to say why workers volunteered, to analyze political motivation, to describe what tasks they performed for their candidates, or to name their social characteristics. On the basis of our knowledge of these campaigns, there is little reason to believe that these characteristics of the 1962 crop of congressional campaign volunteers were materially different from those in other campaigns.

An important study of campaign workers which bears on this point is that of Dwaine Marvick and Charles Nixon, who collected attitudinal data from party workers in the state assembly districts of Los Angeles in the 1956 general election campaign. Some of these findings are worth noting here, since they appear to provide insight into the social structure and motivations of volunteer political workers. Marvick and Nixon found four elements. (1) Types of campaign workers can be distinguished by the roles they play in the campaign organization; i.e. skills, personalities, predispositions, and other characteristics tend to project individuals into particular campaign roles. (2) The composition of political organizations at the local level (one step above which are the congressional district organizations) are closely related to the social characteristics of the community. (3) Volunteer workers closely reflect the upper echelons of party membership in the community; i.e. Republicans tend to represent majority religious groups, upper socioeconomic status, more prestigious occupations, higher social and educational backgrounds, longer community residence, and higher income. (4) Volunteers in both parties were middle class, and neither presented a true cross section of community class structure.[13]

Marvick and Nixon reported that the motives of the Los Angeles party volunteer workers were generally altruistic:

Concern with public issues, strong party loyalty, and feelings of community obligation were the explanations widely said to be "very impor-

13. Dwaine Marvick and Charles Nixon, "Recruitment Contrasts in Rival Campaign Groups," in Dwaine Marvick, *Political Decision-Makers: Recruitment and Performance,* ed. Dwaine Marvick (New York: Free Press, 1961), pp. 193–217.

tant" by Democrats and Republicans alike; making business contacts, being close to influential people, and furthering personal political ambition were the explanations least acceptable. Sizable groups included being a friend of the candidate, making social contacts and friendships, enjoying the fun and excitement of campaigns and feeling that politics was a part of their way of life. [P. 208]

From personal observation and the evidence found in this study we believe that volunteer congressional campaign workers of 1962 clearly fall within the context of the Marvick-Nixon description. Most political volunteers have little to gain personally from their participation. A representative volunteer devoted to defending veteran Congressman Walter Judd's seat in Minneapolis' reapportioned Fifth District stated:

I'm here because I respect Dr. Judd. He has been a good congressman and they are trying to do him out of his seat by changing the district. We have over 200 people working right here in this office to prevent it. I've never worked before, but I don't like what they are doing.

Without a doubt the fifty or more volunteers reported to have worked for Congressman Judd's victorious opponent, youthful State Senator Donald Fraser, would have expressed similar sentiments of personal loyalty and firm belief in the justice of their candidate's cause. In summary, the volunteer workers volunteer because of their identification with the candidate and his cause rather than out of loyalty to or devotion to the political party.

Campaign Finance

When dealing with political money, one must distinguish between party finance and campaign finance. Party finance includes all the money necessary to keep local, state, and national party organizations and machinery operating between elections. Millions of dollars are required to keep the various party headquarters open, pay permanent staff salaries, conduct research, and engage in public relations. The levels of expenditure vary greatly from state to state and range from hundreds of thousands of dollars for maintenance of downtown office suites and staff to the minimal amounts needed to pay for a storefront and a part-time secretary. Local party finance is equally varied, depending upon the level of the activity of the local party apparatus.

Both major political parties find it difficult to maintain a steady flow of income in the periods between elections. This is particularly true of those party units not having a recent record of success at the polls; but an incumbent party also finds it difficult to sustain the level of interest sufficient to pry open the pocketbooks of the faithful. Yet a viable party organization cannot simply disband headquarters operations between elections. These are essential to the health of the party, for it is nearly impossible to gear up for a new campaign at almost any level without a minimal organizational base. Depending upon the condition and aspirations of the party unit, state and local party leaders and executives, like their counterparts at national party headquarters in Washington, must therefore seek funds to pay for the day-to-day cost of operating the party machinery.

Campaign finance is the collection and expenditure of money for political campaign purposes during an election period. It may or may not be centralized in particular units of the party apparatus, and it is most frequently a shared activity including interest groups, volunteer and citizen committees, individual donors, borrowing, and above all the resources of the candidate and his immediate associates. In this section we deal specifically with that money collected and spent on behalf of the 1962 congressional candidates. For most of them campaign finance was an episodic, single-shot operation and did not involve a continuing need for extended contributions before or beyond the election campaign itself.[14]

Any discussion of campaign finance at the congressional district level must necessarily take cognizance of the problems inherent in a study of political money. The chief of these is that loopholes and flexible interpretation of loosely drawn campaign and party finance laws make it impossible to account accurately for many dollars that are actually spent. Only a dozen or so states have financial reporting and disclosure laws with safeguards stringent enough to guarantee some degree of accuracy in official reporting. Moreover, unrealistic expenditure limits in federal statutes force most congressional candidates to disperse effort and responsibility for campaign finance so as to make meaningful reports difficult. Furthermore, such reports as

14. More complete discussions and treatment of party and campaign finance will be found in the publications of the Citizens' Research Foundation, Princeton, N.J., and Congressional Quarterly, Inc. The most thorough treatment of political finance remains that of Alexander Heard, *The Costs of Democracy: Financing American Political Campaigns* (Chapel Hill: The University of North Carolina Press, 1960). See also Cotter and Hennessy, pp. 173–90; Bone, pp. 404–31; Ogden and Peterson, pp. 197–223; and V. O. Key, Jr., pp. 489–519.

are required are filed at state capitols and make systematic compilation difficult.

This discussion of congressional campaign finance is drawn from two primary sources: questionnaire responses from the candidates in this study and reports filed with the Clerk of the House of Representatives as compiled and published by the *Congressional Quarterly*. Within the limits set by available data we shall consider fund-raising and campaign expenditures first in the primary nominating process and then in the general election campaign itself.

FINANCING CONGRESSIONAL PRIMARIES

With regard to the financing of primary campaigns, Alexander Heard has noted:

> The ability to raise money for *nomination* campaigns . . . is crucial. Here, political careers are launched or thwarted. Here, persons with access to money find their greatest opportunity to influence the selection of public officials, and therefore the conduct of the public's business. Party labels automatically attract dollars as well as votes. An aspiring politician is more exposed to the influence of the political financiers before he gets on the ticket than after. [P. 321]

Heard's observation is probably more true of presidential, senatorial, and gubernatorial candidacies than it is of congressional ones. The number of self-starters and the number of defeated nonincumbents in this study who exclusively financed their own primary campaigns strongly suggests that congressional candidates are less influenced in their decisions to run by promises of financial assistance than are candidates at other levels. That is not to say, of course, that some candidates do not make or receive financial commitments before announcing. In this study, however, most did not.

Table 4.5 suggests that candidates for Congress rely heavily upon their own resources or upon those of immediate friends and associates in financing primary campaigns. Democrats appear to have dug deeper into their own pockets than did GOP primary contestants, who received preponderant support from friends and associates. Marginal candidates in both parties received more support from friends and associates than did the losers. Organized nonparty groups are relatively unimportant, although labor furnished limited financial assistance to some Democrats. To a lesser extent GOP primary contests were aided by medical groups seeking advocates in opposition to medical-insurance legislation.

Table 4.5

Sources of Primary Campaign Funds for Losing and Marginal Candidates

	Losers		Marginals	
	GOP (N = 88)	DEM (N = 51)	GOP (N = 18)	DEM (N = 19)
Personal and Family Funds	28%	54%	22%	21%
Friends and Associates	61	26	67	42
Organized Groups				
Labor		12		16
Medicine	2		5.5	
Party Organizations	9	8	5.5	21

The evidence of Table 4.5 concerning party support of congressional candidates in primary elections may appear surprising. Indeed, one of the maxims of the primary election system requires neutrality of party officers and organizational units during primary contests. Moreover, the table suggests that Democrats were far more active in support of their marginal candidates in primaries than were Republicans and that losers of both parties received, in equal proportion, party support in their efforts to win primary nominations. Our investigations show that some of these primaries were "token" contests, while others were in districts in which endorsement of primary candidates was provided by law or party custom. It also reveals the wider organizational base enjoyed by Democrats in fielding candidates.

In no instance was it found that national party committees lent direct financial support to primary contestants. Rather, it came from state and local party units and ranged in form from party-sponsored fund-raising affairs in uncontested primary situations to party endorsement and support in others. In summary, Table 4.5 indicates that the financing of primary election campaigns in the congressional nonincumbent contests is largely a matter of the candidate's own resources and those of his immediate friends and associates.

Financing the General Election Campaign

Once the primary is over, the winning congressional nominee must begin in earnest to raise funds and solicit support for his general election campaign. The time in which to accomplish this goal is short, and his success depends on a number of factors. The most important of these is the skill of his own managers and organization at fund raising. Another, of great significance, is the primary election calendar in the candidate's own state. A handful of states hold primaries in September, allowing eight weeks or less for the entire campaign effort. Other candidates are more fortunate in having four to six months in which to develop support.

At the outset nearly all candidates find to their dismay that little or no support will be forthcoming from their party's coffers. Many respondents indicated that they were totally unaware of the financial conditions of the party and simply assumed that campaign funds would appear from that source. After the election some of these were quick to blame defeat upon one or more levels of the party hierarchy, when in fact they had only been tripped up by problems endemic to the party system itself.

It is nearly impossible to say what an "average" general election campaign for a nonincumbent congressional contest costs. It has been pointed out earlier that financial reporting laws are loosely drawn and unrealistic in scope, so that violations are wholesale and compliance in all too many instances is an empty gesture. The Federal Corrupt Practices Act limits candidates for the House to campaign expenditures of $2,500 or to an amount calculated by multiplying three cents by the total number of votes cast for the office in the previous general election but not to exceed $5,000.

Certain expenditures are exempt from this limitation: state filing fees or assessments, which are levied against the candidate; personal subsistence or travel allowances; and materials expenditures such as postage, printing, and stationery. All congressional candidates, winners or losers, are required to file with the Clerk of the House an itemized statement of all contributions received and expenditures made by him or by any person acting in his behalf with his consent or knowledge. State laws are not affected by the federal statutes unless the state prescribes a smaller maximum expenditure.

If a political committee does not extend across state lines but operates only within a congressional district, federal law does not require reports of receipts and expenditures from political campaign committees. No federal executive department or agency has ever been designated to require submission of reports or to levy inconsequential penalties. The effectiveness of the legislation lies in its disclosure provisions. Since the Congressional Reorganization Act of 1946 and the development of various reporting services, national attention has been focused on campaign costs and reporting at the congressional level.

Obviously, aside from the loose-jointed nature of political activity itself, the loopholes in federal statutes and the wide variety of state laws together make it difficult to determine the costs of congressional campaigns. The multiplication of campaign committees permits candidates easily to overcome any legal ceilings on expenditures made within a district. And finally, the availability of direct services covered as business expenses adds to the difficulties of determining the real cost of campaigns.

In recent years the national party organizations have been increasingly concerned with raising and spending money for congressional and senatorial contests. Republicans in the late 1930s, following their landslide defeat in 1936, unified their national fund raising by establishing the Republican National Finance Committee. This body, elected to reflect the political and financial geography of the party, also includes the state finance chairmen from most of the states. Since the unified approach is dependent upon a quota system, the inclusion of the state financial chairmen provides necessary liaison and cooperation.

The quota system broke down during the 1964 election, as Senator Goldwater's supporters proved that national money could be raised independently of the unified system and as the congressional Republicans struck out on their own to raise funds for their campaigns. By 1966, however, efforts were again being made to unify money gathering through centralized control of the intake through the National Finance Committee. Eleven regional networks were created to finance national and state committees, and the Republican proclivity for unified fund raising began to reassert itself.

In 1962, however, the collapse of centralized funding had not become manifest. Money raised through the Finance Committee was allocated to the three campaign committees according to budgets submitted by them in advance. The National Committee did not provide funds to individual candidates (except on rare occasions), and the Senate Campaign Committee used its share for senatorial contests. Only the National Republican Congressional Committee distributed funds from national sources to congressional candidates.

Funding for the Democratic national party is ordinarily channeled through both the Democratic National Committee and the Congressional Committee. In 1961, however, an agreement was reached among Vice-President Lyndon Johnson, Speaker of the House Sam Rayburn, Congressional Committee Chairman Michael Kirwan, Senate Campaign Committee Chairman Vance Hartke, and Democratic National Treasurer Matthew McCloskey which called for the National Committee to raise all funds at the national level and to dispense them to the two Hill committees in two lump sums totaling $600,000 per year. In addition the agreement called for the payment of $10,000 monthly to each committee for operating expenses. In return it was understood that the Senate and House Committees would not conduct separate fund-raising dinners. This agreement was operative for the first time in the 1962 congressional campaign.[15]

Traditionally campaign funds on the Hill had been channeled to those Democrats who were: incumbents of long standing (southerners), incumbents and/or districts with a history of financial support for certain key Democratic committee chairmen who occupied positions which permitted them to control awards and emoluments (Kirwan, Chairman of the Public Works Committee), and incumbents or nonincumbents in favor on the Hill but not necessarily loyal to the White House. President Kennedy, through this agreement, was attempting to gain some control over political financing of congressional candidates in an effort to build support for his programs and policies.

Under provisions of the McCloskey-Kirwan-Hartke agreement, Democratic Committees in Washington distributed a reported $97,700 in amounts of $500 or more to eighty congressional candidates in the 1962 midterm campaign. Disbursing agent for the bulk of the funds was the National Congressional Committee, about one-fifth of the total being distributed directly by the national party headquarters.

15. This agreement was in effect until 1966, when the White House and the Democratic National Committee decided to discontinue participation because of dissatisfaction with the arrangement. This was due largely to disagreement between the National Committee and the Hill committees as to the amount of support to be provided incumbents as opposed to nonincumbents. The former were supported by the Democratic National Congressional Committee and the latter by the National Committee and the White House, which sought to promote candidates for Congress who were willing to run on national issues based upon the President's legislative program. This 1966 controversy was identical with the one that originally brought about the agreement in 1962. Kirwan's role in the House Campaign Committee has been oriented to the internal policies of the party on the Hill and the many ties between the incumbents and expenditures for public works over which he maintains strict control. *Congressional Quarterly Weekly Report,* 24 (January 28, 1966), p. 284.

The largest party contribution to a Democrat was $4,000, while many candidates received a nominal $500. The average contribution made by the Congressional Committee was $1,063, while the downtown committee contributions averaged $1,458. Both Democratic committees jointly assisted the campaigns of three candidates in close marginal contests with total contributions of $2,500, $3,000, and $4,000.

Contributions of Republican party committees in the amount of $500 or more were reported to be $198,600 and were given to 196 candidates almost exclusively through the Republican National Congressional Committee, except for $15,100 reported received from the Republican National Committee by a few candidates. Average contribution from the Congressional Committee was $1,037 and from the GOP National Committee, $755.

The leadership of the Congressional Campaign Committees decide to whom they will lend support. They have limited resources and many campaigns which need financial aid and tactical advice. Both with incumbents and nonincumbents the committees attempt to parcel out the available money in a manner that, in the opinion of the officers and staff, will do the most good. They rely to a large extent on subjective judgment of a candidate's chances. These judgments are based upon whatever evidence is available concerning the chances for victory. Neither the candidate who will clearly be a victor nor the one who has little or no chance will ordinarily be given substantial financial support. If, however, the district is marginal (i.e. was won or lost in the last election by 5 percent or less of the votes), both parties will classify it as a target and will channel whatever resources are available into it. The actual flow of funds through congressional campaigns in 1962 was far larger than officially reported amounts. These figures report only those party contributions in excess of $500. In many instances party support of candidates was closely coordinated with the contributions of interest groups such as business, labor, medical, and senior citizens.

In all, seventy-six committees reported spending $18.4 million during the calendar year 1962, much of it devoted to the midterm congressional and senatorial contests. *Congressional Quarterly* estimated probable actual spending during that year of nearly $100 million by all groups for all offices.[16]

The Democratic pattern of support to fewer than one-fourth of all

16. Special Report No. 30, July 26, 1963, p. 1191.

the candidates indicates some success in the operation of the McCloskey-Kirwan-Hartke agreement, inasmuch as nearly all marginal Democratic candidates received some support from the national party committees. This backing was in stark contrast to the minimal national support of the nonincumbents as a group.

Despite the continued agitation among the party leaders over *who* distributes money to Democratic candidates, and despite the rather uniform but modest support provided its candidates by the GOP national party committees, financial assistance for congressional candidates is severely limited. In the final analysis the money goes to the candidates and contests which in the judgment of party leaders will "do the most good." At best these men must rely upon educated guesswork in determining to whom the funds will be allocated. Even so, only 54 percent of the nonincumbents in 1962 received some support from their respective parties at any level.[17]

It is impossible, as noted earlier, to gauge accurately the costs of congressional campaigns. We quickly abandoned a preliminary attempt to ascertain the amount of money received and expended by the candidates. In many cases they had little to do with campaign finance operations in their campaign, and those who did take part in fund raising were often reticent to discuss these attempts. Defeated candidates were more willing to discuss finances because they usually had raised much of their own money and, because they were without paid staff, often completed the required reporting forms themselves. Even so, few respondents answered questions relating to finance. Those who did presented some interesting patterns of expenditures and receipts. We cautiously present the results, not as a factual statement of campaign finances in the 1962 election, but as a limited contribution to the overall understanding of political finance.

Respondents were asked, "Do you believe your campaign was adequately financed?" Among all losers, 19 percent of the Republicans and 18 percent of the Democrats responded affirmatively. Among the marginals, 29 percent of the Republicans and 35 percent of the Democrats felt that enough money was available, although some noted they could have used more. The preponderant response, however was that campaigns were underfinanced; 81 percent of the GOP losers and 82 percent of the Democrats claimed inadequate financing.

17. These data were compiled from candidate reports of contributions of $500 or more to the Clerk of the House of Representatives. Based upon reports published in the *Congressional Quarterly Weekly Report,* 21 (July 26, 1963), pp. 1248–65.

Among the marginals, fewer candidates claimed to be short of funds (71 percent of the Republicans and 65 percent of the Democrats).

Those who claimed adequate financing reported average campaign costs of $29,450 (Republicans) and $26,400 (Democrats). Those respondents who did not believe that their campaigns were adequately financed reported smaller expenditures—$16,820 (Republicans) and $22,600 (Democrats). The marginals had higher averages in every group; adequately financed Republicans averaged $30,600 and Democrats $33,000, while those who were underfinanced reported averages of $36,500 (Republicans) and $26,300 (Democrats).

When asked to estimate the amount of additional money necessary to win, Republican losers guessed that an average $20,800 would be needed. Democratic losers suggested an average of $29,010 in additional funds. The GOP marginals estimated their additional needs at about the same level as the average Republican loser, while Democratic marginals were considerably less, with an average of $15,285. The range of estimates for all these losing candidates was from $2,000 to $250,000 in additional monies. It hardly needs to be noted that in many races no amount of money would have been sufficient to guarantee election. Many of the candidates in both parties lost for reasons having little or nothing to do with financing. Some representative comments from respondents suggest that many candidates were realistic in their appraisal of their chances:

No amount of money would have won this one.

I cannot attribute my defeat to lack of funds.

No amount of money would have produced victory in light of the GOP trend.

Even with an additional $75,000, I doubt that I could have won this election.

Others, however, clearly attributed their defeat to lack of funds:

There is no question in my mind that a speaker and $4,000 would have won the election.

I could have won if the Congressional Campaign Committee had given me another $1,500.

If I could have had enough money to balance my opponent's franked mailings into the district and could have saturated the district to overcome his name familiarity, I could have won.

COMPARATIVE SOURCES OF CONGRESSIONAL CAMPAIGN FINANCE

Political campaign money is collected from many and varied sources. It would be difficult to find any two campaigns that received financial support from the same types of sources. The candidate can always rely upon his own resources and those of his friends and family, and

Table 4.6

Major Sources of Campaign Funds for Losing and Marginal Candidates

(Arranged in Decreasing Order of Value to Candidates)

	Losers		Marginals	
	GOP	DEM	GOP	DEM
Most Important	C	C	C	F
↑	B	B	D	C
	D	D	B	B
	E	F	E	E
↓	F	E	F	A
Least Important	A	A	A	D

KEY.   A = Congressional Campaign Committee
   B = Your own resources and savings, borrowing and family lending
   C = Borrowing on notes with others, private contributions from friends and supporters
   D = State, district, or county (party) committees
   E = Volunteer, citizen, or other independent groups
   F = Other (Labor, medical, etc.)

he can usually expect some support, minimal as it may be, from his party's congressional campaign committee. In an effort to determine both the sources and the levels of campaign expenditures, we asked each respondent in this study to cite the sources of his funds and tell what proportion each source played in the total estimated cost of his campaign. A rank-order listing (Table 4.6) shows the comparative weight of each major source of campaign funding for marginals and losers as a whole.

Most Republican losers received the bulk of their campaign finances in contributions from private individuals, from state or local party organizations or officials, or from personal funds. Democrats received funds from the same sources but were also helped to a limited extent by labor or senior-citizens groups and by money raised through personal loans. Common to all candidates is the low status of the support provided by the National Congressional Committee of each party, more than matched in the case of Democratic marginals by the lack of support of state, district, and local echelons of their party. If Table 4.6 shows nothing else, it indicates the personal nature of the general election campaign for most losing candidates and the modest role played by political parties in the midterm contests, in which the parties ostensibly have the most at stake. Obviously the decentralized nature of the party system exacerbates the financial isolation of the congressional candidate. Despite this situation, where national policy questions are deeply felt, as is the case with organized labor in all congressional districts, financial aid is forthcoming to support some candidates—usually marginal ones. In other words, the political constituency of organized labor is clearly located in the congressional contests in the Democratic party. The overall role of organized labor in the financing of congressional campaigns was nevertheless relatively minor, as noted in Tables 4.7 and 4.8. These two tables also show quite clearly the relative "spread" of financial support for congressional nonincumbents. Few candidates, with the exception of marginal Democrats, received overwhelming support from any single source.

Using five categories, respondents' comments were classified by broad levels of campaign support. Immediately it is apparent from these tables that "no support" was available for many candidates from the expected party sources; 50 percent of the Republicans and 70 percent of the Democrats received no support from national party sources, but only 33 percent of the Republicans and 28 percent of the Democrats failed to receive some support from state or local party organizations. The selectivity of the national party groups is clearly shown here: they were obviously unwilling (and very likely unable) to support hopeless nonincumbent candidates with hard cash.

Comparison of Tables 4.7 and 4.8 shows major differences in congressional committee support between losers and marginal candidates. GOP losers, for instance, received up to 20 percent support from their congressional campaign committee in 47 percent of the cases, while marginals enjoyed this level of support in 84 percent of the cases.

The availability of campaign money is not necessarily the most

Table 4.7
Percent of Losers Receiving Support at Five Levels of Assistance

Source	1–19%		20–39%		40–59%		60–100%		No Support		N	
	GOP	DEM	GOP	DEM	GOP	DEM	GOP	DEM	GOP	DEM	GOP	DEM
Congress, Camp. Com.	47%	24%	2%	5%	1%	1%	0%	0%	50%	70%	119	105
Personal Resources	42	42	20	25	6	12	15	6	17	15	123	106
Personal Loans	7	16	3	9	1	3	0	2	89	70	125	98
Borrowing on Note with Others	6	5	0	0	0	0	0	0	92	95	125	105
Private Contributions	14	31	25	26	18	18	30	14	15	11	125	105
Party Sources	33	33	13	21	12	12	9	6	33	28	125	104
Volunteer or Indep. Groups	30	28	10	12	5	5	3	3	52	52	126	105
Other Groups (Labor, Medical, etc.)	7	16	2	17	1	5	0	3	90	59	126	108

Table 4.8

Percent of Marginals Receiving Support at Five Levels of Assistance

Source	1–19%		20–39%		40–59%		60–100%		No Support		N	
	GOP	DEM	GOP	DEM	GOP	DEM	GOP	DEM	GOP	DEM	GOP	DEM
Congress, Camp. Com.	84%	37%	0%	7%	4%	3%	0%	3%	12%	50%	25	30
Personal Resources	55	37	19	18	0	15	7	4	19	26	27	27
Personal Loans	7	10	7	6	0	0	0	0	86	84	29	31
Borrowing on Note with Others	10	6	0	4	0	0	0	0	90	90	30	32
Private Contributions	6	40	27	21	27	11	30	21	10	7	30	28
Party Sources	17	39	24	13	21	6	3	0	35	42	30	31
Volunteer or Indep. Groups	33	29	7	6	10	6	0	3	50	56	30	31
Other Groups (Labor, Medical, etc.)	18	10	0	7	0	3	0	7	82	73	28	30

important contributor to victory, but it is often the scapegoat of defeat. No amount of money will elect a candidate in a district with a major imbalance between the parties, and in other districts the quality of the candidate is of much more importance than the level of campaign expenditure. Nevertheless an old cliché holds that money is the lifeblood of politics, and it is certainly true that it becomes increasingly more difficult to mount a modern campaign without large transfusions of money. As regional and state one-party systems continue to break down, the need for great amounts of campaign money in congressional campaigns will continue to grow. Competition between two more equal parties will beget added campaign costs. And it is certain that the losers in those closely contested elections will continue to blame empty campaign coffers for their defeat.

In April 1962 the President's Commission on Campaign Costs made its report. This far-reaching study of campaign financing made a dozen recommendations designed to regularize and strengthen party finance. The second of these recommendations proposed tax incentives for contributors to political parties and campaigns, to take either of two forms: a credit against tax due and a deduction from taxable income.

Under the first alternative one-half of the total contribution to specified committees, up to a maximum credit of $10 per year, would be allowed. Deductions from taxable income, the second alternative, would be administered like other similar tax deductions. Under the proposed system, a donation made to a national party committee would be eligible for the proposed tax credit or deduction. Each national committee would be allowed to designate one committee in each state to share the privilege of receiving tax-favored contributions. The Commission expected that a well-managed program of solicitations would benefit state, local, and congressional candidates as well as those running nationwide. Furthermore, the tax-incentive system would apply in off-years as well as election years to provide a steady flow of money for the party organizations. If the system were implemented, safeguards proposed by the Commission should prevent splintering of party organizations and strengthening of one party unit over another.[18]

Although in succeeding years Congress made some abortive at-

18. *Financing Presidential Campaigns, Report of the President's Commission on Campaign Costs* (Washington, D.C.: Government Printing Office, 1962), pp. 13–16.

tempts to provide tax incentives for political parties, the recommendations of the Commission were never given a fair trial.

In a political context, the noun "organization" refers to the structure of parties or to some functional unit of the party apparatus. We commonly speak of "county organizations" or "state organizations"; and during election years we add various levels of "campaign organizations." The student of politics often assumes that all campaigns are a function of these formal "party organizations." As we have noted in this chapter, however, five major elements in congressional campaigns have devolved upon the candidates themselves rather than upon the established and continuing groups that make up the party hierarchy. Campaign management, headquarters staffing, auxiliary nonparty groups, volunteer manpower and campaign finance, all serve to illustrate the independence of the congressional candidate from the regular party. Consequently the congressional candidate, particularly the nonincumbent, must build his own organization once he has received the party's nomination.

As a verb, the words "to organize" are an extension of the noun. As political environments differ, so do campaign necessities. But again, only a few of the nonincumbent candidates for Congress could interpret the verb to describe a concrete extension of an established party organizational effort. More frequently "to organize" was a painfully personal directive, which took on aspects of an obsession. The nonincumbents had to create personal organizations of their own. They had to breathe life into defunct or moribund congressional district organizations. They had to hang meat on the bones of their immediate predecessors as carriers of the party standard in the district. The first traumatic experience for many of them was the discovery that so little organization existed. The first remedy was to establish an organization of their own and bring it to fruition. And for most of them the efforts availed little. The campaign was run and the election was lost. Then the personal organization was disbanded among tears, debts, and debris, to wait a year and a half, until a new candidate assumed the mantle and began the process all over again. These candidates in too many instances were truly stepchildren of the American party system, with the congressional districts serving as only foster homes.

5.
Campaign Organization: The Candidate & His Party

Only he who can say "In spite of all!"
has the calling for politics. —MAX WEBER

MOST congressional candidates are painfully aware of the enormous gap between their personal campaign organizations and those of the established units of the party apparatus at the local, state, and national levels. One need only compare the amorphous lines of most congressional districts to the somewhat rigid political geography of the several levels of the regular party establishment to find one basic reason why congressional candidates, particularly nonincumbents, are isolated. Obviously this is not the case in every district and with every contest. Many incumbents have come to prefer the "organizational gap" over close ties with the party apparatus, because it frees them to put a personal imprint on their district and shape constituent support to their interests, rather than to the party's programs. But if this is true of some incumbents, it is rarely true of the nonincumbent who lacks the opportunity and resources to "go it alone." There is often no single experience in congressional campaigns which so embitters the nonincumbent candidate as the discovery that within his district and party an "organizational gap" exists, one which is ordinarily beyond his power to overcome.

As many as 80 percent of the losers and 75 percent of the marginal losers felt that "inadequate campaign organization" was of considerable or great importance to their defeat (Table 5.1). These candidates directed their discontent first at the local party level, second at the state, and finally at the national party committees.[1]

Table 5.1 reflects respondents' attitudes toward general organiza-

---

1. Charles Clapp, in interviewing incumbent congressmen from both parties, found that "Members of Congress tend to be negative or, at best, neutral when speaking of their National Committee." He also notes, however, that criticism of state and local party organizations is widespread among the incumbents. He quotes many verbatim responses to support these assertions. Charles L. Clapp, *The Congressman: His Work As He Sees It* (Washington: The Brookings Institution, 1963), pp. 352–60.

Table 5.1

*Party and Organizational Problems Considered to be of Considerable or
Great Importance as Obstacles to Victory*

	Losers, General		Losers, Marginal	
	GOP	DEM	GOP	DEM
	(N = 77 to 109)	(N = 62 to 98)	(N = 13 to 20)	(N = 7 to 17)
Inadequate Campaign Organization	79%	80%	72%	79%
Lack of Money	81	77	70	71
Lack of Local Party Support	61	60	53	67
Lack of State Party Support	52	49	28	46
Lack of National Party Support	43	43	15	22

tional factors and levels of activity which losing candidates, both
marginal and others, reported to be of considerable or great importance as obstacles to victory.

We have noted before that congressional candidates run for national
office[2] in a local or sectional setting. With local and state party
leaders preoccupied with gaining or maintaining hegemony over state
house, court house, or city hall, the candidate for Congress develops
his own organization and, for the most part, tries to survive with it
alone. Similarly, when asked to analyze those factors which in their
judgment contributed most to their opponent's victory (aside from the
alleged superior financial resources), most of them, losers and
marginals alike, pointed to their superior campaign organizations.
Table 5.1 also suggests that the higher the level of the party unit, the
less the losing candidate believed its shortcomings to have been an obstacle to victory. Most of the dissatisfaction was directed toward lack
of support from local party organizations. The party differences on
this question reflect the energy with which GOP state and national
organization efforts were concentrated on that party's candidates in
the southern and marginal districts.

Typical comments by defeated Republican candidates noted:

2. We have treated membership in the House of Representatives as a "national"
office throughout, since the House is a part of the federal government and the
service is primarily in the national capital.

There was absolutely no district organization . . . and we lacked money to put together a personal organization.

It is impossible to explain the conditions in this district. The party officials believe it a lost cause and will not help. One man and his family cannot do it alone.

I believe that the state organization *can* organize better to aid congressional candidates. In this election they were preoccupied with the state-wide senatorial race. There is a need for a state congressional campaign group or at least a "friend in court" for the candidates. The whole congressional picture needs state effort.

In a similar vein the Democratic candidates commented on the organizational causes of their defeat:

I was well qualified and up on the issues. I am simply in a heavily Republican district without any real organizational support or financial backing.

I needed Democrats who were workers instead of people who only showed up when pictures were to be taken.

Sufficient money, a well-qualified candidate and full party support could get a Democrat elected in this district. But full party support has not been forthcoming since 1890.

The local county committees felt that Democrats could not win in this state and fell down. I find I can't do everything myself.

Reports such as these, which suggest strongly that candidates do not generally recognize local and state party units as benefactors in congressional campaigns, are invariably met with surprise and disappointment by party officials. These same officials were often the ones who initially contacted the candidates, encouraged them to run. and in other respects carried out their political recruitment functions to the best of their abilities. (See Chapter 3). How could these efforts, together with those of other party officials, garner so little gratitude and engender so much recrimination? The answer lies in part with the problems inherent in a decentralized party organization in a federal system of government; in part in the powerful legacies of local and regional history and voting patterns, which become a burden on the nonincumbent candidate; and in the relationship of the nonincumbent congressional candidate to the established party apparatus.

While there may be, and often are, identifiable party structures at the various layers of an ideal party apparatus, there is no guarantee that such units are, in fact, operating ones. For example, in an off-election-year survey made late in 1961 by staffs of each national committee, only eleven Republican state chairmen in the fifty states were found to be full-time, and of these only seven were salaried. Among the Democratic state chairmen, only eight were full-time, and only seven were paid. The term *organization,* therefore, when applied to the party situation in the states—let alone that facing the congressional candidate—is more often than not a misnomer. As a consequence, the congressional candidate becomes an organizational orphan and must determine for himself his relationship to the various levels and units of the party. While one candidate deals exclusively with a single agency of party authority, another may attempt to work with several, and a third will construct his own. One candidate may retain the temporary allegiance of leaders who persuaded him to consider entering the race at the recruitment stage, while another ignores all party officers because they opposed his nomination in the primary or party convention. Some nonincumbent candidates proceed from nomination to election day without being made fully aware of the campaign assistance available from one or another party organization, although such a situation is not typical for the nonincumbent.

The low level of support provided nonincumbent candidates by state and local party units has already been noted in Table 5.1. The remaining sections of this chapter, as well as the next, are devoted to a comparative analysis of candidate evaluation and the services and programs provided by the national party units and, where appropriate, by state or local party units. The results demonstrate unmistakably that the top levels of each party are most deeply involved in the congressional campaigns.

National Party Organizations and the Congressional Campaign

The structure of the six Washington-based committees of the Republican and Democratic parties requires clarification; although each pair is similar in name, they are not functionally identical in programs and services to candidates. The differences occur chiefly between the congressional campaign committees and, to a lesser extent, between the two national committees at the "downtown" party headquarters.

Four major party committees are based on Capitol Hill: the senatorial campaign committees and the national congressional committees for each party. All other party committees on the Hill are devoted to the "internal politics" of the House and Senate. Their work involves the promotion of internal party regularity; the determination of policy positions; the allocation of standing committee assignments and staff assistance; and the rationing of patronage centered on or about the capitol building, the five office buildings for House and Senate, and the Library of Congress. These committees generally have official status as party agencies of the Congress, are supported by government funds, and have office space provided at government expense. These "internal" party committees include on the House side the Republican and Democratic Steering Committees, the Party Policy Committees, the House Republican Conference, The Democratic Caucus, and the Committee on Committees for each party. The Speaker, majority and minority leaders, and whips obviously are responsible for particular party roles.

Only the national senatorial and congressional committees are devoted exclusively to the "external politics" of the Congress. They are charged with aiding the reelection of incumbents and the election of new members. They are a part of the official national party apparatus, rather than of the party in Congress. These committees are composed exclusively of incumbent members of each party, one from each state having representation in the House.[3] The campaign committees are funded by voluntary contributions from party members and a vast array of individuals and groups associated with legislative interests. They are housed, except for the Republican Congressional Committee, at government expense, but with the exception of the Democratic Congressional Committee, they have no staff members on the federal payroll.

The congressional campaign committees developed historically from the differences between President and Congress during and following the midterm elections of 1866. These elections saw the post–Civil War Congress and President Andrew Johnson bitterly divided on the issues of presidential leadership, reconstruction, and civil rights. The thorny question of presidential or congressional direction of the domestic affairs of the nation led to a split of the congressional parties into at least four factional groups: Union Democrats ("Copperheads") and Conservative Unionists, both of which supported the President; the Union Party, embracing the Radical Republicans; and

3. The national senatorial campaign committees are similar in most respects to their House counterparts but do not come within the purview of this study.

several veterans' parties. All four groups held midterm congressional conventions, and after its conclave in Philadelphia the Union Party mounted a nationwide campaign to strengthen its control of Congress. It was the Union Party's Congressional Campaign Committee which a year later was renamed the National Republican Congressional Committee, the formal title under which it has operated since that time.[4]

The National Democratic Congressional Committee was formally established in 1882, although short-term efforts were made in 1842 and again in 1866 to promote Democratic candidates for the House. In the latter year Democratic house members organized and campaigned to increase their numbers so as to rally support for President Johnson, who was at that time threatened by the impeachment drive of the Radicals in Congress. The Democrats worked to gain new House members through their own campaign much as the Union Party's Congressional Committee did.

In their origins and early efforts both congressional campaign committees were highly programmatic, but as they evolved, they came to serve the interests of their respective parties, with little reference to political programs, platforms, voting records of incumbents, factional difficulties arising from presidential nominating contests, and differences with the occupant of the White House. With actual leadership in the hands of senior incumbents of each party, the committees have taken a more conservative tone. This conservatively "neutral" coloration of the party campaign committees is in some respects a species of "nonpartisanship" within the parties, a situation which clearly distinguishes the Hill committees from the downtown national committees. As a consequence, some incumbent congressmen of both parties, secure in their own constituencies, are serious embarrassments to their own downtown national party organizations. The latter, by their nature, must try to forge national coalitions, accommodating

4. This section on the history of the congressional campaign committees is drawn from Herbert Agar, *The Price of Union* (Boston: Houghton Mifflin, 1950), pp. 454–58; Wilfred E. Binkley, *American Political Parties, Their Natural History* (New York: Knopf, 1959), pp. 254–55; Clarence Cannon, *Democratic Manual for the Democratic National Convention of 1964* (Washington, D.C.: Democratic National Committee, 1964), p. 12; Paul A. Theis and Henry M. Maggenti, compilers, *One Hundred Years: A History of the National Republican Congressional Committee* (Washington, D.C.: Republican Congressional Committee, 1966), pp. 10–21; and Hugh Alvin Bone, *Party Committees and National Politics* (Seattle: University of Washington Press, 1958), pp. 127–28.

different factions and interests for the purpose of winning support for party platforms and national tickets. Obviously these efforts may be at variance with the views of some incumbent members of Congress. Political survival on Capitol Hill is considered a separate problem from the winning of presidential elections, and the congressional committees and national committees have become keenly aware of their different missions.

Today the National Republican Congressional Committee has far outstripped its counterpart on the Democratic side in the scale of its operations, its services to candidates, and its influence within its own party. Several factors account for this situation, the most important of which is that the principal locus of national power for the Republicans since 1932 has been in the Congress. For only eight of these years have the Republicans occupied the White House, and for only four have they controlled both houses together. Nevertheless, in the eighteen congresses between 1932 and 1966 the average GOP membership in the House was 173, ranging from a low of 89 members in 1937 to a high of 246 members in 1946.

During these years of Democratic majorities the burden fell to Republicans in Congress—the only institutionalized elected spokesmen for their party in the nation's capital—to provide opposition to Democrats and a voice for their cause. As a consequence, the Republican National Finance Committee, in conjunction with the Republican National Committee, came to provide generous funding for its Hill allies. Throughout this period the Congressional Campaign Committee also conducted fund-raising programs and established a durable financial base of its own. It has been helped enormously by a series of hard-driving chairmen and highly professional staff members. It has a small but well-trained staff of at least thirty people which in election years is increased to fifty or more.

Many close observers have noted elements of hostility between the Hill committees and the downtown, or national, committees. This is particularly evident in the Republican party where latent hard feelings exist between staffers of the two committees over the expanding roles of the congressional committee, sometimes at the expense of the national. They are usually able to cooperate as election day nears only because the party out of power has more to gain from cooperation. The antithesis of "divide and conquer" is "unite or be conquered." But disagreements persist, and cooperation often breaks down. It is difficult for those connected with the national committee to accept the thesis expounded by their Hill counterparts that policy making rests with the congressional leadership. And the latter refuse to consider alternatives to this proposition. Even so, there is a degree of cooperation as campaigns get under way. There has been, in recent years, some exchange of personnel between the two committees, and the successive chairmanship of both committees by Leonard Hall and William E. Miller moved them toward a closer liaison. At a very minimum, the Republican Committee's leadership meets together occasionally, and frequent telephone calls between the staff members serve to keep each informed of the activities of the other. Personal friendships and contacts serve to further cooperation.

Under National Chairman Ray Bliss the GOP National and Congressional Committee leadership met weekly with the leaders of the House and Senate to formulate party positions and discuss strategy. This proved to be a useful coordinating device and helped to reduce the traditional friction between the groups.[5]

The Democratic Congressional Committee is, by contrast, a vest-pocket operation, in principle devoted to the election or reelection of Democrats to the House but in practice largely directing its efforts toward incumbents. From 1936 to 1954 the Democratic Congressional Committee was operated by Victor H. "Cap" Harding, who was a hardworking and knowledgeable party pro who held the title of Executive Director. Harding literally maintained the up-to-date political history of many of the nation's congressional districts in his head and operated as a one-man adviser, field man, and savant for Democrats on congressional politics. Upon his death in 1954 the mantle fell to his son, Kenneth Harding, who, with the addition in recent years of one full-time assistant, Edmund L. Henshaw, has directed the affairs of the committee. Both Harding and Henshaw are government employees, having patronage assignments as Deputy Sergeants-at-Arms of the House. With little financial support from the national party except during the period 1961–65 and no additional professional staff, the Democratic Congressional Committee by choice and by tradition has played a modest role in providing assistance to nonincumbent candidates for Congress.

In its fund-raising efforts as well as its services, the National Democratic Congressional Committee staff has largely, but not exclusively, devoted its energies to personal errands, liaison work, and the primary

5. John Bibby and Robert J. Huckshorn, "Out-Party Strategy: Republican National Committee Rebuilding Politics, 1964–66," in *Republican Politics: The 1964 Campaign and Its Aftermath for the Party,* ed. Bernard Cosman and Robert J. Huckshorn (New York: Praeger, 1968), p. 216.

task of helping incumbents get themselves reelected. While it was dominated by long-time Chairman, the late Representative Michael Kirwan (Nineteenth District, Ohio), incumbent beneficiaries of the Democratic Congressional Committee, in some measure, reflected Kirwan's own political constituency in the House, where he was chairman of the important Subcommittee on Public Works of the Committee on Appropriations. The Congressional Committee's campaign budget averages $500,000 but in 1962 was combined with the Democratic National Committee's midterm campaign funding program for candidates.

The operations of the Republican and Democratic National Committees in presidential politics have been extensively studied in recent years, but there has been little attention devoted to the role of these committees in congressional and senatorial elections, either in presidential years or at midterm. Our purpose here is to examine briefly the role of the two national committee headquarters in midterm congressional elections.

Although the national party organizations in midterm election years do not reach the peaks generated by presidential years they do expand considerably over those years in which there is no national election of any kind. In 1962 both national committees, each with from 80 to 120 full-time employees, operated through divisions devoted to women's activities, nationality and minority groups, young activists, and various occupational groups. At each committee these special units worked closely with the major divisions handling publicity and public affairs, political organization, and research.

The Republicans in 1962 were favored with more stability and continuity in national-committee staffing than were the Democrats. Several of the top executives were veterans of ten years or more of service to national political committees, either downtown or on the Hill.

Despite the prevailing strength of the Democrats in Congress and their control of the Executive Branch, the Democratic National Committee staff displayed considerably less continuity and was plagued with problems of transiency and internal management conflict. While at any one time during the 1960s the Democrats undoubtedly had in their headquarters as many talented political executives as did the GOP, the problems of internal coordination and administration at times made it difficult to provide basic services to candidates and party units outside Washington. This problem has been repeatedly commented upon by members of the Washington press corps who monitor national political affairs as well as by scholars knowledgeable in party affairs.

We noted earlier that there is a certain antagonism between the "Hill" and the "downtown" committees. Partly this results from the different missions of the two groups—the national committees being charged with electing presidents and the congressional committees with electing congressmen. The great rivalry between the leadership of the two groups for power positions has made it difficult to overcome the communications gap between them. Two recent efforts illustrate the problem.

During the 1950s, under the titular leadership of Adlai Stevenson, Democratic National Chairman Paul Butler made notable progress in forging a set of position papers for the party out of power. These statements were developed by task forces of the Democratic Advisory Council and usually represented the "national" positions of the presidential wing of the Democratic party. Butler was unable to get the cooperation of the Democratic leadership on the Hill, except for Hubert Humphrey, and the papers clearly showed the lack of cooperation between the two groups. They did, however, serve an important purpose, since they attracted wide publicity and allowed the party out of power to focus the public's attention on itself.[6]

A more recent example of the same sort of out-party strategy was the creation of the Republican Coordinating Committee after the 1964 election. Spurred by much the same set of circumstances that brought about the Democratic Advisory Council, the Republican Coordinating Committee differed in one substantial respect. The congressional leadership cooperated with the national committee leadership and the Republican governors in bringing it into being and in working out internal problems to see that it worked. The Committee functioned for the entire period between its creation and the 1968 national convention. Through a series of task forces it produced some three dozen policy statements which received wide publicity and general distribution throughout the party apparatus.[7]

Successful "unity" creations, such as these two recent examples, have not been noticeably successful in American political history. The outparty turns to them because it needs a unifying force, and it needs publicity to compete with that automatically guaranteed the president. But as Butler found out, merely developing such an organization does

6. Cornelius P. Cotter and Bernard C. Hennessy, *Politics Without Power: The National Party Committees* (New York: Atherton, 1964), pp. 211–24.
7. Cosman and Huckshorn, pp. 218–23.

not automatically produce unity. The Republicans overcame some of the basic difficulties inherent in such groups by reaching compromises which permitted both major segments of party leadership to participate. Their success may mean that such groups will become a permanent fixture of the party out of power.

We have noted the modest scope and role of the Democratic Congressional Committee in the nonincumbent contests. This fact highlights the vastly greater DNC responsibilities to these candidates. The two national committees differ greatly in this respect.

The Democratic National Committee in 1962 constructed its candidate-support program upon two foundations. First, it relied upon the experience gained, during the 1950s, when the basic campaign literature and organizational techniques aimed at the nonincumbent were perfected. Second, it mobilized some of the skilled personnel from the Kennedy campaign team of 1960 and undertook to apply this experience to the congressional election. Some members of the team operated out of the White House, while others were already on or were added to the national committee staff. A new set of brochures was developed on the legislative achievements and, because of the rough treatment accorded the Kennedy programs in the Congress, on the legislative promises of the administration. This campaign literature emphasized Republican "obstructionism" and prominently featured the proposed Medicare program under social security, which failed to pass Congress by a slim margin during the summer of 1962.[8]

Since the National Republican Congressional Committee controls the purse strings for congressional candidates, the Republican National Committee assumes a supplemental role—that of supporting the campaign with research, publicity, and field assistance. It also, of

8. Indeed, while the national committee's campaign literature was silent on southern obstructionism, the National Democratic Congressional Committee aided at least five incumbent conservative southern congressmen in their reelection efforts. The "Conservative Coalition" support scores for these five were 69, 79, 88, 90, and 94 percent of the roll calls. The average support score of Southern Democrats for this same eighty-seventh Congress was 58 percent. One of the five noted above was defeated, losing by 49.5 percent of the vote. The others were reelected by margins of 55 percent for two and 62 and 64 percent of the vote for the others. Each of these candidates was opposed by a strong GOP challenger. In justice to the Democratic candidates it should be noted that their Kennedy support scores for the eighty-seventh Congress averaged between 55 and 60 percent; on the other hand, all Southern congressmen together averaged 73 percent of the roll calls in support of the key votes on the Kennedy program.

course, lends assistance to gubernatorial and senatorial candidates and others who desire aid.

This discussion of the congressional candidate and the Washington-based party committees has two clear implications. First, that the midterm battle for the Republican party is a challenge to which the well-equipped and highly capable National Republican Congressional Committee, oriented toward a conservative constituency, responds with alacrity. Clearly this drive flies in the teeth of the national committee's effort to "organize the unorganized" and to encourage candidates who might compete with the Democrats for the middle bloc of the American electorate who respond to programs and policies of a more liberal nature.

The second implication is that the midterm battle for the Democrats is a challenge to which the party responds with two separate but related programs. Incumbents receive backing from other incumbents, acting through the National Democratic Congressional Committee, and the strongest support goes to those who are philosophically conservative. Nonincumbents, on the other hand, must seek the support of the Democratic National Committee staff, which is chiefly interested in the marginal seats. The DNC provides a full range of supporting services for those candidates believed to have a chance of election.

The Congressional Candidate and
His State Party Organization

The relationship between formal legal structures and the function and behavior of political parties is too well known to belabor here, but its imprint is nowhere more clearly seen than in the relationship of state party organizations to congressional elections. Although all states provide recognition of political parties in their election laws, there is wide variation among them in the manner of selection and composition of state party central committees.[9]

9. In general there is no authoritative published source of information on comparative state party law and organization. Both the Clerk of the House of Representatives and the Librarian of the Senate periodically publish pamphlets which detail the manner of selecting delegates to the national party conventions, the deadlines and calendars for primary and general elections in the states, and state law pertaining to nomination and election of the President. Recently a start has been made, based upon a survey completed by professors

There is wide variation among the states in the manner of the selection, composition, and functions of the state party committees. In some states they are composed of all the county chairmen sitting ex officio as the state central committee. In others the committee is elected in the direct primary from some electoral district—the county, the state senatorial, or the congressional district. In still others the state committee members are elected by a state convention. These varying means of election and units of representation tend to decentralize power at the state party level just as national committeemen cause the same trend at the national level.

Just as obviously, however, control of the state central committee usually is synonymous with control of the state party apparatus. Most of them perform a significant legal role (and their power is prescribed by law), including the preparation and call for state conventions; deciding the time of the primary elections; canvassing and certifying election results; supervising party primaries; and, in those cases where death or resignation removes a candidate before election day, appointing a replacement. It serves as the executive committee for the state party, and its chairman is the official party leader.

The state chairman is usually elected by the committee from among its membership. He is generally a leading figure in the party, although not always the best qualified to serve as chairman. The chairmanship has in many states led to elective office, or at least to nomination for one. In most states the chairman is a powerful party figure. In the Republican party all state chairmen are members of the National Committee.

In recent years outstanding state party chairmen with extensive experience in national affairs or with special skills in political organization have been chosen to serve as chairmen of the national party committees. In the mid-1960s both committees were headed by such men: John M. Bailey has served as Connecticut State Democratic Chairman since 1945 and was National Committee Chairman from 1961 to 1968; and Ray Bliss came to Washington to head the Republican National Committee in 1965, after fifteen years as a highly effective Republican State Chairman of Ohio.

---

of political science and public administration in the fifty states. The Research Division of the Republican National Committee publishes a quadrennial compilation of state laws governing delegate selection and calendars of primaries and conventions. Also see Richard S. Childs, "State Party Structures and Procedures: A State By State Compendium," mimeographed (New York: National Municipal League, 1967).

Fully two-thirds of all respondents stated that their State Central Committee failed to give adequate support to congressional candidates. There were some notable exceptions, where effective and dynamic state party leaders received fulsome praise, but the overall picture was bleak. Nationally, it was clear from interview responses and personal observations that most state committees evinced little interest in congressional races. Especially did this situation hold true of the nonincumbents.

Clapp found that incumbents reacted in much the same way.

> For the most part, state party organizations are relatively unimportant in the campaign plans of members of Congress, though it appears that the congressional races are receiving somewhat more attention than formerly from state chairmen and state central committees.

He noted that in some states finance committees are making some contributions to the campaigns of incumbent congressional candidates but, for the most part, this is rare. He also noted that criticism of these party units among incumbent congressmen was widespread.[10]

Many incumbents prefer to run their own campaigns and do not desire active support by the state party. They are happy to receive funds if any are available, but in many states none are forthcoming, since the party organization ordinarily can fund none but its own state campaigns.

The real difficulty comes from the failures of state committees to find ways and means of fitting congressional campaigns into the broader scope of "important" statewide campaigns. These organizations are concerned with the election of statewide officers: senator, governor, attorney general, and the like. They must appeal to the voters on the basis of ever-present state problems of taxes, education, health, welfare, and highways. And although tied closely to Congress, these are not problems with wide appeal among congressional candidates. Since they are problems of state concern, many voters realize that solutions must be initiated at the state level. The congressional candidate is more apt to concentrate on issues of federal taxes, federal road programs, foreign policy, and his own view toward the incumbent president.

As noted in Table 5.1, fully one-half of the respondents in both parties believed that lack of state party support was an obstacle of great or considerable importance. Republican marginals apparently received more assistance from state party groups, since only 28 per-

10. Clapp, pp. 354–55.

cent considered party and organizational problems at the state level to be major obstacles to victory. But among the Democratic marginals, 46 percent held this view. This difference suggests that effective state party organizations were spotty or that individual state groups were highly selective in distributing campaign largess.

Numerous candidates for Congress stated that they had never set foot in the state party headquarters and had only perfunctory contacts with state party officials. This situation was deplored by many non-incumbents. One stated:

> I believe that the state organization CAN organize better to aid the congressional candidates. In this race they were preoccupied with the senatorial race. There is need for a state congressional campaign group or at least a "Friend in Court" for the candidates. The whole congressional picture needs state effort.

The inconsistency between the structure of the state committees and their failure to take an effective part in congressional campaigns are apparent. A committee made up of local party officials, even selected from congressional districts in some states, might be expected to actively support a candidate to represent those jurisdictions. But the failure to adequately answer the question of whether a congressman is a local or national officer causes the state committees to concentrate on those who are quite obviously state or local candidates. This is not entirely the fault of the state party organizations. The failure of the incumbent congressmen to make use of the state party structure has added to their disinclination to treat congressional campaigns as a part of their responsibilities.

Our respondents did not mince words in describing their relationships with state campaign organizations. Typical comments were as follows:

> The state had no coordination and no contact with congressional candidates.

> The state headquarters were separate from the Governor's campaign headquarters and there was a lack of liaison between them.

> The only thing I requested of the state committee was the updated list of town committee members and this was provided. There was no assistance volunteered. There is no strong state central committee in _____, as you probably know.

> The state committee did provide mailing lists. We got all the help we asked for and good cooperation. However, in this state you sort of run your own show out in the country.

The state headquarters provided little help, if any. The convention hurt us beyond repair, both because of the candidates chosen and because of the manner in which they were chosen. God save the Democratic Party from any more state conventions like the last two in this state.

The state committee was completely and *exclusively* oriented with the state ticket. In fact, when the President came into the county to speak, the congressional candidate merely got a bow, while the entire state ticket spoke. If they had given me the money they spent on postage for junk, I probably could have bought more newspaper ads for my own campaign.

Republican candidates fared little better with their state organizations. One, from California, was indignant because his state committee was exclusively devoted to the gubernatorial campaign. "Our state central committee was of absolutely no value to anyone except Richard Nixon for Governor. On the average the women's work was best—Young Republicans of no value." One midwestern Republican succinctly stated that his state committee "didn't give a dime or a damn." A southern candidate, noting that his state organization concentrated on the race for governor, also noted that his most effective campaign work came from local women and from Young Republicans.

Many a nonincumbent is not aware of state organizational weaknesses prior to filing. His ambition is uncorked and his euphoria is stimulated by the good wishes of his friends and acquaintances. But ambition and euphoria do not readily translate into hard organizational support and cold cash. If he is lucky, his state organization will treat him as a part of a candidate's team. If he is typical, he will receive little state support and may turn in desperation to the local party groups within his district.

The Candidate and the Local Party Organization

Both precinct and county party units are the stuff of which local organizations are made. Each state is divided into voting districts called precincts—each containing a legally prescribed number of voters, a voting place, and election officers. The precinct is the base upon which our party structure rests. It is not only the place where people vote for candidates and referenda, but also the party unit closest to the people. Precincts, varying in size from a few hundred to a few thousand voters, represent the only political party district that is not simultaneously a constituency. No legal officer is elected from the precinct to serve its interests in any representative or executive body—it exists only as a party unit. Except in urban areas, the only elected precinct official is the committeeman, who represents the precinct as the party officer near at home. In the large cities in urbanized states the party voters often elect a ward committeeman as the basic party officer. He, in turn, appoints the precinct captains (to distinguish them from elected precinct committeemen) to take charge of their respective precincts and report to the ward committeeman. It is upon this base that party machines have been built.

The precinct leader is responsible for the registration of voters and for efforts to get the voters to the polls. The image of the precinct leader was tied to the role of the city precinct captain in the old days of machine politics. The precinct captain was usually undisputed boss of his precinct—controlling some patronage, dispensing favors, providing information, and serving as rallying point for the forces of the party. The traditional picture of the precinct captain as someone who expends great efforts to supply the poor with coal to warm their bodies and food to feed their stomachs is not applicable to the activities of today's precinct committeeman. He often has no organization to work with, no patronage to distribute. In fact, he does well if he maintains a minimum degree of contact with the voters on his list. A cursory examination of selected precinct operations suggests that many precinct leaders, if not a majority, are not able to maintain up-to-date precinct lists except in those states where the law requires it. These are nevertheless the goals of "good" party organization; the parties have simply not provided the wherewithal to meet the goals that have been set for them.

At the county level the key individual is the county chairman. He is usually the representative of the local party organization on the state central committee, and in some states he serves as delegate to the state convention. If his party is in power, he may receive some patronage to distribute; he is also usually called on to direct the party's campaign activities within his own jurisdiction. Sometimes he is responsible for local party recruitment for county and city offices, as well as for people to assume campaign responsibilities. In actual fact county leaders spend much of their time trying to meet state finance quotas and locating "attractive" candidates to run for county offices. The county chairman can be an officer with considerable power and responsibility, but with over 3,000 in each party, their roles and their attitude toward their responsibilities vary widely.

Random comments suggest that a number of Republican candidates attributed the ineffectiveness of local support to a "poor party image" which was unattractive to the voters. Moderates and liberals assigned it to rampant conservatism by party elders, while conservatives believed it to result from years of me-tooism. Both groups agreed that, ideological considerations aside, local Republican officials were too often colorless, defeatist, and/or unimaginative. Urban Republicans complained of inadequate or nonexistent party organizational work with ethnic and minority groups and of the lack of sustained effort on the part of the Republican establishment to register voters.

Democrats in the South were critical of the Kennedy administration and spent considerable time trying to disassociate from it. Northern and western Democrats, on the other hand, suggested that a part of their problems could be attributed to old-line Democratic leaders who did not mesh well with the Kennedy organization.

Local party support for marginal losers provided an interesting contrast. When compared to the 34 percent of all losers who cited lack of local support as a factor of great or considerable importance, the 64 percent of the marginal candidates provided a significant contrast. What could account for such a discrepancy? If reversed, it could be explained as a reflection of the additional assistance provided marginal candidates at all party levels. Such, however, was not the case. The marginal candidate, who might be expected to be far more satisfied with his local support, was actually much more dissatisfied with it. One possible explanation appears in a comment by a marginal candidate in the Republican party, who stated in an interview:

I got absolutely no help from the party people at home after it became known that the congressional committee believed I might win. I guess they thought I was getting lots of help from out-of-state and didn't need any from them.

Interest in congressional campaigns by district, county, and city committees, as well as by responsible party officials, would appear to be most parochial. A few states still retain the congressional district committee to provide exclusive assistance to candidates for the House. The respondents in this study, however, did not credit these few district committees with any campaign role. Local party committees, usually more concerned with local elections for mayor or sheriff, are ill-prepared to provide much more than moral support to congressional candidates. This situation does not, of course, always hold. Local committees in New York City, for instance, are often very active in behalf of congressional races, but even there wide variances are noticeable. Primary fights sometimes leave political scars at the local level, and local officials are especially vulnerable to such political injuries.

Political types at the local level are often amateurs trying to rebuild a shattered party machine or are old party wheelhorses who have built power and repute on city and county but not congressional victories. In rural areas this amounts to "friends and neighbors" politics, and outsiders (that is, congressional candidates) are not always welcome. Furthermore, the party system at the municipal level has been de-emphasized in the name of nonpartisanship. All these considerations contribute to the ineffectiveness which the congressional candidate encounters in the party system at the local level. The net effect is to compound the isolation of the nonincumbent and to force him further into a personalized campaign.

Many of the losing congressional candidates were well into the campaign before they fully realized the general weaknesses of the ward and precinct political organizations. So preoccupied were they with unexpected problems of campaign management that the need for a strong base at the precinct level was often overlooked. Yet, as noted in Table 5.1, a significant majority of respondents considered weaknesses at that level a more significant obstacle to victory than those at the state or national levels.

Without a doubt the viability of local political organizations has much to do with the success or failure of contenders for public office. We do not, however, have survey data to support any generalizations about off-year congressional election campaigns. A closely related study, however, sheds considerable light on the problems existing between local party groups and congressional candidates in a presidential election year. Katz and Eldersveld carefully selected eighty-seven mixed sampling units in Wayne County, Michigan, and examined the relationship between party leadership and political activities and its impact upon the electorate.[11] If valid for the presidential year of 1956, this study should be even more significant for an off-year election, where the candidates suffer lower visibility.

11. Daniel Katz and Samuel J. Eldersveld, "The Impact of Local Party Activity Upon the Electorate," *Public Opinion Quarterly*, 25 (Spring 1961), 1–24.

Katz and Eldersveld found that precinct leaders are beset by the same types of difficulties as are the leaders of voluntary organizations. In what is considered one of the most highly organized political areas in the nation they found that precinct leaders functioned inefficiently and rarely performed all the duties assigned to them by the state organizations or in party manuals. In fact, "The great majority of voters did not even know that the parties have local workers in their own neighborhood" (p. 24). Moreover, precinct leaders are frequently ignored by other party functionaries in a typical campaign year:

> Party organization will often by-pass the precinct leader, as in fundraising activities, membership drives, and even registration efforts. Such by-passing is both an effect and a cause of weak precinct organization. Since the precinct leaders, with their partial involvement and marginal time, are not the most reliable sources of help, special campaigns and activities will be sponsored and carried out by higher levels in the organization. [P. 6]

An index of leadership appropriate to local party organizations showed that "only 14 percent of the Republican group can be characterized as strong leaders, compared to 30 percent of the Democrats." Nevertheless, it is clear that strong local leadership can make a difference in "lifting" the level of voter participation at the precinct level in a presidential election over the predictable levels related to social and occupational characteristics in the precincts. The Wayne County study noted that "when a political party neglects its organizational activities in an area in which the other party has a strong leader it will suffer in consequence at the polls. . . . With all other relevant factors held constant," the study noted, "the strength of Republican leadership was significantly correlated with voting behavior; the strength of Democratic leadership was not" (p. 15). Katz and Eldersveld concluded that a well-established local party organization has more difficulty in increasing its share of the vote than does a minority party in response to equal leadership activity and effort (p. 24).

That the nonincumbent candidates believed that they suffered at the polls is suggested by some of their comments:

> Under the circumstances and considering the setbacks I doubt that anything different would have been possible. I feel that if we had had time to build an adequate independent precinct organization we could have done much better.

> I would forget all about the local county Democratic organization and provide a closely-knit full-time staff of three to five full-time people,

three men and two women. . . . Congressional candidates must have more than lip-service support from the combined efforts of the Democratic State Central Committee and the Democratic National Committee and this involved a campaign manager or press representatives in each Congressional district working for the national (congressional) ticket, because the county committees are preoccupied with county candidates and the state candidates with their own problems.

I would get a grass roots organization first, because the precinct organization is very essential and does not exist in my district. I would broaden the base of the organization and start earlier.

I had excellent help from dedicated people on my staff and in my organization. I never worked harder in my life. Basic party organization is sadly lacking and if we wait until much before the next election to try to improve this, we will lose many votes which we now have.

One final point in this examination of the candidate and his local party organization bears emphasis. That is the prominent place occupied by organized labor in providing organizational support and skill at the local level for Democratic congressional candidates. The role of labor in recruitment and finance has been discussed earlier, but for many Democrats labor was of direct assistance in voter registration drives, precinct organization, and "get-out-the-vote" drives. Republican candidates repeatedly noted that their opponents received campaign assistance from labor, either in support or in lieu of local party organization. One GOP marginal noted, "Organized labor was responsible for most, if not all, of his get-out-the-vote effort." Democratic candidates often acknowledged their debt to labor groups. This is not to say that Republican candidates received no outside support; but most of what they received from medical and business groups was in the form of financial assistance rather than organizational aid.

There is an almost total detachment of the state and local party apparatus from the organizational needs of the nonincumbent congressional candidate. Without the resources to go it alone, the nonincumbent congressional candidate finds that the organizational gap becomes wider the closer he gets to the local party organization.

The precinct and other local voting districts have been enshrined in American political folklore in symbolic, albeit paradoxical, roles. On the one hand the precinct or ward is the seat of "grass-roots democracy" and "citizen political action." On the other, it is portrayed as the source of political corruption and bossism and all that is invidiously political about local government. Both images were derived from earlier periods in American history, and neither is precisely relevant today. The repeated pleas of congressional nonincumbents would suggest that they would be happy to see the local party live up to either historical role, since either would presumably fulfill the needs of the candidates to a greater extent than the grass-roots organization now does.

6.
Auxiliary
Candidate Services

*A politician must often talk and act before
he has thought and read. He may be very
ill-informed respecting a question; all his
notions about it may be vague and inaccurate; but speak he must.*
—T. B. MACAULEY

POLITICS, like the oldest profession, requires little previous training and experience of its practitioners. Certainly, political candidacy at most levels of government has less to do with one's qualifications than it does with the many intangible qualities associated with influencing people and attracting voters.

Other professional groups—teachers, doctors, lawyers—have evinced their concern by raising professional standards and by establishing controls over entry into their professions, thus raising the standards and the prestige of the professions and establishing patterns of formal training. At the nonprofessional level, craft unions have regulated entrance into skilled occupational fields by means of apprenticeship programs and high initiation fees. Whether a bar association or a barber licensing board, the thrust of these regulations has been toward exclusiveness, increased specialization, tightened access to membership, and higher economic benefits for those members who qualify.

Even if political practitioners realized the need for such career training and advancement, American politics does not lend itself to professional development in any realistic sense. To be sure, as our discussion of political recruitment has indicated, congressional candidates are expected to have achieved some measure of success in other fields before transferring their interests to the political arena. But because of the continuous instability in the lower levels of political involvement, the encounter with a first congressional campaign is to many candidates a traumatic and unsettling experience. Even incumbents seeking reelection have difficulty converting their legislative experience and expertise into tangible voter appeal. The usual programs and measurements for the improvement of the professions do not, therefore, apply to the world of practical politics. Any formal training programs designed to "professionalize" politics, and especially its campaign aspects, faces problems which have traditionally been difficult to overcome. Both national party organizations have taken halting steps to educate and train the politicians who march under their respective banners. At a bare minimum, this constitutes an effort to protect the party's good name. In the process it might also help to elect some of the party's candidates. And that, after all, is the party's true aim.

Auxiliary candidate services are those activities, programs, and materials which fill out the organization and message content of the campaign, as well as providing special emphasis and support for individual candidates. They are developed and performed by the continuing party headquarters organizations primarily at the national level. Auxiliary services include research and publications; voting records; candidate training programs; personal advice; speech materials; field services; speakers; special group activities; and public-opinion polls. These services have in common a heavy emphasis upon the techniques and products of the communications media. They are also directed to the candidate as a means of bridging the informational and organizational gap between the congressional district and the upper party echelons.

We have noted earlier that congressional candidates seek election to a national office in a local or sectional political environment. The incumbent congressman has already had the opportunity to establish constituent contacts and services and has selected the local or district-wide issues which relate to national policy questions. He can take these steps regardless of official party doctrine, and typically he gains a "lead time" of several years over his opponent. For example, the incumbent congressman regularly seeks to avail himself of every opportunity to gain local support by taking credit for projects, appointments, and programs which apply to his constituency; if he is of the same party as the president, the White House cooperates in insuring that he gets local credit. The nonincumbent candidate, on the other hand, seeks the assistance of party agencies which will help him nationalize his campaign and remove it from the severe limitations of local politics. Auxiliary campaign services, organized by the national party headquarters, help these candidates to overcome this handicap. They are not always appreciated, but they are there if the candidate wishes to take advantage of them.

Table 6.1

Percent of Losing and Marginal Candidates Designating Auxiliary Candidate Services of the National Party Committees as Most Useful

	Republicans		Democrats	
	Losers	Marginals	Losers	Marginals
Research and Publications	56%	45%	55%	52%
Voting Records	75	45	69	40
Candidate Training				
Programs	44	25	61.	48
Personal Advice	32	31	21	16
Speech Materials	24	0	58	0
Speakers	9	4	15	29
Field Services	9	14	11	23
Special Groups	6	6	10	7

Note: Respondents were asked to check those services that were "very much" or "somewhat" useful and these two categories have been combined as "most useful" in this table. Columns total more than 100 percent because of multiple responses.

Table 6.1 shows the percentage of losing and marginal candidates who rated the basic auxiliary candidate services of the respective national party committees as most useful (See Appendix A). Respondents did not clearly discriminate between the services of the Hill and the downtown committees, and their responses have been grouped together in this table. It should be noted that reports of auxiliary services offered by state party organizations were rare and have not been included here.

Research and Publications

In July 1962 a letter arrived at the headquarters of the Republican National Committee addressed to Chairman William E. Miller. This particular letter, one of hundreds received each week, announced that the writer had just received the Republican nomination to run for Congress. He expressed his appreciation for the honor and resolved to do his best to return the seat to GOP control. The letter concluded:

I would be most appreciative if you and your staff could send any research and campaign materials which might be helpful in my campaign.

While I feel qualified to discuss some important issues, I think it is only realistic to assume that _____ has a more thorough understanding of them because of his long incumbency. I would make good use of any publication that might help me to put my best foot forward in the campaign.

There was nothing unusual about this letter or the request it contained. Scores of such requests arrive in the early days of any campaign year. This particular letter probably crossed in the mails with communications from several GOP officials in Washington, including Chairman Miller, congratulating the candidate upon his victory in the primary and offering the very services he sought. Very probably the candidate's request was routed to the Congressional Campaign Committee at the Congressional Hotel on Capitol Hill.

Within a few days the candidate received packages of material from both party committees, representing the combined efforts of the publicity, research, and public relations experts of both the downtown and Hill committees and ranging from party periodicals to organization manuals and brochures on particular issues. Throughout the ensuing campaign a steady shower of publications descended upon the candidate from the Washington-based committees and in a few cases from his state central committees. In this way candidates became initially acquainted with the party line on issues, with organization, and with party analysis of the opposition candidate's record. Unless a candidate had unusual personal connections in Washington or had run for Congress before, none of these materials was available to him until after the primary election or state nominating convention.

Political research as conducted by the national party headquarters deals with the accumulation of information and data—a neutral and objective task in itself—for the selective use of the party and its candidates in campaign situations. Aside from historical considerations, the chief justification for research by a political party is to provide information and ammunition required to influence voters and to capture public offices. Since few candidates have either skilled staff or financial means to conduct research operations, they must rely upon the established national party headquarters.

An incumbent congressman can rely on members of his own staff for a considerable amount of assistance with research. He will be familiar with the impact of major federal programs and of projects in his own district. Furthermore, incumbents benefit from policy statements prepared by the respective policy committees on the Hill (including the Democratic Study Group). These are ordinarily directed toward national policy, but their sheer mass and complexity makes them less valuable for nonincumbents in a new campaign experience.[1]

Obviously nonincumbent challengers do not share these research resources. They must rely instead on the established national party organizations. Though, in recent years both parties have taken pains to increase the quantity and quality of their research efforts, both parties—particularly the Democrats—tend to underrate the product and undernourish the research operation in comparison to other functions and divisions of national party headquarters.

The Research Division of the Republican National Committee is highly respected, and its publications have been cited favorably by scholars, authors, and the press. Understaffed for many years, the GOP Research Division has nonetheless retained some of the better political-research talent in Washington. Its biennial statistical reports on general elections have a reputation for frankness and accuracy that is the envy of other political-research agencies in Washington.

In 1962 the Research Division of the Democratic National Committee operated under the administrative direction of the Deputy Chairman for Public Affairs. It was better staffed and better financed than the GOP committee but garnered little recognition within the party or press establishments. A rapid succession of directors after the Butler era of the 1950's plagued the Democratic research operation and prevented any degree of continuity. The average tenure of directors has been less than eighteen months during the past several years. Furthermore, prior to 1968 the Divison operated in the shadow of the major research resources of the federal government and the White House, a fact which considerably weakens any commitment to political research.

The political research divisions must produce results useful to the party's candidates or its leadership. Little of the research product reaches the public directly; it is compiled for the use of others, some of whom may choose to disseminate the material more widely. Both the Washington press corps and the publicity and public-affairs staff

---

1. For an excellent review of the activities of the Republican Policy Committee, see Charles O. Jones, *Party and Policy-Making: The House Republican Policy Committee* (New Brunswick: Rutgers University Press, 1964). Although the Policy Committee does not directly channel its research productivity to candidates for campaign purposes, the results of its efforts are useful to them and to the National Congressional Committees.

of the two national committees make use of the divisions' work; in a sense the research staff produces the ammunition, while the public-relations people direct the fire.

Except for nominal clipping, filing, and record keeping, the National Democratic Congressional Committee performs little research. The *Congressional Record* is clipped for the more important pronouncements of incumbent GOP congressmen, and these clipping files are furnished to challenging candidates. The vast resources of the government are also available for referrals of reports, hearings, and other publications. These latter are more accessible to incumbents who are familiar with the operations of government. For the most part, nonincumbent Democratic congressional candidates rely upon the assistance provided by the National Committee's Research Division and the Public Affairs Division.

The GOP National Congressional Committee, in keeping with its status on the Hill, maintains a respected research organization with a permanent staff. It compiles information for use by its own public-relations staff and provides spot research service to Republican congressmen and to those candidates who request it. In general, political research falls into two categories: that directed to candidates and materials directed to organizations. The candidate-directed material focuses on voting records, fact books, prepared speeches, issue analyses, and position papers. Organization-directed research, on the other hand, takes the form of "how-to" manuals and handbooks for precinct workers, campaign managers, and others involved with directing the campaign. These materials deal in detail with basic political organization, registration, get-out-the-vote drives, purchase of radio and television time, and similar activities.

CANDIDATE-DIRECTED RESEARCH

Even though policy questions and political issues may have little actual bearing on election outcomes, as the following chapter suggests, both the party organizations and the candidates must approach the campaign as though these elements counted heavily. As a consequence, both national party organizations concentrate on issues, particularly those of sharp partisan appeal. For the party in power such publications justify its record; for the opposition they provide an opportunity to present alternatives and well-aimed attacks on administration policy.

To accomplish these ends, both national committees biennially publish a fact book which serves candidates as a basic policy document. The Democratic National Committee has published its *Fact Book* every two years since 1954, when the publication was inaugurated under the chairmanship of Paul Butler; it is one of the least known but most widely used publications of the Committee. The 1962 *Fact Book* was researched and written by the staff of the Research Division, and a printing of 10,000 copies was distributed to party leaders, candidates at all levels, and the working press. A 144-page document describing the accomplishments of the first "Kennedy" Congress, it attempted to develop a positive statement of accomplishment and purpose.

The *Fact Book for Republican Campaigners—1962* was different in purpose and aim. For the party out of power, especially in a critical midterm election, the strategy must necessarily be one of attack. The GOP publication set about to demonstrate the Kennedy record of "failure, inconsistency, and unfulfilled promises." For example, the second page of the 69-page document stated:

The disparity between the words and the deeds of the New Frontier in foreign policy increases the risk of war through miscalculation. It becomes progressively harder to stop the Communists with stern warnings and shows of strength when they see that the deeds of the New Frontiersmen consistently fail to jibe with their words.

The domestic policies of the Kennedy administration were contrasted in two columns headed "goals" and "performance." As might be expected, the performance rarely measured up to the goals in this highly partisan document. Much use was made of disparities between words and deeds of members of the administration, with generous use of quotations from columnists, radio and TV commentators, and public speeches by prominent Democrats.

Both committees also published "fact sheets" and "position papers" which set forth factual information or were devoted to pressing issues and policy "flare-ups." The Democratic National Committee's Research Division, for instance, issued seven "fact sheets" between January and September 1962. Two of them were devoted to issues, while the others were concerned with demographic and election information.

The Republican National Committee printed six position papers concentrating on issues, the equivalent of the DNC's "fact sheets." They dealt with the national debt, foreign policy, civil rights, social security, and the like. These papers provided material for speeches and press releases by and for Republican candidates and party units. Excerpts often found their way into state committee newsletters and other party publications.

Candidates were generously furnished by both parties with speech cards and speech kits. One of the best of these, published by the Democratic Study Group, was the deck of sixteen pocket-sized speech cards summarizing particular areas of Democratic policy on a historical basis, including the record of the Kennedy administration.

Republican efforts in speech preparation tended to center on special occasions, such as the traditional commemoration of Lincoln's Birthday, but some speech material was prepared for general campaign use. Spot research assistance was available from both party headquarters, and generally the Research Divisions were charged with retrieval of information and preparation of special material on any subject.

One of the more useful candidate-oriented research services was the voting-record kit sent by each party to its nominees for Congress. Once a candidate was officially nominated, he received a set of voting records, attendance records, clippings, and speeches from the *Congressional Record.*

The voting-record books compiled by the Democrats are the more elaborate of those prepared by the two parties and extend back to the 1950s and earlier for landmark pieces of legislation. A major product of the DNC Research Division, the voting-record books in 1962 were in their third consecutive series. Voting records were rated as one of the most important and useful of the auxiliary candidate services by the respondents to this study, particularly the losers. They came closer than most campaign material to forcing the opposition candidate to "stand on the record."

Both parties publish year-round party newsletters which provide a good transition point in this discussion of candidate-voter-oriented research and organization-strategy-oriented research. The newsletters serve both purposes and are directed at both groups. During 1962 *The Democrat,* published once each week as a tabloid newspaper, was light on issue content, tending instead to emphasize party news aimed at maintaining and stimulating party loyalties.

The party newsletter with the most longevity is the *Congressional Committee Newsletter,* written and published by the Republican Congressional Committee. This highly readable and heavily partisan political document has been published each Friday by the Public Relations Division of the Hill Committee and has become a staple for

Washington correspondents looking for leads or quotable materials. The second weekly publication in 1962 was the National Committee's *Battle Line,* a four-page news sheet designed for incorporation into speeches and press releases.

ORGANIZATION-DIRECTED RESEARCH

The second major category of research production was geared to the party apparatus and to officers, as well as to candidates. Largely of a service nature, it was directed toward improved campaign strategy or organizational efficacy. Very little of this material reached the public or was used in campaigns; it was designed for strategic purposes.

Candidate-Training Programs

There is no established method of training candidates to run for public office. Whatever training a nonincumbent congressional candidate receives is usually learned on the job or inherited from some earlier candidacy for another office. Few respondents in this study had previously run for the House, those who had some prior campaign experience having run for the state legislature or county or municipal office. An earlier campaign for a lesser office is not necessarily a fruitful source of instruction for the broader context and demands of a congressional campaign. The issues are different, the constituency is often more complex, the style is more demanding, and the organizational problems are of greater magnitude. Because there is no accurate way to appraise a candidate's ability or need for training at the beginning of a campaign, about all that can be done is to bring him, along with his fellow nominees, to Washington to attend candidate-training schools. Having realized the need for some form of training program, both parties have taken halting steps in recent years to carry out a training mission.

A political campaign school is designed to bring candidates for the House into close personal contact with experienced party leaders and campaign managers, with a view toward preparing them for the campaign and informing them of those services available from official party agencies. Extensive preparation is usually devoted to planning these conferences, and candidates and managers are encouraged to participate, although at their own expense. A party may sponsor only a single training session, to which all are invited, or it may spread several such meetings over a period of time, each devoted to a particular group of candidates or a singular campaign problem.

In June and again in July and September 1962 the Democratic National Committee was host to newly designated primary nominees for the House and Senate in a series of three candidate schools. Immediately after the primary elections in a dozen to eighteen states, the winning candidates received invitations to come to Washington for campaign conferences. Control of the executive branch and Congress provided Democrats with a preeminent advantage in putting together programs for the three conferences. Cabinet officers, White House aides, administrative officials, and congressional leaders, all took part. Members of the National Committee staff and key Kennedy campaign advisers explained techniques of campaigning and services available from the various party units. Members of the Cabinet and congressional leaders discussed issues related to individual departments and attempted to evoke understanding and support for administration programs among the candidates. Each candidate was offered an opportunity to have his picture taken with the President, and most of them accepted.

The Republicans held a single candidate school in July, at the Marriott Hotel across the Potomac. Candidates and managers were invited to hear spokesmen of the National Committee and the Congressional Campaign Committee and to meet the personnel of the two organizations. The program was organized by the Congressional Campaign Committee, while the arrangements were directed by National Committee personnel. The three-day meeting was conducted in the form of seminars for candidates and managers. Experienced personnel from the committees spoke on matters related to their speciality. Candidates exchanged campaign tips and sought advice as individuals. Samples of literature and campaign materials were available and on display. Party leaders mingled with the participants offering encouragement and assistance. Major addresses were delivered by Senator Barry Goldwater and Governor Nelson Rockefeller.

Seminars and meetings, at both campaign schools, were largely descriptive rather than pedagogical. It is not possible to relate such a program to each individual congressional district or campaign. About the most that can be accomplished is to disseminate information on available services and general advice on campaign techniques. For instance, it is useful for candidates to be given advice on the purchase of television and radio time; the timing of newspaper advertisements; and fund-raising methods. These are matters of common interest, but they are not problems of common solution. The most that can be done in a "campaign school" is to point up problems, offer advice, and create an aura of conviviality and party faithfulness. Democratic candidates were given a touchstone of enthusiasm which only a White House visit could provide.

No state central committees undertook formal training conferences for candidates. Some offered advice and assisted with campaign problems, but none actually scheduled formal training sessions. The Minnesota Republican State Central Committee, for instance, assumed many ordinary campaign burdens that normally fall to candidates and offered continuous professional advice. In a letter to the authors (August 4, 1965), Robert A. Forsythe, State Chairman during the campaign, stated:

Our field staff, which is highly professional and well trained, worked with the incumbent congressmen and congressional candidates in every district. They helped schedule caravans, meetings and a host of other things in behalf of candidates. In some cases, the field representatives of the party were close to the congressional candidates as strategists. I am thinking particularly of the Minnesota Seventh Congressional District and Odin Langen's victory. After that election Langen's Democratic opponent said that the biggest factor in his defeat, outside of Langen himself, was the Republican field representative.

We tied the congressmen in on campaign literature, radio spots and featured them at the Minnesota State Fair booth. We also helped them in finances, although again not as much as we should have.

The Republican organization of Minnesota was not the only one to try some rudimentary campaign-assistance programs for congressional candidates. That program was, however, one of the best. The Democratic state committees in Michigan, Indiana, and Pennsylvania were also strong, and each ran some type of candidate-orientation program. The overall response of the candidates to questions concerning state efforts, however, was highly critical.

Respondents in both parties were enthusiastic in their reaction to the training conferences held in Washington (Table 6.1), the Democrats, on the whole being considerably more favorable than the Republicans. This discrepancy resulted partly from the fact that the single Republican school fell in early July, when several state primary elections or conventions had not as yet been held. Furthermore, control of the presidency enabled the Democrats to schedule a greater number of glamorous political speakers who were more easily available for a series of meetings, thus avoiding the problems inherent in a single one.

Personal Advice

Personal advice to candidates and managers is always in great supply although not always of high quality. During campaign time, however, as the problems of the campaign press in upon the candidate and his staff, the number who seek advice from political experts multiplies many times over. Many of these experts on the staffs of the national and congressional campaign committees have been in national politics for a number of years. Even though personnel turnover on the staffs is often high, those in key positions are remarkably stable. It is to these individuals that most questions from candidates are directed.

During the 1962 Republican campaign from 3,500 to 4,500 telephone calls came into the National Committee's switchboard each month. Of these, about fifty a day were channeled to the Campaign Director, A. B. (AB) Hermann. The Executive Director, William S. Warner, received nearly the same number from the party's leaders and candidates across the nation. Both these men, as well as other division directors, were in close touch with the Hill committees and key congressional leaders. Most calls were from people seeking advice on special campaign problems. How is a campaign budgeted? What new fund-raising ideas have been developed? How can scurrilous attacks be answered? What "name" speakers can be furnished for fund-raising dinners and other events? Where can campaign materials be procured? How can special appeals be directed at senior citizens, young voters, doctors, lawyers, Indian chiefs? The questions are as varied as they are endless. Many of them are answered intuitively, while others can be answered only from experience.

Respondents, when asked about the value of "personal advice," were generally negative; 71 percent of the Republicans and 55 percent of the Democrats among the losers judged that advice from party officials was of little or no use in the campaign (Table 6.1). Marginal candidates were hardly more sanguine in evaluating headquarters advice. Personal observation would suggest to us that much of the advice offered to candidates and campaign subordinates was worthwhile and generally useful. The negative response in some cases merely represented the fact that the respondent himself had asked for no advice, although in some instances his campaign manager had. On the whole, however, these findings support the general feeling of isolation noted by many congressional candidates in 1962.

Speakers

At some time during any campaign almost all candidates frantically raise the question of "name" speakers with national party people. Most field men, as well as others representing the Washington headquarters, are repeatedly subjected to the "speakers question." Candidates and managers profess to see many advantages in being boosted by a well-known speaker with a national or regional reputation. Depending upon his renown, the speaker, it is believed, may attract attention and money to a candidate's campaign. To the nonincumbent, seeking visibility and opportunities for fund raising, these advantages place a premium on arranging for one or more outside speakers.

From the point of view of the national party organizations, however, these requests (or demands) are very difficult to fill. All candidates want a speaker of national reputation, of high standing with the party, and with some meaning to the voters in the district. The better-known the speaker is to the average voter, the greater is the potential benefit to the candidate. Congressional candidates quite naturally tend to view their own contests as key party battles —which rate a visit by no less a person than a top man: the president, vice-president, governor, senator, or national chairman. Furthermore, each hopes to attract a man whose ideological views will fit comfortably with his own.

Conservative Republicans were particularly fortunate in that Senators Barry Goldwater and John Tower, both in the forefront of the conservative movement, were very active in the 1962 campaign. Goldwater appeared in eleven of the respondents' districts, while Tower spoke in twenty-four, more than any other single individual in either party. These appearances were highly valued by the respondents, many of whom went out of their way to praise the famous men who were available by choice or by assignment to speak in their behalf.

Among the respondents, 53 percent of the Democrats and 48 percent of the Republican losers claimed speakers from outside their states. Democrats listed thirty-four separate speeches by senators, twenty by members of the Kennedy Cabinet, fifteen by staff members of the Democratic National Committee, and eight by the President himself. Despite these efforts, the evaluation by candidates of the usefulness of speakers to their campaigns invariably showed disappointment. Only 9 percent of the Republican losers and 6 percent of the Democrats considered speakers to have been of "very much" assistance to their campaigns.

During congressional campaigns each national party headquarters tries to coordinate the many requests and demands for speakers which press upon leading public figures in each party. The speakers' bureaus of the national committees have long since discovered that most engagements for speakers, if served at all, must be honored by congressmen, subordinate party officials, or in the case of the party out of power, a former presidential assistant. The time of leading party figures is extremely limited, and many of them are engaged in campaigns of their own. Much of the time of field representatives and national campaign coordinators is spent explaining these facts of political life to disgruntled candidates and managers.

Major party leaders are often hesitant to involve themselves in a congressional contest, lest an unfortunate turn of events damage their own personal prestige or political position. Nevertheless, in 1962 both President Kennedy and former Presidents Eisenhower and Truman took active parts in the campaign.[2]

President Kennedy, after several weekend sorties, planned to undertake a major speaking tour in behalf of congressional Democrats but cut it short on October 20 because of the developing crisis over Soviet missile emplacements in Cuba. The President, in Chicago for a speech, cancelled the remaining engagements on the tour and returned to Washington. His decision could hardly be questioned in

2. Nonincumbent Democratic candidate Richard Hanna, running in the newly created Thirty-fourth District of California, was so elated with the presence at a major dinner of former President Truman that he mistakenly introduced him as "former President Hoover." Hanna, recovering nicely fom the blooper, went on to defeat his conservative Republican opponent in the November election. "The True Story of an Election," a sixty-minute film produced by Churchill Films, 6671 Sunset Boulevard, Los Angeles, California.

light of the ensuing two weeks at the brink, but several Democratic candidates complained of the damage done their campaigns by the President's inability to keep engagements in their districts.

Former President Dwight Eisenhower, initially reluctant to enter the campaign, was finally persuaded and undertook a series of tours which eventually covered twenty-three states and produced thirty-four speeches. These were more frequently given in behalf of entire state tickets, rather than for individual congressional candidates. Though some—such as his St. Paul-Minneapolis speech in behalf of incumbent Walter Judd—were arranged to benefit one particular candidate, most were general speeches, which included only a passing reference to the congressional candidate or the incumbent congressman in the district.

Even though a speaker sent to represent his party may not meet the candidate's demands for celebrity, the national party organizations nonetheless make every effort to furnish as renowned a speaker as possible. Most key party spokesmen were willing to allow the speakers' bureaus of the national committees to schedule speeches for them once dates and places had been cleared through their own offices. Ordinarily the speaker must be acceptable to the candidate in whose behalf he is appearing.[3]

Relationships between congressional candidates, particularly incumbents, and the national committees are not always friendly either during or after an election campaign. One bone of contention mentioned by numerous candidates regarded the arrangements for speakers. Their experience was corroborated by Charles Clapp, who reported that one incumbent had noted:

When I came to Congress—even before—I went to the National Committee and offered to be of assistance to the Democratic party. Dur-

3. Some prominent men in both parties did not allow their speaking engagements to be scheduled by the speakers' bureaus. During 1961–63 Senator Barry Goldwater, the most sought-after speaker in the Republican party next to General Eisenhower, would seldom allow the National Committee to arrange speaking engagements for him. Most requests for the Arizona senator went directly to his office, and those received through other channels were referred there. For a leader of Goldwater's importance, and especially one in great demand, it made a good deal of sense to completely control his own herculean speaking schedule, however much trouble this arrangement might have caused GOP headquarters planners. Similarly, Senator Humphrey, among others, booked his own speaking engagements, at times contrary to requests received by the National Committee. At all points the White House staff played a strong role in "placing" speakers where it was politically expedient.

ing a recent presidential campaign, they sent me out to make 26 speeches in five or six states, in the course of which I expended $680. After the campaign I decided it was reasonable to ask the committee to reimburse me for these expenses, since it had insisted in the beginning that I would be reimbursed. I sent in my statement and said, "I am $680 in arrears," and they replied, "Well, what about it? We are $1,500,000 in arrears." Finally, after I raised a row I received a reply from an employee of the committee saying, "Congressman, don't you know that you should have collected your expenses from each place that you spoke?" Now, that was ridiculous. In the final days of the campaign I spoke in as many as five or six places some days. Usually I knew no one in the community.[4]

After the 1962 campaign other complaints were forthcoming from losers and marginal candidates alike:

I asked for speakers but received no reply.

With the exception of _____, who did a marvelous job at a "Womans' Day" in August . . . I received no assistance on speakers; yet we made a request for such assistance and speakers within one week of the primary election. The real problem is that I was never told whether or not I would get a speaker—to this date I have not received a firm answer to this question—and I think this is an unnecessary burden to place on the candidate. If the committee does not feel the district should have a speaker, the candidate should be told and not left dangling in mid-air.

They always came to the district nearby. It was tragic that our district with approximately 750,000 inhabitants was ignored. We were unable to get a prominent figure for our congressional dinner.

They did not even have a national Democrat at the National Corn Picking Contest. Why? I would like to know. We called everyone in Washington and could not get past any of the front desks. Why?

We were "let down" in this regard.

Governor _____ wouldn't come. He was the only one who could have helped.

Goldwater and Nixon came but local and state candidates were even denied the privilege of sitting on the same platform.

These responses are understandable coming from candidates who had just been defeated; the national committees could not possibly have filled every request for assistance. Nevertheless, the problem of speakers indicates another aspect of the unhappy relations that

4. Charles L. Clapp, *The Congressman: His Work As He Sees It* (Washington: The Brookings Institution, 1963), p. 359.

often exist between congressional candidates and the national party organizations.

The Republican National Committee maintains records of all speeches scheduled during each campaign period; during the period from June 1, 1962, to election day, 163 speeches were scheduled in 130 congressional districts.[5] Not surprisingly, the Republicans relied heavily on their incumbent members of Congress in 1962. Twenty-one members of the House and ten senators provided speeches in states other than their own. Congressmen, who must run for reelection every two years, are usually hard-pressed to find the time to provide assistance to other congressional candidates. Most of those who did contribute time as speakers did so at little risk, being reasonably sure of re-election. The speakers' bureaus must place heavy reliance on speakers who are not themselves running for office.

Among all marginal losers 54.6 percent were furnished an outside speaker by the national committee. In marginal Republican districts 62.5 percent benefited, while marginal Democrats fared less well, with 45 percent. Since only 43 percent of all Republican candidates were furnished with speakers, it becomes apparent that the marginal candidates did receive special consideration.

Geographically congressional candidates in the Midwest received the greatest proportion of benefits from outside speakers.[6] With 33 percent of the contested seats, these candidates received 42 percent of the outside speakers. Of the other three regions only the West had more speakers than its percentage of the seats entitled it to. With

5. These data on speakers were collected through the cooperation of Mrs. Vera Ash, long-time director of the Speakers' Bureau at the Republican National Committee. The Democratic National Committee also includes a speakers' bureau, but its records were not available for analysis.

6. Arriving at a meaningful geographic distribution of the states is always a thorny problem. Too many divisions result in too few distinctions, while a restricted number of areas may not take into account regional differences. We have categorized the states by area as follows:

South: Alabama, Arkansas, Florida, Georgia, Louisiana, Mississippi, North Carolina, South Carolina, Tennessee, Texas, Virginia.

Midwest: (including the Border States) Illinois, Indiana, Iowa, Kansas, Kentucky, Michigan, Minnesota, Missouri, Nebraska, North Dakota, Ohio, Oklahoma, South Dakota, West Virginia, Wisconsin.

West: Arizona, Idaho, California, Hawaii, Montana, New Mexico, Colorado, Alaska, Oregon, Utah, Washington, Nevada, Wyoming.

Northeast: Connecticut, Delaware, Maine, Maryland, Massachusetts, New Hampshire, New Jersey, New York, Pennsylvania, Rhode Island, Vermont.

16 percent of the seats, the western congressional candidates utilized 17 percent of the speakers (see Table 6.2).

In response to the questionnaire, 53 percent of the Democrats noted visits from speakers from outside the state; 48 percent of the Republicans were successful in attempts to get speakers—somewhat surprising in view of the shortage of GOP officeholders in 1962. The advantages to the party in power were quite apparent from the roster of Democratic speaking engagements. Candidates listed thirty-four separate speeches by senators, twenty by members of the Kennedy Cabinet, fifteen by staff members of the Democratic National Committee, and eight by the President himself. Other commitments were met by members of the White House staff and by Democratic congressmen.

Table 6.2

Geographic Distribution of GOP Speakers Arranged by the Republican National Committee

	No. of Seats (435)	No. of Speakers (187)	No. of Multiple Speakers (37)
South	106 (24%)	40 (22%)	7 (19%)
Midwest	142 (33%)	79 (42%)	14 (38%)
West	70 (16%)	32 (17%)	6 (16%)
Northeast	117 (27%)	36 (19%)	10 (27%)

Only 9 percent of the Republicans and 6 percent of the Democrats considered speakers to have been of very much help during the campaign. The more significant finding, however, was that 71 percent of the Republicans and 61 percent of the Democrats considered speakers of no help at all. There were indications that some of the disappointed nonincumbent losers had placed too much reliance on single visits by nationally known speakers and failed to balance these isolated events against the overall insurmountable problems of their campaigns.

Finally, it should be noted that some candidates not only did not seek assistance from speakers but actively opposed any "outside" help. These candidates believed that voters were sensitive to "interference" from Washington, both in government programs and in political campaigns. One Republican noted:

I told the congressional committee that I did not want any help. The people up here don't cotton to outside people coming in to tell them how to vote. An outside speaker or outside money would have hurt my chances more that either would have helped.

Others were influenced by the judgment of state or local party groups in deciding to forego assistance from the national parties. A Democrat reported, "I could have asked certain national men myself, but County HQ insisted on reserving this right to themselves. So no one save Mr. _____ and state candidates appeared."

Party response to the problem of speakers emphasizes again the decentralized nature of the American political system. The national committees seek to coordinate speaking engagements, but they must always operate within multiple limits laid down by the local and state organizations, by the cadre of possible speakers, by the parallel Hill campaign committees, and by the desires of the candidates themselves.

Field Services

It is a common misconception that candidates in the field benefit from continuing liaison with "expert" representatives of the national party organizations. These field men supposedly offer advice on campaign techniques, scheduling, speaking engagements, and other elements of the "good" campaign. Unfortunately, from the candidate's point of view, the assumption is virtually groundless.

In 1962 the Republican National Congressional Committee's field operations, under the direction of Chauncy Robbins, employed only three full-time field men to cover the entire nation. All of them were members of the RNCC's permanent staff assigned to field operations. Five or six additional field operatives volunteered their services, either without pay or, at most, for expenses.

The Democratic National Congressional Committee has long needed field services but has never been staffed adequately to carry them out. Only a few top staff people from the National Committee offices worked in the field in 1962, and these were associated with the entourage of the President or cabinet members as "advance men."

Ideally a permanent field force could furnish information relating to individual districts, prospective candidates, effective local campaign gambits, and general intelligence that might be helpful to the candidate. With so few men to cover the 435 election districts in the House, it is not possible to rise to the potential.

That these services did not measure up to the ideal was illustrated by the candidates' reactions to them. As noted in Table 6.1, few candidates in either party considered the national organizations to be at all helpful in providing field services. About 70 out of every 100 candidates received no field assistance at all.

This fact is worth further consideration. National party officers are unable to provide the field service they would like for congressional races. This lack represents an area over which they have little control: there are some inherent problems which prevent them from engaging in field activities to the extent that they might wish. First, the perennial shortage of funds precludes the employment of a field force large enough to service more than a small number of races. More important, however, are the problems of training and the episodic nature of elections. Training for field men must necessarily evolve from experience in the field. There is no method of training an individual to be a political field man; he must develop whatever skills are necessary from exposure to politics and experiences in campaigns. Yet these very requirements restrict the number of such men available for this kind of work. Furthermore, lack of security and periodic employment severely reduce the number of people who are willing to be employed for field responsibilities. Consequently, as an election year nears, the party organizations must hire whoever is available or assign regular headquarters staff personnel to field activities. Neither of these alternatives is particularly satisfactory. The first results in a hit-or-miss system of employment, while the second takes experienced campaign operatives away from important ongoing activities.

Special Group Activities

Voter groups are made up of people with similar backgrounds, with ethnic or religious identities, or with other common sociological or psychological determinants. Although no one has satisfactorily measured the impact of these groups on voting behavior it is apparent that there is a causal relationship between the groups and the way they vote. Data from the University of Michigan's Survey Research Center suggests that there is a high correlation between voting behavior of certain groups—labor unions, Catholics, Negroes, and Jews—and the Democratic party. Persons closely identified with such groups tend to vote Democratic to a greater extent than do persons with weak group identification.[7] Group participation in politics is shaped to a large extent by public expectations of what the group believes. That is, regardless of the degree to which a particular group becomes active in a political undertaking, the public believes that it is active and united.

Political leaders and candidates tend to view politics as a series of separate appeals to particular voter groups. The voting behavior of Negroes, Poles, women, farmers, young people, and other discernible social or ethnic groups are probed, measured, and analyzed for predictable trends in behavior. But prediction, like hindsight, is not enough in politics.

Both national committees normally have several subdivisions that deal with special voter groups. Thus in one campaign, senior citizens and labor may be predominant while in another farm groups or minorities may figure largely. At times such divisions completely disappear from the organizational entity while new ones grow to replace them. Periodic campaigns in behalf of medical insurance have caused various doctors' or healing-arts divisions at the two committees to rise, only to fall once the issue had run its course. In 1962 the impact of Medicare on the national committees caused the reactivation of senior citizens' programs associated with each. And the lack of important labor or farm issues caused those two areas of special-group activity to languish. A special organization unit, the famed Southern Division, at the Republican National Committee was at its zenith during the 1962 election campaign— seeking by means of regional appeals to enhance GOP prospects in the South. The budget for "Operation Dixie" far surpassed that of any other campaign division.

Considerations of space led us to limit the number of campaign units to be included in the questionnaire. We chose to leave out those traditional divisions of party interest covering labor and farm interests. We also chose not to include the Southern Division of the Republican National Committee because it was pertinent to a single section of the nation—one with few Republican candidates. We restricted our query to three campaign units: women's divisions, minorities, and youth groups.

7. Angus Campbell, Warren E. Miller, Philip E. Converse, and Donald E. Stokes, *The American Voter* (New York: Wiley, 1960), Ch. 12.

Both national party committees have been seeking for years to delineate acceptable and viable roles for women and women's groups in national politics. Some have argued that the role of women in party affairs should not differ markedly from that of men; politics and political activity, it is maintained, do not differ between the sexes. Others, however, suggest that there are special duties that can best be performed by women and for which they are more inherently qualified than are the males. For their part, women have long believed that they are looked down upon and exploited by the party leadership. They cite examples of apparent discrimination to support their view. For instance, the Republican National Convention acted in 1952 to add certain state chairmen to the membership of the National Committee; since men are traditionally state party chairmen, some women argued that the move was designed to dilute the influence of women in party affairs. And within the national committees themselves, staff rivalries for financial support, program leadership, and other factors often take shape between the womens' organizations and other units.[8]

Women as a special voter group were not very helpful to candidates in 1962. Almost 70 percent of the respondents in both parties questioned the value of the women's groups. The few female candidates understandably gave them credit, but few men did so.

In view of the energy, money, and talent that is channeled into the women's operations of the national party organizations, these responses are somewhat startling. Aside from the possibility that many respondents who had women working in their campaigns did not associate them with the national party organizations, the statistic points up the nature of the world of politics and government. Both the actual and the would-be wielders of power are predominantly male, and this fact translates into voter appeals and evaluation of campaign assistance.

It would seem axiomatic that the political parties, repeatedly having proclaimed their intention of capturing the Negro vote, would maintain effective machinery for doing so. Yet the Minorities Divisions of the two national committees have been financially starved and until recently officially ignored. The Democrats have tended to take the Negro vote for granted since the New Deal era, while the Republicans have forfeited it as a small reward for considerable ex-

8. Cornelius P. Cotter and Bernard C. Hennessy, *Politics Without Power: The National Party Committees* (New York: Atherton, 1964), pp. 149–54.

penditure. Both parties, in seeking to enlist the support of southern voters, have difficulty reconciling these efforts with the growing political power of black voters in the North and South. The attitude that "the Negroes will always vote Democratic" has permeated the upper echelons of the parties and has assured the Minorities Divisions their awkward positions within national party councils.

Neither of the congressional party committees assign staff exclusively to minority voters. Particular candidates may benefit from the activities of field men working in Negro areas, but their assignments are not based solely on the minority status of the voters. Rather, it reflects the overall chances of the candidate in a district which contains Negroes. Essentially the same is true of the state committees. A few appeal directly to the Negro populace in areas of heavy voter concentration, but again this effort is a by-product of a marginal district which contains Negroes. In other words, the controlling factor in local party programs is not that there are Negroes in the district but that the district with Negroes in it is, or might be, a marginal district.

The National Committees, on the other hand, do have formal Minorities Divisions. As with other headquarters operations, neither of them has sufficient nourishment to be very active between elections and consequently strain to do better during a campaign. In 1962, for instance, the Republican high command provided only one man, the director, to run the Minorities Division. For much of the election he was not even provided with secretarial assistance. There is little a single individual, regardless of his talent, can do under such circumstances. During the 1962 campaign Clay Claiborne, the Director of the Division, spent most of the campaign in a single state in which a major Republican officeholder was thought to be in political trouble.[9]

Not surprisingly, few candidates received any assistance from the Minorities units of the two parties. Only 4 percent of the Republicans and 3 percent of the Democrats received "very much" aid from this source.

Each national party headquarters houses respectively the National Young Republican Federation and the Young Democratic Clubs of America. The careers of both John F. Kennedy and Senator

9. Claiborne, spent six weeks in Louisville, Kentucky, seeking to lend assistance to Senator Thruston Morton's reelection campaign. Partly through Claiborne's efforts the Senator's vote percentage in Negro sections of Louisville approached 50 percent.

Barry Goldwater stimulated the youth of both political persuasions into active political work as no two politicians had done in recent years. Although both national committees had young people's units in operation in presidential contests for the past few campaigns, it was not until the era of Paul Butler at the Democratic National Committee that the Young Democrats received a regular berth on the staff. Despite the effectiveness of their work with the Kennedy presidential campaign of 1960, the Young Democrats, like other special group units at the National Committee, were provided with little financial support and recognition for the 1962 congressional campaign. This neglect was in the face of their faithfulness in assuming tedious responsibilities in many state campaigns and in individual congressional campaigns.

The Young Republicans are apparently better organized and appear better integrated into the national party structure than the Young Democrats. Nonetheless, by the time of the 1962 general elections the YRs were already split decisively between the conservative Goldwater supporters and the "Old Guard" moderates who had been in control of the national Young Republican organization for some years. Much of the conservative strength resulting from this division was channeled into the Young Americans for Freedom, a separate organization not affiliated with the party but sharing many offices and members with the Young Republicans.[10] The aftermath of this dispute was the election of a member of the YAF as national chairman of the Young Republicans in 1963. The resulting splits in the YR organizations on campuses across the country have never fully healed since that date. The infighting was already proving an embarrassment to Republican candidates in the 1962 elections because the conservative activists made known their desire for Senator Goldwater to receive the Republican nomination in 1964.

The results of these difficulties in the Young Republican establishment were evident in the responses to the questions concerning the evaluation of headquarters aid. All but one of those included in the 6 percent who said that the Young Republicans were "very much" helpful were identified as conservatives. This identification is to some extent subjective but is corroborated by an inspection of the campaign literature of the individual candidates.[11]

10. Cotter and Hennessy, pp. 154–58.
11. As a part of this project a reasonably complete collection of campaign literature of individual candidates was compiled. It was especially helpful in revealing issue positions and personal data.

The advantages of support by the Young Democrats was not valued by a single candidate. There were some who received some assistance from the YD's, but few singled them out for thanks for their campaign activities.

These results present an interesting contrast. The candidates were much more prone to acknowledge the worthiness of campaign efforts from other divisions of state and national headquarters. They found publications, research, speech assistance, field support, and candidate schools to be useful in the development of their campaigns, but services directed to particular groups of voters by particular campaign divisions were not at all well received. None of the three groups emphasized (women, minorities, and young people) were credited with important campaign roles. It is not possible to identify the reasons for their ineffectiveness, although they would appear to differ from one group to another.

Public-Opinion Polling in Congressional Campaigns

The study of public opinion and opinion measurement has undoubtedly become more sophisticated during the past few decades. It is certainly not the "real ruler of America," as suggested by James Bryce in 1921,[12] but neither is it an insignificant factor in American politics, as argued by some critics. Polls have come to occupy an important place in American politics, and for the most part the opinion industry has carved for itself a responsible role in political campaigns. The art or science of polling first began making an impact in presidential races. Public fascination with the "scientific" measurement of voter choices made polls a sure winner in the journalistic sweepstakes. As their reputation for accuracy has grown, their public-information role has become a significant part of our political system. Nevertheless, their most important role is in campaign strategy.

No poll will enable a candidate to change his personality or his stand on issues. Transformations of this magnitude are not the province of the opinion analysts, and that is as it should be. However, the findings of competent opinion polls can enable a candidate to modify and select his campaign strategies so as to take maximum advantage of his time and money; those issues which appear to have

12. James Bryce, *Modern Democracies,* vol. 2 (New York: Macmillan, 1921), p. 122.

the most appeal to voters; and the campaign techniques that may have the greatest impact for him. Even these changes in strategy may not win an election, but they can have a dramatic effect in marginal or other close races.

As opinion polling has matured, it has broadened its role in the political arena. Presidential elections and presidential candidates no longer represent the sole interest of the pollster. Louis Harris has noted this broadening of the role of the political poll:

> Survey research is a powerful instrument of intelligence and counsel for the candidate running for office, whether for mayor, congressman, U.S. senator, governor, or president. During the 1962 campaign it is likely that over two-thirds of the men running for the U.S. Senate had polls conducted for them, probably three-quarters of the candidates for governor employed polling from a professional organization, and about one congressional candidate in ten used survey research in his campaign for election.[13]

Harris' estimate of the number of congressional candidates employing opinion polls in 1962 is at variance with the actual number reflected by the responses in this study. Instead of one-tenth of the House candidates estimated by Harris, 30 percent of all losing candidates reported that opinion polls were taken in their districts. This disparity suggests that politicians and pollsters may not define *opinion poll* in the same way. To some it means a straw vote conducted by a newspaper and based perhaps upon random reader response to mailed ballots or coupons. The accuracy of such polls is quite appropriately suspect, since they are not governed by strict sampling techniques or design. Nonetheless, to naive candidates as well as to newspaper consumers such polling constitutes the "scientific" measurement of voter attitudes conducted by a professional opinion-polling organization. The responses of most of the losing candidates suggest that their use of the word *poll* conformed to the latter definition. If so, the Harris estimate is considerably below the actual number of polls that were commissioned in 1962 at the congressional district level.

Surveys of public opinion are useful in politics at two levels. Party organizations or officials have begun within recent years to use them as recruitment and candidate-evaluation devices, while can-

13. Louis Harris, "Polls and Politics in the United States," *Public Opinion Quarterly,* 27, no. 1 (Spring 1963), 3–8.

didates have used them, to a much greater extent, in the development of campaign strategies.

The preprimary phase of polling activities encompasses the recruitment of candidates, the identification of more meaningful issues, and the assessment of party and candidate images. Information on public attitudes toward each of these factors can be valuable to party organizations as they move into an election campaign. At the very least, such a survey will enable the party leaders and candidates to chart a course between their ambitions and their limitations.

A prerecruitment poll can provide the party with data that will enable it to identify and, it is hoped, recruit candidates who have a high degree of voter identification and whose public image needs but little buffing. They may also generate useful information regarding voter acceptance of candidates, familiarity with names, and even particular advantages enjoyed by one candidate over another. Follow-up questions may indicate the comparative initial "acceptance" of several candidates in contrast with those of the opposition party; the qualities the voters in a particular district or area hold uppermost in their evaluations of political men; and questions designed to elicit voters' perceptions of candidates which must be met and might be corrected.[14]

The second use of precampaign polls is as a tool to identify those issues which might prove beneficial or detrimental to a candidate once he is selected by his party. Party leaders, in looking ahead to the general election campaign, need to know which candidate might be successful against the potential opposition. To do so, the leadership needs to assess public issues in order to avoid candidates who might be identified in the public mind with possibly damaging attitudes. For example, in 1966 the results of a poll in New York State led to the by-passing of certain candidates because

---

14. Representative questions are the following taken from a poll contracted for by a Republican State Committee:

Here is a card which lists some possible Republican candidates for Congress from this district. Which one of these do you think you would vote for in the primary?

How well do you know each of the following names? By that I mean can you identify each person, or what he has done or what he is doing?

In your own words can you tell me what qualities you look for in a man when you are deciding which candidate you will vote for in the primary election?

they were too closely identified with the 1964 Goldwater campaign.

Campaign strategists rarely know in advance which issues will attract voters and which ones will repel them. At times there are serious misconceptions of voters' attitudes toward a given issue, and a campaign public-opinion survey can point these out. One poll sponsored by Oregon's party leaders corrected general notions that problems in the timber industry were a prime concern to the people. The results showed that only 9 percent of the people were aware of such problems, and only 3 percent felt that the issue would affect their vote in any way. When asked in what way it would affect their vote, respondents came to a standoff, with only 0.5 percent favoring the Republican candidate, while the same number came out for the Democrat. The party leaders then agreed that the problems of the timber industry was not an exploitable issue. This survey provided them with an additional factor to consider in the recruitment of a candidate to carry the GOP standard.

Finally, surveys can be used in preprimary campaign planning to assess the current public image of the party or its leaders. Since the 1940s and 1950s the Republican image has been shown in many national surveys to be one of "big business," while the Democrats are believed by the voters to favor "labor" or "the little people." One confidential poll of sixteen states in 1956 revealed that in only two did the voters disagree with the first of these assertions, while the second held true in all but one state. Knowing the extent and intensity of such opinions can be advantageous, and party leaders and candidates need to know of these matters in advance.[15]

Once the candidates are selected, campaign strategies must be developed and carried out. Political leaders in safe districts where an incumbent is being defended may be able to make accurate judgments on strategic matters by simply relying upon those tactics which have been successful in the past; sometimes it is not necessary to plan even so much. In close contests, however, a more careful assessment of the factors which go into the voter equation is necessary. The primary method of making such an assessment is the public-opinion survey, which is used to gather data necessary for making campaign judgments. Such information will ordinarily take three forms: (1) broad population data, to enable major voter

15. A corollary use of an opinion survey was suggested by two GOP congressional candidates who reported their use to determine, among other items, what national Republican leaders would draw larger crowds for fund-raising functions preliminary to the 1962 campaign. Both resulted in the invitation of Senator Barry Goldwater to statewide party events.

blocs to be identified; (2) issue data, to define those areas of debate that will attract the widest possible support; and (3) candidate data, to point out strengths and deficiencies in the image of the man.

One of the most important uses of survey data has been the identification of group patterns that make up the social and political fabric of a district. Such social analysis will indicate racial and religious patterns, ethnic and nationality group centers, occupational classes, and other constituency distinctions by area. When these data are combined with voting patterns from prior years, they enable candidates and managers to estimate the strategies that might be incorporated into winning a majority vote for the candidate. If polls are carried out throughout the election period at given intervals, the candidate's weaknesses with particular groups of voters can be analyzed and corrective action can be attempted. There is no evidence that any substantial number of House candidates in 1962 were able to take advantage of polling to gather data of this sort about their districts.

The second use of strategy polls is to identify those issues which might prove beneficial or detrimental to the candidate or the party. Many issues are localized so that national opinion surveys do not reflect the most appropriate or politically salable position the party may want to take. At the same time, however, issues are seldom confined to the boundaries of one district; they extend throughout the state or region. Consequently a statewide poll is often helpful to a congressional candidate in developing his own campaign issues. If, for example, a statewide poll reveals that unemployment is a major concern to the voters, the same concern is likely to predominate in some of the congressional districts. Other representative issues that emerged in particular localities in 1962 were public as against private power, grazing and timber control by the national government, the development of oceanographic sciences, and agricultural problems.

A Republican candidate reported that the survey contracted for by his State Central Committee showed that Medicare was not an important concern in the minds of most age groups normally sensitive to the question. Consequently he played down the issue as much as possible.[16]

A third area of information which can be used as an element in

16. A similar survey for the Republican National Committee showed that there was little voter concern with the issue of the "Kennedy Dynasty" in 1962. The national leadership had little control over the use of such issues by local and state candidates but, subsequent to the poll, made little use of this particular issue in national campaign materials.

strategic campaign planning concerns the candidate's public image with the voters. It should not be forgotten, however, that no poll of candidate images will determine the outcome of a nomination contest. It is therefore helpful to a candidate to estimate what the voters think of him personally. Especially those candidates who have obvious personal, financial, or professional advantages are enabled by polls to take cognizance of their own strengths.

These are the major areas to which opinion data can be usefully put. It is not enough for a poll to reflect which candidate might win the election; polls must be related to potential electoral behavior and related to past voting statistics if they are to be useful in campaign planning. Those polls which attract public attention are ordinarily designed for journalistic purposes and a newspaper audience. They, and "confidential" polls which have been leaked to the press, can have a considerable impact upon an election campaign.

Although polls can be useful to candidates seeking to inaugurate a bandwagon movement, a more common effect is a reduction of productive campaign work by volunteer workers. If the candidate is shown by a poll to have a reasonable chance of success, his campaign workers may slacken their efforts on the assumption that their services are not really needed to assure victory. One Republican noted that the poll taken in his district three weeks before the election "looked so good that it contributed to the general overconfidence from which we suffered." Another Republican candidate stated that "these polls were taken by a leading metropolitan newspaper and the only effect the results might have had were to tend to diminish aggressiveness during the latter stages of the campaign, since all polls except the final one showed me comfortably in the lead."

A more likely effect of a leaked or published poll is to cause workers and contributors to turn their backs on the candidate shown to be trailing. A number of Democratic losing candidates commented bitterly upon the results for their campaigns:

Lou Harris for State Central Committee—it showed that I wouldn't get 30% of the vote and a lot of "big" people left me or didn't get interested. The poll hurt me a great deal—I received over 42% of the vote— running by myself—with little aid from anyone and this against a twelve-year incumbent and a Republican landslide.

People who might have given did not give as they felt it would be wasted money.

Harris poll leaked and was disastrous to my cause.

It made it impossible for me to get campaign contributions I could have received had it not been for the poll. It was very detrimental to the campaign in general. It was also inaccurate by 12–13 percent in primary, and by over 10 percent in the general election.

Polls have not been particularly useful in developing campaign strategies in the past, although more and more candidates are depending upon them for that purpose now. Lewis Dexter noted in 1954:

> *Under present sampling procedures, polls of candidate popularity are not likely to be of use to political campaigners,* because the samples are too small to permit any helpful inferences about where the candidate is weak, where he is strong, who is in doubt. Of course, polls often report on the attitudes of groups and regions. But politics is operated geographically by wards and precincts and by groups which are much more refined than those upon which polls report. . . .
>
> Polls of candidate popularity, as they are conducted for newspaper purposes, do not yield information nearly as valuable as that provided by the analysis of voting statistics, corrected and checked by information from precincts and groups. Obviously, anyone studying campaign strategy will in default of other information utilize what is available in the polls; but he should be extremely chary of recommending anything on the basis of most polls alone. It would be possible, without sacrificing the journalistic interest of polls, to make them somewhat more helpful for campaign planning.[17]

The past decade has brought to fruition some of the changes proposed by Dexter. Polling organizations have, to a greater extent than before, carried their efforts to the congressional district level. Polls are now used in selected "key" precincts to ascertain the candidate preferences of special population groups or particular swing areas. They have also been used to identify the potential impact of selected issues.

It is not possible to say that congressional candidates today make better use of opinion polls as strategic devices than did their predecessors of a decade or more ago. But it is reasonable to conclude, in view of the growth of polling in politics, that candidates today are more apt to use polling in their campaign efforts.

Some Democratic candidates in 1962 were furnished with, or had

17. Lewis A. Dexter, "The Use of Public Opinion Polls by Political Party Organizations," *Public Opinion Quarterly*, 18, no. 1 (Spring 1954), 55–6.

access to, the Harris Poll conducted by numerous state central committees. The Democratic National Committee, cooperating with the
AFL–CIO's COPE, contracted with the Harris organization to run
polls in selected districts and states. In some instances the results were
leaked to candidates, while in others the DNC notified the candidates
of the results in order to bring campaign deficiencies to their attention.
Some of the poll results found their way into print, with the results
noted earlier. Harris ordinarily included all state races—gubernatorial, senatorial, and congressional—but on occasion, especially in
marginal districts, the poll was confined to a single district.

The Republican National Committee used the services of Opinion
Research Corporation of Princeton, New Jersey. Headed by Thomas
W. Benham, that organization has done issue research and campaign
polling for the National Republican Party for a number of years. In
1962 it prepared a midcampaign survey of voter attitudes toward the
GOP, the Kennedy administration, members of the Kennedy family,
and issues ranging from farm prices to civil rights. The results were
presented to the Republican National Committee meeting in July and
later to the National Committee staff. Although taken before the
campaign really got under way, the surveys provided candidates with
an overall view of public attitudes toward the Republican party and
the opposition. Because they were not localized, they did not provide
much assistance to the individual candidate for Congress.[18]

An opinion poll of some type was taken in 30 percent of the
districts in 1962 (Democrats, 33 percent; Republicans, 28 percent).
Among marginal candidates 39 percent had polls available to them,
the GOP a slightly larger percentage (40 percent) than the Democrats (38 percent). The Democrats, on the whole, had the benefit of
more polls because of the National Committee's contracts with the
Harris organization. Both parties were more willing to invest in
surveys in marginal districts since these represented the greatest potential for political gain.

Table 6.3 shows the candidates' assessment of the effect of polls on
each campaign.

The 1962 polls had little or no effect on the campaigns of 37 percent of the losing candidates and 44 percent of the marginal losers.
Their polls either confirmed the approach being taken or were timed

18. The Republican National Committee did not contract with a polling or
survey organization for individual contests except in the case of National
Chairman William E. Miller, who was in a close race for reelection to Congress
in upstate New York.

Table 6.3
Effects of Polls on Campaign

	All Losing Candidates			Marginals		
	GOP (N = 36)	DEM (N = 35)	ALL (N = 71)	GOP (N = 14)	DEM (N = 11)	ALL (N = 25)
Little or *No Effect*	42%	31%	37%	36%	55%	44%
Some to a *Considerable Effect*						
Allocation of Funds for Ads, Radio, TV, etc.	25%	14%	20%	14%	35%	24%
Campaign Organization	22	20	21	14	27	20
Campaign Staffing	8	0	4	7	9	8
On Selection and Emphasis on Issues	42	37	40	36	45	40

Percentages total over 100 because of multiple choices.

so that the impact upon the campaign was minimal. One Republican's comment exemplified those included in this group:

> The poll was so badly handled that tabulated results were not considered truly representative and wholly dependable. Also, by the time results were available my campaign was in its last stages. The poll showed that I would win.

Among those who were able to use poll data to some or to a considerable extent most were aided in the selection of issues to emphasize; 40 percent of the respondents in this group stated that poll data had reinforced their choice of issues, caused some change in issue emphasis, or served as the vehicle through which their issues were selected. Among those whose choice of issues was strengthened by the Harris Poll was a Democrat who noted:

> . . . confirmed choices already made. Medicare for the aged, federal aid to education, and area redevelopment.

Several candidates noted that they decided to change the emphasis which had been placed on certain issues prior to the poll taken in their district:

> The poll pointed up the attitudes on federal aid to education which already were fairly well known. This issue was played down.

> I used the October 1st poll to determine last two weeks of speeches.

> We had been over-emphasizing Medicare. The poll showed that 80 per cent of the respondents wanted it.

Finally, some candidates in both parties used survey data in the initial selection of issues. A Republican stated that the effect of his poll was "Very great. We emphasized issues with which the majority of voters supported our position." A candidate on the Democratic ticket stated that his poll was made "solely to determine the issues to be used." No candidate admitted that he changed his position to bring it in line with poll responses. But these data were clearly influential in many decisions as to which issues to emphasize.

As shown in Table 6.3, the second-largest group of respondents acknowledged making changes in their campaign organization as a result of their polls. These changes were usually in the form of renewed efforts to appeal to a particular section of the district where the survey revealed relative weakness, a strengthened effort in particular population groups, and an increased emphasis on getting out the vote.

Decisions to increase campaign emphasis in areas of weakness were described by several candidates:

We decided . . . to focus on strongest Republican district rather than the Democratic district.

There was some shift to what the poll showed was a "weak" county.

We planned a helicopter tour of the district in the last week to gain attention and to become better known.

Others sought to enhance their appeal with groups of voters who were shown by the polls to be islands of weakness. A Democrat, for instance, reported that he spent a great deal of time during the last few days of the campaign in trying to organize support among senior citizens groups which were shown by the survey to be somewhat apathetic. A Republican increased his efforts in blue-collar areas, while another "tried to organize Spanish areas to offset the projected loss of the Polish vote in the opposition's stronghold."

Finally, some candidates in both parties noted the need to "get out the vote" because their polls showed that a larger than normal vote would improve their chances. One Democrat made this a family project:

The poll found I was down 10 points—Seven of my children and I went door to door to thousands of homes to try to improve this. We passed out cards and literature.

Table 6.3 shows that 8 percent of the GOP respondents in this group reported some staffing changes as a result of a survey. One of these individuals noted that he added three cochairmen to recruit local volunteers in certain areas of the district after his poll showed a general weakness in those areas. Another employed some Spanish-speaking campaign workers to go door to door in Mexican-American areas. In each case these were marginal districts.

The respondents were also asked whether or not poll data had an effect upon the allocation of funds for advertising and the media; 20 percent of the respondents and 24 percent of the marginals acknowledged that survey results had caused a change in emphasis toward political advertising. Most of them increased their allocation of funds for this purpose during the latter stages of the campaign. Others were unable to divert funds to this purpose although such diversion was indicated by the polls. One Republican stated that his poll showed a need for Spanish-language billboards but that his fund shortage precluded his buying them.

Most candidates said that their campaign strategists advised greater use of radio spots and television after seeing the results of the polls. Some then assigned sizable amounts of campaign money for this purpose:

My poll indicated that my problem was to become known; consequently, we spent 80 percent of our limited campaign funds on radio, television, and newspaper ads.

The high cost of media advertising was a constant threat to the campaign planning of numerous candidates. The cost of the polls themselves was a major expenditure for the candidates and was the principal factor in the inability of many of them to engage survey organizations to begin with.

The cost of statewide or districtwide opinion polls varies according to the area, the reputation of the company, and the extent of the poll desired. The average candidate was unable to say what his poll cost, although most complained that the price was substantial. Many Democrats relied upon the Harris Poll conducted under a contract with the Democratic National Committee. As shown in Table 6.4, however, a wide variety of practices was employed to pay for surveys.

Polls were financed from three major sources. First were those paid for by a unit of the party—typically the state or county committee—and they usually encompassed more than the congressional race. Some Democrats noted that the local labor union organizations cooperated with the party units in paying for the surveys.

A second group relied on friends or volunteer groups, or its members paid the cost from their own pockets. Some of these were "piggyback" surveys, in which the congressional race was simply attached to a statewide poll and a proportionate amount of the cost was charged to the candidate's organization. A few candidates in both parties arranged with academicians to conduct polls at relatively nominal cost.

In a few instances a local newspaper contracted for a poll, and even though the primary purpose was journalistic, the results were used in evaluating the candidate's campaign position.

It is impossible to evaluate the precise uses to which poll results are put. Within the limits of our knowledge, many candidates were able to make good use of poll results while others could not. Some, quite obviously, sift from the data those bits of information which lend support to what is already being done while ignoring others that suggest a change in style.

Table 6.4
Methods of Financing Public Opinion Polls

	Losing Candidates			Marginal Candidates		
	GOP (N = 34)	DEM (N = 34)	ALL (N = 68)	GOP (N = 12)	DEM (N = 12)	ALL (N = 24)
Poll Paid From Candidate's Own Funds	18%	9%	13%	17%	17%	17%
Poll Paid From Staff Funds or by Volunteers	38	21	30	33	25	29
Poll Paid by State Central Committee or County Committee	35	43	39	50	42	46
Newspaper Poll Only	6	18	12	0	8	4
Don't Know How Poll Was Financed	3	9	6	0	8	4

The pent-up frustrations and the resigned indignation of the non-incumbent challenger when he finally realizes the narrow range of assistance to be offered by the national, state, and local party authorities was concisely stated by one Democratic candidate, who noted:

> No one is much interested in the congressional race until about a month before the election, then it is too late to get your campaign underway. My loss by less than 5 percent was a personal triumph as far as I was concerned. I got virtually no help from any party groups or officials. It was my personal followers who rounded up the votes.

Faced with this grand isolation, the nonincumbent candidate must put together a personal organization, using what party structure is available to him but depending largely upon his personal initiative. These efforts, unlike those of the candidate quoted above, often suffer from inadequate financing, haphazard organization, and lack of direction. They are sometimes unable to effectively meet unexpected campaign contingencies and react to crisis with obvious panic. Time devoted to organizational problems must be sandwiched between the candidate's early-morning greetings at the factory gate and late-evening receptions at the Kiwanis Club. When time is found, it is often borrowed from other campaign efforts, and seldom is the loan repaid.

On occasion the judgment of a candidate is incredibly bad. One Republican described an afternoon spent in a parking lot at the county fair, during which he took time to put one of his campaign stickers on his opponent's car because it "would make him so mad." It is doubtful that the effort reportedly devoted to this bit of childishness was as important as the loser apparently thought.

If this story has a moral, it must be that no matter what the national, state, and local party organizations do for their candidates, there is no real guarantee that the man will have the personal qualities or the campaign organization necessary to make maximum use of the aid. That, however, is no reason for the party organizations to reduce or minimize their auxiliary campaign services. All too few of them provide even a minimum level of assistance, and all too many congressional candidates are left to fend for themselves. It is our suggestion that even in a decentralized party system such need not be the case.

7.
Issues in the Congressional Campaign

*Political campaigns are designedly made
into emotional orgies which endeavor
to distract attention from the real issues
involved, and they actually paralyze what
slight powers of cerebration man can
normally muster.*
—JAMES HARVEY ROBINSON

SOCIAL scientists engaged in research on the role of issues in American politics must sometimes conclude that they are grappling with phantoms. Not only is there disagreement over what constitutes an "issue," but there are immensely disparate views as to the sources and effects of issues upon political behavior. A number of distinguished scholars have considered some phase of the problem, but few have launched a thorough, broad-scale attack upon it. Indeed, most studies have approached the subject from the point of view of the voter rather than of the candidate or the political organization.

The Survey Research Center at the University of Michigan has satisfactorily established the general absence of doctrinaire political philosophies among voters and at the same time shown that those voters are motivated by partisan commitment.[1] Berelson, Lazarsfeld, and McPhee have compared "style" issues with "position" issues, using the two terms to distinguish between those issues of ethical or moral tone and those of more concrete and specific definition. The former are often difficult to particularize but refer to indirect, material considerations, embracing such matters as corruption in government, civil liberties, and candidates' personalities. Position issues, on the other hand, relate to potential or actual tangible gain for some group in whose interest the issue is propounded; examples are taxation, farm prices, and labor-management relationships.[2]

1. Angus Campbell, Philip Converse, Warren Miller, and Donald Stokes, *The American Voter* (New York: Wiley, 1960), Ch. 10.
2. Bernard Berelson, Paul Lazarsfeld, and William McPhee, *Voting* (Chicago: The University of Chicago Press, 1954), pp. 183–85.

Another team of scholars—McCloskey, Hoffman and O'Hara—concluded that distinct differences of viewpoint about public issues exist between the leaders of the two major parties but that only moderate differences are apparent between the leaders and their followers.[3]

Others have discussed issue development and effect within a particular stratum of political life. Professor Frank Sorauf, for instance, studied the role of local issues in state legislative contests in Pennsylvania.[4] And the authors of The Legislative System considered a whole network of role orientations which affect the issue response of those state legislatures studied.[5]

At the congressional level Charles Clapp reports on the attitudes of incumbent congressmen toward issue development as it relates to their efforts to be reelected and to project a favorable image.[6] Occasionally a political memoir contains a reference to issues as affecting a particular political career, but by and large these represent assertions of belief rather than statements of fact.

Finally, a number of writers have written of presidential campaigns in which issues are often more clearly drawn and have much greater chance for widespread dissemination and political impact.[7] None of

3. Herbert McCloskey, Paul Hoffman, and Rosemary O'Hara, "Issue Conflict and Consenses Among Party Leaders and Followers," American Political Science Review, 54 (June, 1960), 426.
4. Frank J. Sorauf, Party and Representation (New York: Atherton, 1963), Ch. 6.
5. John C. Wahlke, Heinz Eulau, William Buchanan, and Leroy C. Ferguson, The Legislative System: Explorations in Legislative Behavior (New York: Wiley, 1962), Part 4.
6. Charles L. Clapp, The Congressman: His Work As He Sees It (Washington: The Brookings Institution, 1963), pp. 372–79.
7. Although the following is by no means an all-inclusive list, these works include: James M. Burns, The Deadlock of Democracy: Four-Party Politics in America (Englewood Cliffs, N.J.: Prentice-Hall, 1963); Paul F. Lazarsfeld, Bernard Berelson, and Hazel Gaudet, The People's Choice (New York: Columbia University Press, 1944); Theodore H. White, The Making of the President 1960 (New York: Atheneum, 1961) see also the 1964 and 1968 volumes in this series; Frank J. Sorauf, Political Parties in the American System (Boston: Little, Brown, 1964); V. O. Key, Jr., Politics, Parties and Pressure Groups (New York: Crowell, 1964); Richard E. Neustadt, Presidential Power (New York: Wiley, 1960); Samuel Lubell, Revolt of the Moderates (New York: Harper, 1956); and various editions of the American Government Annual (New York: Holt), for discussions of particular issues. Many political biographies and autobiographies contain discussions of issues by candidates and those closely associated with them.

these sources, however, treat issues as they relate to congressional campaigns. And none of them consider issues developed by non-incumbent candidates.

Issue Orientation of Defeated Candidates

In any serious discussion of issues in politics and the relatively minor role they are alleged to play in campaigning, one is faced with a paradox. There is a widely held belief that issues do not win campaigns but that it is with issues, and issues alone, that campaigns have meaning and take place at all. Issues provide the occasion for candidates and parties to publicly state their case, to agree or disagree, and to provide ideological, economic, historical, or other reasons to support their positions. If issues are the stuff of political campaigns, the grist which candidates must grind, why are they not more important as factors in victory or defeat at the polls? Indeed, self-government and representative democracy are defined in terms of access of voters and candidates to questions of public policy, so that these may be ventilated and debated and choices provided among candidates for public office.

Moreover, in the perspective of history, it is what men "stood for" that distinguishes them from their forgotten opponents, rather than other matters considered so crucial to victory at the polls by most observers. On the one hand, democracy pays tribute to the power of ideas in its willingness to permit public choices of who rules and represents. On the other hand, when listed as factors influential in the actual behavior of those to vote, issues ran a poor fourth behind organization, finance, and candidates' qualifications.

Candidates reported in this study that issues played a relatively minor role as obstacles to victory or reasons for their opponents' success at the polls. Neither group rated issues of great importance in the campaign. They were much more apt to credit pragmatic campaign organizations and financial programs as major factors in the outcome. Nevertheless, the relatively low status of issues as salient features of congressional campaigns does not mean that the candidates did not talk about substantive matters at all. They did discuss various subjects which they considered to be issues in the campaign.

Candidates were asked to "rank, *in order of emphasis*, the five issues in your opponent's campaign which were most damaging to you." They were also asked to rank, *in order of emphasis,* the five

Table 7.1

Percent of Candidates Reporting Estimates of Issues Considered Most Damaging to Their Opponents

Type of Issue	Losers		Marginals	
	GOP (N = 128)	DEM (N = 106)	GOP (N = 24)	DEM (N = 20)
Policy	41%	53%	50%	50%
Ideological	9	6	4	15
Constituency	17	14	16	15
Personal	20	9	13	0
Various	5	7	4	10
No answer or None	8	11	13	10

issues in their own campaign which caused the most damage to their opponent. The term *issues* here was purposely left open-ended, to elicit what the respondents considered them to be.

Responses in ten areas were sought, and a furnished checklist included such broad levels of issues as local, national, and international policy; constituent services; and matters of personal nature. It should be pointed out that most candidates emphasized only two or three major issues in both their utterances and in campaign materials. About 10 percent of the respondents reported a spread over more issues, making systematic analysis of the comparative emphasis of their campaign issues difficult. Others raised questions of personal

Table 7.2

Percent of Candidates Reporting Estimates of Issues Considered Most Damaging to Themselves

Type of Issue	Losers		Marginals	
	GOP (N = 128)	DEM (N = 106)	GOP (N = 24)	DEM (N = 20)
Policy	16%	32%	29%	45%
Ideological	12	17	0	25
Constituency	33	26	25	25
Personal	15	8	21	0
Various	9	6	8	0
No answer or None	15	11	17	

need, such as campaign finance and management problems, as if these were also public issues. Such responses were discarded.

Using the rough classifications described here, responses and comments of losing and marginal candidates were regrouped and tallied in general categories of policy, ideology, constituency, and personal matters. Tables 7.1 and 7.2 illustrate the comparative weight of these issues conceived by the respondents as being "most damaging" to themselves and their opponents. From these responses we are able to estimate the saliency of issues to the respondent in the 1962 congressional elections.

POLICY ISSUES

Campaigns directed to policy issues are perhaps the ideal in popular concept of the democratic electoral process. An exchange of candidates' views on specific areas of public policy is considered both a means of public enlightenment and the most desirable method of informing voters in an election campaign. Policy debate embraces the term "issues" in its basic sense and illuminates the candidate's grasp of the broad field of public policy, his deftness in handling controversy, and his style of operation. Although it is quite likely that one's policy stance has less to do with the outcome at the polls than have many other factors in a campaign, the challenger candidate feels he must make a strenuous effort to master the "issues" facing a potential congressman as one means of proving his qualification for office. And the efforts of the national committees are largely aimed at supporting this need on the part of candidates.

Ideally the policy-oriented campaign can be distinguished from other varieties of campaigns by its recognition of and emphasis on factual information and the relevant historic, social, or economic aspects of the issue at hand. At the very least, the policy-oriented campaigner would eschew sloganeering and minimize simplistic labeling of complex issues. Thus, in responding to the Medicare issue of 1962 with cries of "creeping socialism," a candidate is giving an ideological response rather than addressing the issue itself. If he does not proceed from this point to the real question, he is evoking heat rather than shedding light on a complex social, historic, and economic question.

Actual policy statements among candidates in the 1962 congressional campaign covered a wide range of questions: foreign policy, generally centered around the Cuban threat and the disposition of the missile crisis late in the campaign; the perennial question of the extent of American involvement in the containment of Communist nations; and the extent of aid to underdeveloped nations. Domestic questions were less prominent except in the area of constituency issues. Regardless of emphasis, the policy-oriented campaigns were clearly differentiated from others by the level of the candidate's responses and their judgment on the areas considered most damaging to their own and to their opponents' campaigns.

It is no surprise to find that policy questions were dominant in the candidates' estimates of the issues most damaging to their opponents; 41 percent of the Republican losers and 53 percent of the Democratic losers felt that policy issues were most damaging to their opponents (Table 7.1). Only 16 percent of the GOP losers and 32 percent of the Democratic losers believed their opponents' use of policy issues to have been damaging to them (Table 7.2). Among marginals, 50 percent in each party felt that policy questions were most effective against their opponents, but they differed considerably when considering the effects of policy issues on their own campaigns (29 percent of the Republicans and 45 percent of the Democrats).

The similarities between the candidates of the two parties on vulnerability to "policy issues" suggest that candidates of both parties saw real advantages in the use of policy issues. On the other hand, on the receiving end, the Democratic candidates—losers and marginals alike —attested to more damage on policy matters than on any other type of issue.

Because they were representatives of the incumbent party in both Congress and the White House, with previously untried leadership in the person of the President, the Democratic party and administration had a record to defend. Its candidates were therefore more sensitive to GOP attacks upon that record. This circumstance delineates in a general way the issue vulnerabilities of "defenders" even though they were challengers for congressional office.

Among Democratic candidates the specific issues reported most frequently as damaging were government welfare and medical care programs, the Cuban missile crisis, high taxes, and the involvement of the Democratic party with organized labor and alleged labor-policy trade-offs. Republicans felt most vulnerable to Democratic charges relating to alleged GOP neglect of major social legislation, including Medicare and Aid to Education, tax loopholes, and equivocal stances on foreign aid and the Peace Corps.

Although some candidates' responses may represent little more than rationalizations of defeat, it is believed that the reaction to policy issues was substantially accurate and indicates both its substantive and tactical role in the campaigns of losing and marginal candidates.

Just as policy issues may at times tend to be long on facts and short on rhetorical impact, so ideological issues may be short on facts and long on passion or rich in symbolism. An ideological campaign issue is calculated to evoke maximum emotional response with a minimum of hard data, and those largely of a philosophical nature. Ideological issues in American politics yield easily to stereotypes, sloganeering, and the tyranny of labels, so that little more than their utterance is required to "prove" their point. Ideological issues by their sweep and impact drastically simplify the difficult questions which an opponent concentrating on policy might propose or defend by more deliberate, rational campaign argument. They are also as much a part of political campaigning in America as are the symbolic elephant and donkey. When effectively used in conjunction with policy issues, they can have maximum effect on political audiences.

With little difficulty most candidates can slip into heated ideological disputation to carve out a place on the liberal-conservative spectrum. Obviously some candidates are temperamentally more prone than others to the use of ideological campaign issues. Others may use these issues to capitalize upon a prevailing ideological sentiment. A Republican candidate, who in 1962 was already supporting Senator Goldwater's drive for the presidency, commented upon the ideological emphasis of his campaign:

The only reason the Republican party has not been able to win this seat has been that we have always run me-too candidates. This is a conservative district and I was certain that a conservative candidate could win it. The fact that I didn't win doesn't mean the district is not conservative. I am sure that it is.

Even though this candidate ultimately received 44 percent of the vote, he remained convinced that the ideological complex of his strategy and estimation of the district was correct. Several other conservative candidates volunteered comments of this nature, indicating their inability to accept the judgment of the voters as a possible criticism of the ideological slant of their campaigns.

Several Democratic "peace" candidates flaunted deeply held beliefs in the faces of many voters who clearly held contrary opinions. Having won nomination in heavily one-sided districts, these "peace" candidates admitted that their cause was not popular and that its advocacy was unrealistic in terms of electoral choices, but they held to it stoically throughout their campaigns. In brief, these candidates engaged in "peace education" before mass audiences as few minority groups are able to do.

Several candidates, in the face of widespread expressions of relief and approval of the President's action in the Cuban missile crisis, did not hesitate to make known their opposition to that action. One elderly Republican candidate, reflecting upon his campaign experience, noted:

> I was the first candidate in years in the district who was not a right-winger. That's true of the Democratic candidates too. Both parties always nominate right-wingers. But I slipped into the primary and won the nomination on my good name and when it came time to campaign I knew I didn't have a chance anyway so I decided to tell the people things they didn't want to hear. I even came out against Kennedy's Cuban stand because I thought it was a dangerous grandstand play for political purposes. It was a lot of fun and gave them their first real choice between a conservative and a right-winger they ever had. They still picked the right-winger but I bet they stopped and thought first.

It should be noted at this point that in analyzing candidates' responses to the questions on issues, no effort was made to refine the respondent's terminology. Terms such as "liberal," "conservative," "socialist," and "right-winger" were accepted and classified in the sense that candidates used them, using everyday meanings. Democratic candidates tagged with being "ultra-liberal," "pink," or "socialist" were hard put to understand what the implications might be when added to the charge of adherence to Kennedy's New Frontier. Similarly, Republican candidates who were bruised by ideological charges reported being tarred with "right-wingism," "Goldwater conservatism," or "John Birchism." The latter term was difficult to refute; one candidate reported, "He said I was a Bircher and even though I'm not, I couldn't convince anyone of that fact from then on out."

Virtually all the candidates claiming effective damage to their opponents on ideological issues stated that they had not used terms stronger than "liberal" or "conservative." If we accept these denials, we must assume that the more immoderate ideological efforts were those of incumbent congressmen. Most of these nonincumbents would have agreed with the Democrat who rather piously noted, "I sought to keep the campaign on a high level by discussing my liberal approach to governmental problems." In spite of expressed good intentions, however, many were "forced" to abandon the high road to engage their opponents with weapons of their own choosing. One example was particularly striking. A Republican candidate was highly incensed that his opponent throughout the campaign tagged him with the reputation of another GOP candidate in an adjacent congressional contest, who was admittedly a member of the John Birch Society. The respondent claimed that his defeat was caused by these attempts at guilt by association. This anecdote also illustrates the impact of ideological issues in general—that on the receiving end they ranked much higher in the estimate of "damage" than the same issues did as weapons of offense.

Ideological issues ranked low when estimated as damaging to opponents (Table 7.1). Only the Democratic marginal candidates believed that ideological issues were more important when used against their opponents. The Republican marginals and the losers of both parties were far less certain of this alleged "damage."

ISSUES OF CONSTITUENT SERVICE

A theme familiar to all observers of political campaigns, and one to which congressional campaigns are no exception, is the assertion that "Candidate ——— can do more for you." By "more" is meant a range of activities loosely classified as constituent services. Among these are a myriad of congressional franked mailings inviting the voter to request informational pamphlets published by the government departments and distributed by the Government Printing Office. The now classic booklets, "Infant Care" and "Your Child from One to Six," have long been sent to voters by congressional offices following birth announcements in local papers. Constituent services also include a host of activities which staff members for incumbent congressmen call "casework." This includes favors, inquiries, introductions, and requests to unsnarl the web of agency decisions in almost every conceivable area of government activity. Constituency services respond to pleas for draft exemption and military reassignment; immigration and naturalization problems; job requests; and the ever-present demand for agency contacts and/or influence for businessmen and other activists in the congressman's constituency. Voters are led to expect a schoolboy record of perfect attendance to House Roll Call votes as proof of fidelity to the high office of congressman, and as final evidence, a record of sponsorship of or influence upon major pieces of legislation and public-works projects affecting the folks back home.

A youthful candidate scored an eastern Republican for his alleged legislative inactivity:

During _____'s two terms in Congress he submitted 320 bills and resolutions with not one ever being enacted (but with most of them getting maximum publicity coverage) . . . the worst *strike-out* record in Congress.[8]

A Democrat listed the following five constituent issues as those most damaging to his opponent:

1. In thirty years in Congress he never introduced a bill or any legislation.
2. He has never done anything for his Congressional District.
3. He has lost touch with local issues and local economic conditions.
4. As a result of reapportionment, he no longer lives or spends any time in the District.
5. His preoccupation with Republican Party matters, as a major GOP spokesman and official, often requires him to vote against the interests of his own District, such as Rural Electrification, Social Security, Farm Price Supports, Water Pollution, etc.

As many as 26 percent of the Democrats and 33 percent of the GOP losers felt that constituency matters, of which the above list is a good example, were the most damaging type of issue used against them. Unlike the sensitivity of losing candidates to policy issues, nonincumbents believed that their major disadvantage was on constituency matters.

Republican losers felt that constituency matters were their Achilles' heel. This sensitivity points up once more the advantages enjoyed by the incumbent candidates in their errand-boy capacity. The incumbent can point with pride to his own seniority and to his assignments on House committees as vital to the interests of the voters; he can emphasize the full range of constituent services he has provided.

The nonincumbent has the choice of ignoring constituent issues

8. Fair Campaign Practices Committee, Inc., *Report: The Fourth Biennial State-by-State Study of Smear: 1962* (New York: Fair Campaign Practices Committee, 1964), p. 9.

or of attacking the incumbent with regard to them. Such an attack provides the occasion for campaign strategies relying upon attendance records; assessment of legislative output; roll-call votes on local questions; and other easily measured indices of political and legislative capability. Campaigns based on issues of service or constituency in this study almost always occurred between candidates matched as incumbents and nonincumbents, rather than between two newcomers to the congressional races.

As weapons of offense, nonincumbents attacked the voting records of opponents, asserting that their stands on selected issues were not of service to the district or were "obstructionist" or "do-nothing." Obviously, service issues as used by incumbents are positive in nature. They are designed to convince the electorate that incumbency, being "on the job," is itself a notable reason for reelection. They assert that prior experience warrants return because of the value to the constituency of the congressman's knowing his way around Washington and his familiarity with the problems of the district as these relate to the federal government. Incumbents continually cited the benefits of personal seniority, since in this area the challenger is at an automatic disadvantage. Incumbents cited membership on committees of importance to the home district. A midwestern Democratic loser complained, "I simply couldn't overcome his [the incumbent's] membership on the House Agriculture Committee, so important was it in this farm district." A Republican stated, "He said that _____ got its new Post Office because of his seniority on the Post Office Subcommittee."

The refrain of the nonincumbent on constituent issues is directly tied to any chinks that might be found in the armor of the incumbent. One such chink that was emphasized by many was the question of legislative authorship of bills. Both Democrats and Republicans sought to prove that the incumbents were unable to "get bills passed." When several of the incumbents did have substantial legislative records of direct benefit to the district, however, the handicap was difficult to overcome. One loser noted, "I couldn't explain away the little projects which he had been responsible for over the years."

Since news media and academic observers often emphasize policy and ideological differences between candidates, it was surprising that service issues ranked so high. Since the national party organizations emphasize policy and ideological issues, except for voting records and federal "impact" data generated by the Democrats, it remained for the candidates to develop whatever constituency issues they could.

PERSONAL ISSUES

Personal attacks or character allegations questioning the personal attributes or qualifications of candidates have occupied some part of political campaigning since the first free election. It is this threat of exposure of one's personal life which keeps many people from embarking on political careers, since in the final analysis there is no guarantee that the most upright of candidates may not be falsely charged.

Sometimes these personal issues may dramatize qualities or qualifications for office which might actually be considered as legitimate issues. It may be argued, for example, that an elderly incumbent no longer possesses the physical or mental stamina needed to qualify for the demanding work of a congressman. Although such a charge can under certain circumstances be in bad taste, it can still be a legitimate issue. On the other hand, personal attacks may be inserted in a campaign to smother authentic policy differences between candidates or to "paper over" the lack of such differences. At times personal issues constitute a subliminal undercurrent in a campaign, while on other occasions ridicule, name calling, and overt character attacks may be used openly. Sources of personal campaign attacks are elusive at times, and their authorship is frequently anonymous. These issues are not designed to educate the voter but simply to win support by shaking his confidence in the opposition.

The long-term congressional incumbent is especially vulnerable to personal attacks. His personal indiscretions, whether real or imagined, usually take place in Washington, and meaningful refutation within the bounds of the electoral district is difficult. The annals of political biography and descriptions of political life are rife with examples; some candidates are berated for advanced age, while others face charges of disloyalty to their country. Because there is no way to prevent even the most trivial personal matters from becoming matters of contention, it is obvious that some campaigns will not be concerned at all with significant issues of public policy.

The most notable feature of the personal issues reported in 1962 (Tables 7.1 and 7.2) was the sensitivity of Republican candidates. In considering the issues most damaging to their opponents, one-fifth of losing GOP candidates leaned heavily on personal matters, in contrast to less than one-tenth of the Democratic losers. Similarly, nearly twice as many GOP losers felt that personal issues had been most damaging to themselves. Among marginal candidates the contrast was even greater.

Since most issues of a personal nature were used as offensive tactics, it might be well to examine some of the individual charges made in the campaign. Among them were seventy-six specific charges which constituted unfavorable personal issues or reflected adversely upon the opposing candidate. These fell into three separate categories: the personal characteristics of the candidate, his beliefs, and his personal associations.

Attacks upon personal characteristics and qualifications appeared to dominate many of these campaigns. Charges were sometimes clandestine, conveyed through suggestions and whispers. At other times they were aired through the more formal media of newspapers, radio, and television. Some focused on age or personal appearance; others on occupation and even on marital status.

The age of a candidate was an important issue in several campaigns. The allegation was usually made that the incumbent was too old, senile, or both. This charge was often leveled by Republicans against Democratic incumbents and is particularly noteworthy since, as noted in Chapter 2, the Republican candidates were an average of ten years older than were their Democratic counterparts. On the other hand, one Republican discovered much to his dismay that he had to defend his youth. Some, it was argued, had not lived for a long enough time in the district to assure adequate understanding of its problems, and a Democrat felt it necessary to respond to the charge that his birthplace was outside the state.

Occupation was sometimes an effective point of attack. One Democrat from a rural district found himself on the defensive because of his occupation—attorney at law. Another, a Republican housewife, found it difficult to overcome the jests of her opponent that her place was in the home. Two academic candidates, one from each party, found their occupational role as college professors a personal charge of a disadvantageous nature.

One issue, closely related to occupation, was the matter of personal inexperience. A Republican loser argued that the incumbent's lack of military experience made him an ineffective member of the Armed Services Committee. Another carefully documented his own business experience and compared it favorably with that of his opponent. Most such issues reflected varying degrees of desperation.

The category of personal qualities included unsubstantiated charges of cowardice, ignorance, and immorality. Republicans appeared to rely on such issues more than did Democrats. One of these said that his opponent was a "tipsy laughingstock on Capitol Hill." American political history is replete with examples of such campaign issues and there is little to be gained by exploring them in greater detail. Closely related but categorized separately were two Democrats whose marital status was attacked. One was expected to defend his bachelorhood (he refused to discuss it), and another was subjected to a whispering campaign alleging that he had "abandoned his family to run for Congress."

Another group believed that ethnic considerations played a role in their campaigns. Some candidates had to defend themselves against charges that their national origins did not correspond to a substantial proportion of the voting populace of the district. One felt strongly that his opponent's Polish name was damaging to his candidacy in a predominantly Polish district.

Another variety of personal issue centered on the relationship of the candidates to unpopular ideological beliefs or groups. These included such charges as "soft on Communism," a recurring theme among Republican candidates for nearly twenty years; Democratic charges of Republican associations with Birchites; and general allegations of GOP "negativism." Four Republicans and one Democrat believed that the "soft on Communism" charge was effective against their opponents. A Democrat felt that his most effective issue was his allegation that his opponent was affiliated with the John Birch Society.

More frequently candidates accused their opponents of being under the influence or control of an interest group or political machine. Typically, Republicans were "controlled" by big business and Democrats by organized labor. Republicans exploited the urban political "machines" of Mayors Daley and Wagner, saying candidates were held in thralldom or were manipulated by these political "bosses."

As in three previous elections, the Fair Campaign Practices Committee in 1962 published a state-by-state study of "smear" campaigns.[9] As might be expected, relatively few candidates felt strongly enough about the personal charges made against them to file formal complaints with the FCPC. Many others felt themselves unfairly

9. Fair Campaign Practices Committee.

treated when in fact they were simply inexperienced or naive political campaigners. FCPC reported that forty candidates in twenty-two states were victims of definite violations of the Code of Fair Campaign Practices which, if applied, would include most of the charges made by the respondents in this study.

The Code establishes the following working criteria of unfair political tactics.

1. Anonymity (including telephone and whispering campaigns).
2. Bogus organizations or publications.
3. Scurrilous attacks on a candidate's personal or family life.
4. Outright vilification.
5. Lies or substantial distortions.
6. Removal of a statement (or photograph) from context so as to reverse or substantially change the significance of the full statement (or picture).
7. Attempts to create or exploit doubts about the honesty, loyalty, or patriotism of a candidate without objective evidence.
8. Exploitation of racial or religious prejudice.
9. False accusations of racial or religious prejudice.[10]

To apply the term *smear* to the personal issues cited by respondents would be inaccurate. It is noteworthy, however, that our classification of personal issues gains legitimacy when compared to those listed in the FCPC code. Without question many significant issues of policy or constituency were trivialized into personal issues, and in the heat generated by ideological questions candidates were frequently led to personal attacks.

Even with massive assistance in direction and manipulation of campaigns provided by advertising and public-relations firms, it is accident rather than design that often led candidates to emphasize personal issues. Most of them reacted to the frustrations of fighting a lonely battle against a seasoned incumbent.

10. P. 2. The *Report* lists two different types of "smears" used in the 1962 campaign. First were those directed at candidates as "stand-ins" for the President, who was not on the ballot. To attempt to tie the local candidate to alleged errors or indiscretions of a higher officer is not new to American politics. In 1962 FCPC found that these issues were generally concerned with either Medicare or Cuba. These two issues, of course, have been treated as legitimate policy questions by us and were listed as such in our issues structure. The second group, although not specifically distinguished by the Committee, obviously included personal attacks in violation of the group's own Code of Fair Campaign Practices. This was most evident from a review of the targets of 1962 campaign smears as discussed on pages 8 and 9 of the 1962 *Report*.

The candidates are not the only ones to influence the level and type of issues used in congressional campaigns. Just as important are the influences of the reporting services in selecting newsworthy questions and, of course, the curiosity and receptivity of voters to nonsubstantive campaign issues. Charles Clapp reported that many members of the House recognized the inability of constituents to understand or even to express interest in substantive questions of policy germane to the work of the congressman. He concluded:

> One result has been to focus congressional attention on the need to present the voter with a favorable picture of the person who represents him, without seeking to educate him extensively on the issues.[11]

Clapp reports a viewpoint common to many candidates. It is confirmed by the experience of the nonincumbents in this study. Several complained that the daily press releases from the offices of their opponents were concerned with preserving or developing images rather than with developing voter education. Although the assertion is difficult to prove by statistical yardsticks, this emphasis is also generated by the need of candidates to permit professional public-relations men to build images rather than to rely solely on concrete achievements.

Issue Emphasis by Marginal Candidates

We have attempted to compare and distinguish those candidates who were running in marginal congressional contests and those who were not. In Tables 7.1 and 7.2 the differences between the two groups in emphasis on issues is clearly shown. Although the categories are not amenable to stricter tests of statistical significance, some simple comparisons enable us to draw some useful 'conclusions. To some extent they represent distinct characteristics of the marginal and losing candidates.

The marginal candidates showed a pronounced orientation toward policy issues. Considering both parties jointly, 50 percent believed that policy issues were most damaging to their opponents, and 37 percent believed that policy issues were most effective when used against them. Moreover, emphasis on policy issues by marginal candidates was considerably stronger than on other types of issues.

11. Clapp, p. 372.

In view of the accumulated evidence[12] that voters are not normally oriented to policy issues, it is interesting, and not a little unusual, that marginal candidates pressed such matters so wholeheartedly.

Illustrative of this emphasis was the comment by a Republican marginal:

> I knew that I had a real chance of winning. _____ had only served one term and an undistinguished one at that. He didn't do any of the things he promised two years ago. Just about everyone thought I would take him. I spent a lot of my time on public relations to discuss our differences in views that I thought were important. . . . Somehow, I didn't get through. Cuba hurt, but it wasn't just that. They just didn't seem to understand the issues or they weren't interested in them.

The experience of this candidate partially explains the ambivalent nature of policy issues and their effects on campaigns. Most candidates were not familiar with the more sophisticated research on this subject and acted out roles within the bounds of what they thought constituted certified campaign technique. Hence the candidates saw broad areas of policy difference and believed that they needed to be exploited and discussed. They lacked information on the effects such matters might have on the voters. They campaigned according to preconceived formulas and were almost universally surprised when the responses were not as expected.

At the same time the incumbent, with more campaign experience plus some years in office, emphasized service issues and those policy matters which tended to associate him with the president or, in the case of the Republicans, with some leading party figure. These appeared to him to be more potentially productive. Both might have been missing the mark, but the nonincumbent was missing it completely.

The evidence shown in Tables 7.1 and 7.2 suggests a greater propensity by marginals to concentrate on issues of policy and service. They underplayed ideological and personal issues. Several of them, not wishing to assume an ideological label, sought to broaden their appeal by placing major emphasis on other matters. The marginality of the district itself might possibly suggest a moderate or middle-of-the-road electorate, to whom an ideological appeal

12. Campbell, et al., Ch. 10; Berelson, et al., *Voting*, pp. 308–11; Clapp, pp. 372–79; Frank J. Sorauf, *Political Parties in the American System* (Boston: Little, Brown, 1964), Ch. 4; Nelson W. Polsby and Aaron B. Wildavsky, *Presidential Elections: Strategies of American Electoral Politics* (New York: Scribner, 1964), p. 11.

might be unwise. Whatever the reasons, the marginal candidates stuck to the "safer" issues of policy and service.

Knowledge of the Issues

Having asked the candidates to list those issues which seemed in retrospect to have been damaging, we foresaw the need to determine whether they would blame defeat on inadequate knowledge or under-

Table 7.3

Evaluation of Candidates' Knowledge of Issues Considered as an Obstacle to Victory

Knowledge of Issues	Losers		Marginal Losers	
	GOP (N = 77)	DEM (N = 62)	GOP (N = 13)	DEM (N = 8)
Of Great Importance	10%	0%	8%	0%
Of Considerable Importance	6	2	15	0
Of Little Importance	90	98	77	100

NOTE: Percentage totals may exceed 100 because of multiple responses.

standing of the issues. To arrive at this conclusion, a multifaceted question was included which, among other matters, sought to direct the candidate to a self-evaluation of his own knowledge of the issues. "In analyzing your defeat, what factors do you feel were your greatest obstacles to victory?"

A number of disparate factors were listed to elicit the candidate's views on the effect of inadequate financing, insufficient and ineffective party organization, and lack of press support. Among these eight disparate items was, "Inadequate knowledge of issues." The respondent was asked to indicate on an accompanying scale whether the item was of little, considerable, or great importance as a cause of his defeat. Table 7.3 shows the results by candidates in general and marginals in particular.

Among the losers of both parties 94 percent believed that inadequate knowledge of issues was of little importance as a contributing factor to their defeat. The remainder perceived this element to be of considerable or of great importance. Marginal candidates were less certain of the effect, an average of 14 percent in both parties suggesting that knowledge of issues might have been of considerable or great import. A comparison of the responses according to party, on the other hand, showed that GOP losers gave much more emphasis to lack of familiarity with issues than did Democrats. A great many of them singled out the Cuban affair as an example of an issue which could have damaging consequences if the candidate had too little familiarity with it. Some of them believed that Democrats as a whole were provided "inside" information about Cuba, while their opposition was forced to rely upon newspaper reports. This point was brought out more dramatically through a separate series of questions relating to issues in the 1962 campaign.

A number of Republican nonincumbents voluntarily discussed the effects of issues on campaigns, and almost all of them gave particular emphasis to Cuba. There was little doubt in their own minds that the long-run effect of the Cuban issue was advantageous to the Democrats. One noted that his opponent's "attachment to JFK only became important to him after the Cuban action on October 22." Prior to that date, he said, there had been no noticeably close association of views between the candidate and the President. Another, unable to suppress his bitterness, reported, "I honestly believe that I could have run against Fidel Castro and the results would have been the same." The image of public confidence in the President created by the Cuban crisis was particularly helpful to members of his party who were campaigning for public office. Most of the GOP candidates, unable to attack the President, claimed instead that he had belatedly adopted a program of action which their party leaders had authored.

It might be worth noting the impact of the Cuban issue upon the campaign as illustrated by reactions from the various major party headquarters. Prior to the dramatic action in Cuba, the Republicans had been on the offensive, basing their attacks on charges of inaction, lack of White House understanding, and poor diplomatic and military intelligence. Many Democrats during those early weeks found themselves on the defensive—privately agreeing with Republican charges but unable to challenge their party leader. During the week prior to the crisis many of those closely associated with the Democratic National Committee and many state campaign organizations were in quiet despair. GOP charges were clearly creating a public impression of inadequacy in United States policy toward the Castro government.

Many Republicans, on the other hand, were jubilantly counting on sizable increases in GOP House membership, confident that public dissatisfaction over the Cuban matter would bring about large-scale defections from Democratic candidates. Congressman Robert Wilson, Chairman of the Republican National Congressional Committee, confidently predicted an increase of forty seats in the House of Representatives. Reports from Republicans in the field—candidates and others—lent weight to these assessments of the impact of the Cuban situation. Many reports cited Democratic disorganization and frustration over the failure to "recognize the existence of Soviet missiles in Cuba." The discovery of such missiles on Cuban territory and the ensuing week of international crisis clearly upset prognostications of party officials on both sides. A Republican party spokesman said that John Kennedy had, for once, done exactly as GOP leaders had been demanding and had in the process blunted whatever chances Republican candidates had possessed. Charges of presidential indecisiveness and inaction appeared hollow indeed after that dramatic ten days while the world seemed to teeter at the brink. The fact that Republicans might have "foreseen" the development was small consolation in the face of the overwhelming public support given the President over his dramatic and successful confrontation with Russia.

In short, the candidates campaigned on issues because it is traditional to do so. To meet the public the politician needs something to discuss. His own psychological involvement in politics is probably based upon a combination of self-seeking, partisan commitment, and ideological persuasion. The latter two are almost certain to evoke strong feelings about the issues of the day. The candidate may have an ideological commitment or he may be directed toward constituency issues. But whatever its cause or intent, his orientation is certain to find an outlet in discussion of issues. Most such discussions were directed toward what we have called "policy" issues.

Candidate Impressions of Policy Issues

Congressmen have often commented that the public is seldom well informed on issues which seem to them of transcendent importance.

The main issues in off-year congressional elections have often appeared more local than national in character. Studies have shown that most voters cast their ballots for reasons totally unrelated to a candidate's policy position. It was, therefore, of more than passing importance that the respondents in this study appeared to emphasize policy issues. The reasons, however, are not clear. The close victory of President Kennedy in 1960 may have caused Republican candidates to approach his administration's first electoral test with more than normal contentiousness. Some of the issues (e.g. Medicare and Cuba) had the advantage of dramatic clarity. Should the elderly have a medical care plan under the social security system or not? Should the Soviet Union be allowed to plant nuclear missiles "ninety miles from our backdoor" or not? These are simple expressions of complicated political issues. They were well tailored for use in a turbulent campaign.

The failure of more than a handful of major pieces of legislation in the first of the Kennedy congressional sessions was quite probably a signal to extend campaign discussions to a number of issues. With President Kennedy's increasing personal popularity the Republicans, looking for some ray of hope, viewed the record of the administration as a flag to greater effort. The Democrats were spurred on by the prospect of increasing their majorities in order to pass the Kennedy program. In the ensuing melee policy matters became the main ammunition. Both parties sought in the 1962 congressional campaign to develop issues viable for the 1964 presidential race.

Some policy matters always receive more attention than others. An inordinate interest in a problem of moment may offer great appeal to a major segment of the voting public. Farm policy was obviously important in the congressional campaigns of the 1950s. Labor policy occupied an important role in those states debating "right to work" laws during the past decade. Social security and medical care for the aged were of particular interest to voters in states with large retired populations. Some two or three issues usually emerge as the predominant focus of discussion.

The folklore of American politics that in off-year congressional campaigns the issues are predominantly local in character is not altogether borne out, however, by the results of this study of the 1962 contest. As noted in Table 7.4, substantial numbers of candidates listed national and international policy issues as being of transcendent importance to their campaigns.

Foreign affairs are inextricably tied to the presidency, and the

Table 7.4

The Saliency of Specific Policy Issues in Campaigns of Losing Congressional Candidates
Percentage of Candidates Ranking the Issues Listed As Damaging to Self or Opponent

	Republicans		Democrats	
	Damaging to Own Campaign (N = 128)	Damaging to Opponent's Campaign (N = 128)	Damaging to Own Campaign (N = 106)	Damaging to Opponent's Campaign (N = 106)
Cuban Missiles	21%	26%	9%	23%
Foreign Policy		20	15	11
Federal Spending		33		33
Farm Policy	3	11		12
Labor Policy		4	5	
Medicare	17	8	42	8
Welfare Programs	18	4	25	
Aid to Education	5	4	11	5

NOTE. Percentages may not total 100 because of uneven responses to a scaled question.

in-party congressional candidate will usually attempt to associate himself with the policies of a popular administration. Out-party candidates, in the age-old style of adversary campaigning, will attack the record of the president and seek to prove that the national interest demands the candidate's own election and support of his party's stance. Two facets of international policy were prevalent in a large number of 1962 campaigns. These were the Cuban missile affair and a catch-all category of "foreign policy" which included United States efforts in various other trouble spots as well as foreign aid.

A poll taken in October by *Congressional Quarterly* reported that Cuba was the most important issue of the campaign with congressmen and editors who were interviewed.[13] Other observers suggested that Cuba was one issue among several dominating the congressional campaign at that time. Among the Republican losers, 26 percent believed the Cuban issue to be most damaging to their Democratic opponents. A few noted that, despite their inability to capitalize upon the issue after the week of crisis, they still believed

13. *Congressional Quarterly Weekly Report,* October 26, 1962, p. 2050.

it had worked to their own advantage. The most prevalent reaction was expressed by one Republican who noted, "I thought I came out all right on Cuba. I had been calling for Kennedy to take action and he did. I simply claimed credit for it."

Without a doubt the Cuban missile affair, involving direct confrontation with the Soviet Union, not only dampened the campaign but also effectively excised about ten days from the last weeks before the election. But Democrats felt nearly as strongly about the advantages they gained in the same crisis: 23 percent believed that the issue of the Cuban missile crisis was most damaging to their opponents. While they had been confused and defensive before the crisis reached its climax, the withdrawal of the missiles was a saving grace. "I was on the defensive throughout the early fall. The period afterward helped me to recoup," reported a midwestern Democrat. In an interview (November 27, 1962) with one of the authors a well-known Republican candidate said:

I had called for the President to go slow in demanding that the missiles be removed. I had gone against the prevailing opinion of my party leaders and was very vulnerable. I really didn't think the missiles were there in spite of what Ken Keating said. I have always been wary of overusing the military and was naturally cautious in this situation. The crisis left me holding the bag. I went to the lake for a few days until I saw where I stood. My campaign never recovered from it.

Like many others, this candidate felt it politically dangerous to engage in debate over so volatile and uncertain a chain of events.

Among Republican losers, 21 percent expressed the belief that the Cuban matter damaged their campaign efforts, and many commented that they found themselves unable to maintain the initiative on the issue after the President's action. Reflecting what became a widespread unshakable belief among Republicans, one noted, "I had been right all along, but the President's dramatic use of his power to cement the election jerked the rug out from under me."

Only 9 percent of the Democrats considered the issue damaging. This included several "peace" candidates, but also many of those who had been vociferous in denying the existence of the missiles. One of them commented: "Cuba—he [my opponent] constantly called for something to be done—after it was done—said too little and too late—press supported him—this was the only issue he used."

The Cuban issue certainly damaged some elements in both parties but appeared to be more helpful to the Democrats during the final days of the campaign. A Gallup Poll reported that 80 percent of the people supported the blockade, and congressional mail ran strongly in favor of the President's actions. The chairman of the Republican National Congressional Committee, Representative Wilson, stated one month after the election that the strong action of the President had cost the Republicans "at least twenty seats."[14] The fact was, however, that no one could say with any precision just what effect the Cuban affair had on the electorate. It is evident that the defeated candidates, admittedly involved, assessed the issue as having considerable impact on their campaigns.

Foreign policy per se usually emerges as a campaign issue; but depending on the international situation at any given time, different aspects of it emerge in different campaign years. Although in 1962 the United States action in Cuba was the dominant foreign-policy theme, other matters of international involvement came to the fore. Among the damaging issues candidates listed were foreign trade, the admission of Red China to the United Nations, nuclear disarmament, the "disintegration of NATO," and especially foreign economic aid. Republicans (20 percent) believed foreign policy issues more damaging as an offensive weapon than did Democrats (11 percent). On the other hand, 15 percent of Democratic losers and no GOP losers felt hurt by general charges in the area of foreign policy.

The remaining six issues noted in Table 7.4 were domestic. The question of federal spending was used with effect by 33 percent of the candidates in both parties, although none of the respondents felt the issue damaged his own campaigns. Republicans, as in past campaigns, cited the dangers of overspending and inflationary problems allegedly brought about by federal programs. Democrats argued, however, that federal spending programs were essential to continued social growth, while those candidates in districts harboring defense industry attempted to show that continued local prosperity was dependent on continued spending. That is, there was a close parallel between candidates' support of spending programs and personal creeds of liberalism. The overall issue emphasis, however, was one of policy orientation.

In 1962 the issues of farm and labor policy played a smaller role than in some recent election campaigns. Agriculture remained a major economic problem, but compared to other years, the farm

14. *Congressional Quarterly Weekly Report,* December 14, 1962, p. 2258.

industry was relatively prosperous in 1962. Farm legislation that year was not designed to break the impasse that has held in agricultural policy for so many years, nor was it instrumental in reshuffling the various components making up the amorphous group termed "farmers." Consequently, although the topic was of importance in selected districts, the attention paid farm policy in the campaign was negligible.

Even though the months preceding the election constituted a period of relative peace between labor and management groups, the AFL-CIO's Committee on Political Education (COPE) was very active in the 1962 campaign. Yet few candidates listed labor matters as important in their campaigns. Most of those who mentioned labor at all related it to campaign contributions that they or the opposition received from organized labor. Most of these were in industrial areas dominated by large labor groups and with a strong labor vote.

In mid-October the *Congressional Quarterly* poll rated medical care for the aged as the most potent issue reported by Democratic congressmen outside the South. In early October the issue took precedence even over Cuba. Republicans did not rate medical care nearly as highly as did the Democrats, 42 percent of whom felt strongly about Republican use of this policy issue in the campaign.[15]

The anti-Medicare campaign was carried out through the activities of the American Medical Political Action Committee (AMPAC), a voluntary unincorporated group, the membership of which consisted of physicians and their wives. Although some AMPAC literature did not emphasize the fight against medical care, it was unquestionably the predominant issue of importance to the group. The AMPAC National Board of Directors, consisting of nine physicians and one member of the Women's Auxiliary of the AMA, is appointed by the latter group's Board of Directors. An AMPAC official, speaking to a Republican candidate's conference in 1962, said that most of the money used by the organization came from contributions from members of the medical profession. The structure of membership fees ran from $10.00 for an active member to $99.00 or more for a sustaining member. Sustaining members, in return for the fee, received a membership card, a subscription to *Political Stethoscope* (an AMPAC newsletter), and a "99 plus" sterling silver pin.

AMPAC reported spending a total of nearly $250,000 in 1962, all of it in support of candidates and campaign activity in forty-three

15. *Congressional Quarterly Weekly Report,* October 19, 1962, pp. 1933–34.

states. In one battle between a liberal Democrat and a conservative Republican challenger in the far West, AMPAC contributed $5,000 to a single campaign. The records of the Clerk of the U.S. House of Representatives showed that at one time during the campaign the American Medical Association transferred $50,000 in cash to the AMPAC treasury.

Respondents in this study were divided along party lines in assessing the influence of AMPAC upon the campaign, Republicans favorably and non-southern Democrats unfavorably. Only one midwestern Democrat, a conservative, received direct campaign support from AMPAC, with $2,000 from an AMPAC fund-raising dinner.

AMPAC's efforts to appear nonpartisan were highly transparent. One piece of AMPAC literature quoted Representative Wilson of the Republican National Congressional Committee: "If it hadn't been for AMPAC, dozens of *our* good candidates wouldn't be members of the Eighty-eighth Congress." Another brochure, released at the same time and in the same envelope, quoted "one party professional": "If it hadn't been for AMPAC, good candidates *on both sides of the aisle* wouldn't be members of the Eighty-eighth Congress." (Emphasis supplied).[16] This would appear to be an obvious attempt to lend an aura of bipartisanship to the activities of AMPAC, even though the evidence suggests that Republicans benefited almost exclusively.

The campaign in support of Medicare was led by organized labor, mainly through COPE, with executive talent supplied by the United Steelworkers of America with the help of a new organization, the National Council of Senior Citizens. The latter was headed by former congressman Aime Forand (D-RI), sponsor of the medical insurance measures of the 1940s. The National Council of Senior Citizens, which claimed a membership in early 1963 of 1.5 million, devoted its considerable energies during the campaign to promoting the President's legislative program on Medicare, the King-Anderson Bill providing for medical care for the aged under

16. This information about AMPAC is derived from three sources: several brochures published by AMPAC, American Medical Political Action Committee, 520 North Michigan Avenue, Chicago, Illinois; *Congressional Quarterly Special Report: 1961–62, Political Campaign Contributions and Expenditures* (July 26, 1963), p. 1192; and "Summary of 1962 Receipts and Expenditures, American Medical Political Action Committee," Office of the Clerk, U.S. House of Representatives. This was also summarized in a Research Division Staff Memo, March 23, 1963, Democratic National Committee, 19 pp., mimeographed.

Social Security. (After the defeat of the King-Anderson Bill in midsummer, NCSC devoted its efforts to supporting candidates who had voted for it and to helping all newcomers in the congressional races willing to make Medicare a major campaign issue). The group also testified before the House Ways and Means Committee in support of the King-Anderson Bill and sponsored workshops and conferences, ostensibly nonpartisan in nature, throughout the country on the problems of the aged and of medical and hospital care. Mass rallies in thirty-two major cities were conducted by the National Council of Senior Citizens, culminating in a Madison Square Garden rally that was addressed by President Kennedy.

Throughout the campaign the Senior Citizens Council was rumored to be the creature of the White House and the Democratic National Committee, and newsmen speculated on the extent of financial support provided by the party. Since the Council filed no report of expenditures, and since the Democratic National Committee was on record for only one contribution to the Council of $5,000, solid evidence is lacking as to the sources and the extent of the financial backing given the organization by the party. Close observers, however, believe it was almost totally supported by organized labor.

Considering the effort devoted to this issue by interest groups on both sides, it was not surprising that large numbers of candidates considered the issue important. Evidence as to the impact of Medicare on the election outcome, however, was somewhat conflicting. Both proponents and opponents claimed to have been successful. A Gallup Poll taken after the election suggested that the issue did not help the Democrats among the older citizens. The majority of those voting supported Republican candidates, regardless of their views on the medical-care issue. AMPAC claimed to have supported fifty congressmen and to have aided over two-thirds of these in getting reelected. The organization would not, however, make public its list of congressmen.

The Senior Citizens Council, on the other hand, also claimed successes. The executive director of the group claimed that it had a major role in the defeats of Congressman Walter Judd and Senator Homer Capehart, both leading opponents of the administration program. Among those assisted by the NCSC were victorious members of both houses, many of whom were marginal, if not safe, incumbents at the outset. These conflicting statements are certainly inconclusive as evidence of the effectiveness of the groups. Without a doubt, no single candidate could claim to have lost or won on the basis of Medicare alone.

Indeed, among the losing congressional candidates a curious pattern asserted itself with regard to Medicare. Even though the Democratic party and President Kennedy made it a major issue, 42 percent of the losing Democratic candidates felt it to have been the issue most damaging to their campaigns. This percentage of candidates was the largest to single out any policy issue in this study, and it contrasted sharply with the percentages in the other candidate groups as shown in Table 7.4.

There are a number of possible explanations for this response. In pushing the medical-care program the Democrats, possibly unwittingly, undertook to attack a significant element in the social structure of small-town and rural America. The physician occupies a position of social prestige and civic responsibility in most communities, and the problem of health care for the aged was skillfully converted by the opposition into an attack on the medical profession itself. It was this latter point that was heavily emphasized by the local and state medical societies in their campaigns against Medicare, with materials carried to doctors' waiting rooms across the nation. And whereas the effects of such attacks might not have filtered directly to election command posts, it was obviously an issue of serious concern to Democratic candidates in the field.

Furthermore, even though in 1962 there were seventeen million persons of sixty-five or over, it is also true that this group exhibits a relatively low voter participation. This fact, combined with the minor interest that younger voters have in medical care for the aged, may have been responsible for the apparent lack of voter support for the issue and the candidates backing it. Whatever the reasons, the Democratic candidates reacted to a surprising degree against the damaging effects of the Medicare issue.

A number of candidates listed issues such as "unemployment benefits," "federal aid to the poor," and "mental health programs." We classified all of them as "welfare programs." As noted in Table 7.4, one-fourth of the Democrats and 18 percent of the Republicans claimed these issues as significantly damaging to their campaigns. Over one-half of these Democrats had to contend with charges of "socialism" because of their support of welfare legislation. And one-third of the Republicans noted that their positions on these issues were too liberal to please their constituencies. No Democrats and only a few Republicans suggested that these issues were damaging to the campaigns of their opponents.

The last issue listed in Table 7.4 is federal aid to education. Only the Democrats, against whom this issue was used, considered the question of significance. Of the 11 percent who singled it out, most attributed their difficulties to the unresolved deadlock on the question of aid to parochial schools.

It may be argued that a candidate cannot meaningfully analyze his own campaign in terms of issue damage. It seems to us, however, that the candidate is in an enviable position to make just such judgments. It was the candidate who fielded questions from countless audiences who usually had to make the decisions as to which issues to emphasize and who was forced to decide which parts of the mountain of campaign material to select. The determination of whether to emphasize local, national, or international issues was the responsibility of the candidate. And he was usually the most knowledgeable within his entourage concerning the reaction of the local press to the issues. In short, we are content with the analysis of issues suggested by the candidates. No one, it would seem, unless he were to conduct an in-depth analysis of congressional elections, is better qualified to discuss the effects of policy discussion upon the campaigns than the losers.[17]

Local Issues in the Campaign

Few observers have examined the effects of local or district issues in congressional campaigns. Occasionally a textbook suggests that off-year congressional elections are more vitally affected by local issues because of the lack of a presidential contest, but generally nothing at all is said. Some research has been carried out on the

17. It will be noted that Table 7.4 does not include the issue of civil rights. On September 29, 1962, President Kennedy, after considerable provocation, ordered the Mississippi National Guard federalized, sent U.S. Army troops to the University of Mississippi, and forced the admission of black students. Politically explosive as these actions appeared at the time, only about a half-dozen candidates, all nonincumbents, cited them as of damaging importance. Almost all of them were Southern Democrats or Republicans, and almost all of them described the issue as "Oxford, Mississippi" or "Ole Miss" rather than as "civil rights."

question of local versus state issues in state legislative politics, but such findings are not pertinent at the congressional level of campaigning. Nevertheless, some respondents expressed the belief that local issues were important and reflected upon "the desire of the people of the district to have a congressman who will spend his time on district and local matters." Although we made no effort to evoke answers about local issues as such, we found that some candidates listed local issues in their responses to the questions about issue damage. Therefore, we have extrapolated two kinds of information from the questionnaires: the percentage of candidates who volunteered mention of local issues as important to their campaigns; and the nature of the local issues used.

It was possible for a single candidate to list any number of separate issues which were damaging either to his own or his opponent's campaign. However, each respondent was asked to list five in each category, and only five spaces were provided for each in the questionnaire. A count of the total number of issues listed by all 234 respondents revealed that there were 1,561 separate items, or an approximate average of seven per candidate. Of this total only 119 were clearly and demonstrably local in character. This figure represents about 8 percent of the total of all issues. Democratic losers were responsible for listing more in each category of campaign damage than were Republicans. Among the Democrats, 11 percent felt that local issues were damaging to their own campaigns, while just 6 percent of the Republicans agreed. Those who believed such issues to have been damaging to their opponent's campaigns were divided 7 percent for the Democrats and 6 percent for the Republicans.

Nonincumbents in both parties clearly recognized the local "pork barrel" issue as being most damaging to their own campaigns. All but one of the Republican issues of a local nature dealt with such questions and projects in the district itself. Half the local issues listed by Democrats were of this type. The following sample of comments is illustrative:

Amount of "pork barrel" appropriations secured in Washington for the District.

His claim of what he had done for the district—Lockheed contract, etc.

His record of successful pork grabber for district.

River development and water shed.

Getting funds for a 40-foot channel.

His ability to get goodies for the district.

Defense contracts in Missouri because of his committee assignment.

His successful appeal to Industrial Committees of the Chamber of Commerce showing public works and A.R.A.

Claim that he stayed in Congress to get the $500,000 appropriation for the Arkansas Frying Pan project.

His ability to help constituents with Federal assistance under programs he voted against.

Other local issues damaging to the respondent's own campaign covered a wide variety of matters. Several candidates were alleged to be part of a local political machine in their districts. Others suggested that personal views or votes on some local matter had been misconstrued to the voters. Several were blamed for rises in local taxes or for triggering tax reassessments at the local level. Only three listed issues of a policy type: "Eighty-cent corn—the farm bill"; "a local option on drinking"; and "school-prayer decision." But this group was also oriented toward federally financed local projects. As might be expected, to the candidates local issues are built upon a foundation of local projects.

The candidates who suggested that local issues were damaging to the opposition were much more versatile and covered a greater range of subjects. Obviously they had no "pork barrel" projects to point to with pride and, as a result, relied on anything at all that could be developed as an issue. A glance at the range of matters listed by the respondents will illustrate this point:

Failure to protect the Alaskan fishing industry.

My proposal for a 9th district Advisory Committee.

Democratic scandals in Chicago.

Loss of missel [sic] contracts.

His refusal to take a stand on the issues of local gambling.

He did nothing about our jet problem [flying over homes].

His project against "sonic booms" over Cleveland.

His record of deficit spending in city government.

The Rockefeller Tax Scandal.

Voted against our Iowa farmers at every turn—REA, farm bill, etc.

Expressways not yet completed.

It is reasonable to assume from these responses that incumbents employed their relationships to district projects as their principal local issues. By the same token, it appears that the nonincumbent, regardless of political party, will try to develop local issues but may be forced to rely on a wide variety of matters, often irrelevant, to attract the voters' attention. Though some of the issues listed by the latter were patently outside the jurisdiction or the influence of a congressman, they were apparently of enough importance to cause the opposition to list them as damaging.

By and large local issues played a minor role in the congressional campaigns of 1962. Congressional campaigns, if this study is indicative, are geared to national issues, and the variances in this pattern are found in those few campaigns directly involving public-works projects. It may also be concluded that those incumbents who emphasized local issues were able to point out their own involvement in securing projects paid in some measure by federal appropriations. At the same time those local issues developed by the nonincumbents tend to be of greater variety, cutting across jurisdictional boundaries.

The study of campaign issues in American politics has been devoted almost exclusively to the impact of discussion of issues upon electoral behavior. Few attempts have been made to systematically analyze the viability or saliency of issues from the perspective of the candidate except at the presidential and state legislative levels. Nor do we yet have a very clear understanding of the role of issues in congressional campaigns. Nevertheless, we have explored some useful data, although we have found few definite answers. Given the profusion of contrasts between various campaigns and the milieus in which they take place, it is even difficult to generalize meaningfully. Congressional campaigning is hectic, fast-paced, and baffling to candidate and observer alike.

We do not fault the candidate for his ignorance of policy issues —rather, if fault is to be assigned, it belongs to the system which forces him to discuss when there are few listeners; debate when there is no real engagement; decry when the need is for enlightenment; and engage in personal attack when substantive alternatives remain unexplored.

The fact that most candidates did not attribute defeat to inadequate knowledge of the issues does not mean that they were fully prepared to discuss them. Many of the candidates were most certainly ill-informed regarding specific questions of policy and ideology. But all of them found it necessary to speak, regardless of their competence to do so. And few of them found time to develop that competence during the actual campaign.

The gap between what a campaign was and what it should be caused much anguish and self-criticism among these losers. They pled for policy debates and were forced into personal recriminations. They spoke against the incumbent's record and were met by silence. They wanted to exploit important social and economic questions but ended by emphasizing niggling and unimportant ones. This wide gap between the conception of what a campaign should be and the actual experience of what it was caused many of them to become discouraged and disenchanted.

The issue orientation of the defeated candidates tended to emphasize policy and service matters. They discussed policies because it was expected of them and because they were sensitive to individual and party differences of opinion. They discussed service because the incumbent (and the opposition was normally an incumbent) was believed to be vulnerable in that respect. They talked principally of national and international matters because congressional campaigns are inextricably interwoven with the presidency and the president. When they digressed to speak of local matters, it was usually with regard to local public works projects. Furthermore, most of the research material and speech material received from national or state sources dealt with national and international questions. The pressing policy questions are framed in the national political environment— not in the relatively obscure problems of various congressional districts. It takes a skillful candidate to attach local relevance to most of these very broad issues.

Marginal candidates appear to have engaged in wider and more carefully considered issues. Aware of some chance for victory, they were more likely to disperse discussion of policy issues over a wider area than did the ordinary candidate. Few of them were willing to risk the consequences of a personal attack upon the opposition and were not attacked in turn.

Therefore, even though congressional campaigns can hardly be said to be designed to enlighten the electorate, the candidates valiantly try to use them to that purpose. Even though the electorate is not listening, the candidates talk as though it were. And even though the election is not decided necessarily on the basis of confrontation and discussion of policy questions, issues and discussion still make up the substance of what is thought of as political campaigning.

8.
The Politics of Defeat

There could be no honour in sure
success but much might be wrested
from a sure defeat.—LAWRENCE OF
ARABIA

THROUGHOUT these chapters we have emphasized those aspects of congressional candidacy which appear to contribute to defeat. The task has not always been an easy one. Elements of victory and defeat are difficult to define and to catalog, and as we expected, we became enmeshed in extended discussions of campaign techniques. While methods are important to any study of congressional politics, they are probably not the overriding determinant of electoral outcome. It is true that an occasional candidate can win a particularly difficult race by employing interesting and unique campaign strategies. But it is also true that the largest percentage of contested seats are decided with little regard for campaign styles or political tactics.

The study of congressional politics has not been treated adequately under the rubrics of either state or national party systems. State organizations center their attention on state and local electoral contests, while the national organizations support incumbent congressmen and national presidential tickets. The congressional nonincumbent candidate occupies a never-never land between the two organizational extremes. This circumstance has been the pervasive theme of this book; it dominates congressional elections just as seniority dominates congressional organization.

Our central and prevailing thesis has been that the incumbent congressman has the advantage over the nonincumbent; and that among the nonincumbents the marginal candidate enjoys greater party support and encouragement. These situations result partly from the district system, which permits nearly three-fourths of the seats to go virtually unchallenged, and partly from the lack of meaningful campaign assistance offered to those who challenge an incumbent from outside the system. Challengers may receive vocal encouragement, but they are seldom in a position to translate it into actual campaign assistance. There are many reasons for this, as we have noted in these pages.

To some, the congressional races may appear to be more local than state or national, but the nonincumbent challengers are often excluded from the local party establishment. The nature of the district system, constructed as it is by state legislative bodies, automatically guarantees a preponderance of districts which are safe for the incumbent. This, in turn, guarantees that the national and state party organizations will pay little attention to those districts, while the local organization ignores them in favor of seeking more parochial political prizes.

The losing congressional campaign is a discrete event: a set of actions and problems and experiences, unique to each candidate, election, and district. There is little or no continuity with the past or with the future. The challenger candidate must work without a meaningful or relevant record of his own and must run with but nominal support from the usual party cadres. The incumbent, on the other hand, not only has the momentum of his own past election victories but also a record of involvement to provide the continuity for his reelection bid. His efforts to retain his 1/435th share of the basic power of the House of Representatives is far less a separate event than it is a mere question mark in his continuing efforts to hold on to his seat.

The incumbent usually has far better sources of funds for his campaign. He is better able to exploit those sources of campaign money, represented by local, state or national interest groups. He is apt to get a greater share of official party assistance, and he is usually in a stronger position to garner contributions from appreciative constituents.

The question of campaign issues is almost always decided in favor of the incumbent, merely by his greater ability to call upon his own experiences in discussing them. He has taken part in House deliberations, and he has a wealth of information, garnered from committee responsibilities (which usually parallel his and his district's interests), on which to draw. The nonincumbent must begin his campaign without benefit of congressional experience and without adequate research facilities or time with which to bring himself up to the level of knowledge of his opponent. Admittedly, the impact of political issues on campaign outcomes is ambiguous, but no candidate—and particularly no nonincumbent—can appear to be uninformed. Even to speak in generalities requires some grounding in fact.

As noted in Chapters 4 and 5, campaign organization is an important element among those contributing to victory. It is particularly important to the congressional candidate who has no continuing organization within the party upon which to draw. Conversely, the lack of a continuing organization represents a nearly insurmountable problem for many nonincumbent challengers—the time is too short, the funds are insufficient, and the resources are unattainable. He must put together an organization that has no antecedent and probably has a limited future. Personnel to man such an uncertain apparatus are difficult to find, and once found are faced with the same insurmountable problems as the incumbent himself. The incumbent, however, can call upon his own personal district organization, the national party agencies, and members of his own congressional staff to serve his organizational needs. These helpers are known to him—often are already on his payroll—and the future is far less uncertain.

Some facets of congressional campaigns are unpredictable to incumbent and nonincumbent alike. In a presidential election year it is difficult to predict, and almost impossible to control, the impact of the names at the top of the ticket on those races falling further down on the ballot. A weak presidential ticket can have disastrous consequences for congressional incumbents of the same party; the Republican campaign of 1964 clearly demonstrated this problem. Another factor constituting a threat is the unpredictability of voter turnout; an unusually large or light vote in any given election can operate to the advantage or disadvantage of one or the other candidate. We made no effort to study the effects of either of these phenomenon on congressional races. We partly chose 1962 because it was not a presidential year. We also placed the effects of voter turnout outside the purview of the study because it is an intangible political factor which varies from state to state and from district to district. Some respondents cited high or low turnout as possible reasons for defeat, but these usually appeared to be efforts to rationalize the defeat rather than to explain it. The fact of the matter is, however, that in many congressional races the outcome depends more upon what others do than on what the candidate does.

Two problems which were discussed in the preceding chapters and which fall outside the control of the candidates themselves are the recruitment of candidates and the effects of primary elections on the ultimate outcome of the general election. Recruitment of congressional candidates has been thoroughly aired in Chapter 3. Most candidates in both parties were recruited by the leaders at some level of the party organization. Relatively fewer, particularly among the marginals, were self-starters. The entry of these individuals into "big-time" politics was outside party control in that they were invited to run by others.

The effects of involvement in a primary battle for the nomination are also beyond the control of the candidates. As noted in Chapter 3, the parties play a relatively minor role in primary election contests, but the primary itself can have a decided influence on the behavior of the candidate. The primary can be a useful and meaningful trial by ordeal of the uninitiated political novice; he can learn some of the problems which will beset him when the general election campaign gets under way, and he may gain the admiration of a wider audience within the party itself by virtue of the fact that he has won the nomination on his own. He has proved to the party pro that he is a vote getter. At the same time he may be severely hampered in the general election campaign by antagonisms generated in the primary. The enemies he makes may be more important to the eventual outcome than the friends. The costs of the primary may severely restrict the scope of his later campaign. And the time necessary to heal the primary wounds may be extracted at his peril from the limited time available to campaign. Nevertheless, if he wishes to gain the nomination, he may be required by forces beyond his control to engage in a costly primary contest.

Carl Friedrich has observed that the "relative role and strength of political parties depends upon the existence of a real prize for which to fight."[1] Nowhere is this more true than at the congressional district level. As we have noted, only 88 seats were classed as marginal by the *Congressional Quarterly* in 1962, and about 300 seats are seldom ever contestable. If the congressional seat is the "prize" in the congressional district, it is little wonder that the parties in those 300 districts play a small role and have little strength. This circumstance may well explain the lack of organizational vigor in those districts which go many years without a meaningful contest for the congressional prize.

We have also noted, however, that few of those 90 to 125 seats

1. Carl Friedrich, *Constitutional Government and Democracy*, rev. ed. (Boston: Ginn, 1950), pp. 416, 419

whose degree of marginality makes them contestable show any signs of party strength or party role in the congressional races. These districts may be marginal, but that in itself is not enough to guarantee that the candidate for Congress will benefit from party support. Incumbents may well ignore the formal party apparatus and may operate solely through personal organizations painstakingly built up over the years and held together primarily through personal loyalty. Nonincumbents, however, may fail to benefit because the good intentions of the parties are manifest but their support is misdirected. The national party organizations may overwhelm the congressional candidate with masses of general materials which he has neither the time nor the staff to use properly. Where he needs professional staff assistance he will, if he is lucky, see a field man once during the campaign. Where he needs pat answers to pressing local problems, he will be deluged with neatly packaged solutions to world crises. Where he is constantly shadowed by insolvency, he may see the bulk of those funds available lavished on those in his party who have already established themselves as winners. And when he turns to the local party leaders, he may find their attention riveted upon the courthouse or the state legislature, where real support will result in real emoluments. The material benefits to the nonincumbent congressional candidates are as scattered as are the parties which dispense them.

Given these conditions, the nonincumbent goes on to defeat in 80 percent of the congressional districts. In the last analysis the non-incumbent is most probably running in a district carefully carved to prevent him from winning. He is seeking a seat which does not neatly fit within the party structure, and he is facing a congressman-candidate who has traversed the road before and probably knows every byway, pitfall, and curve. He gets the wrong kind of assistance, often at the wrong time and in the wrong place. There is, in short, little to stimulate aggressive support by local and state party leaders because the few legitimate congressional "prizes" are distinct from the practical realities of defeat.

There exists, however, a deeper question of democratic theory that needs to be discussed. Does a democratic system of election in a two-party apparatus demand that each party put forth strong candidates who can compete on equal terms? Obviously, all congressional districts will not be equally competitive even if district inequities are overcome at a maximum level. Furthermore, even in a competitive district the incumbent will still retain the advantages of incumbency. But the question is whether or not lack of competition in a substantial number of districts endangers democracy. Our implicit assumption that the answer is positive is based on the probable desirability of a close race in a congressional district. Without such an occasional contest the minority party becomes disfunctional and impotent, and the majority party may well become self-serving and complacent. Neither result can possibly serve democracy well.

In any two-party electoral system, balanced or not, someone is always going to lose and someone is always going to win. Why then, it may be asked, make it easier for the nonincumbents to displace the incumbents? Is not this just a transference of roles between winners and losers? It probably is, but at the same time it must serve to strengthen the party system. A more competitive two-party system in most congressional districts should result in improved quality of debate and should produce a campaign that is more strongly directed toward issues. It is also possible that a greater degree of competition will attract candidates of higher quality, since the prize is open to two parties instead of one; that argument has been used for years in behalf of stronger party recruitment efforts. Furthermore, such a result should hold true for both self-starters and party recruits. Men of true ability are more likely to run in contests where there exists some hope of winning, and party officers are more likely to look for the best candidate available if there appears to be a true chance of success.

In a larger context, as concerns the effects of seniority in the House of Representatives, meaningful contests offering a greater likelihood of success should reduce the number of incumbents and, presumably, the number of senior incumbents, thus opening the power positions in the House to newer and younger members. All these considerations are highly theoretical but do lay the groundwork for a series of recommendations which, if adopted, would greatly increase the chances for victory by nonincumbent candidates for congressional seats.

Some Recommendations

The American party system is too fragmented and the American voter is too lacking in party loyalty for a clean-cut ideologically bifurcated political structure to succeed, even if it proved possible to build one. People who have developed family political loyalties over many generations are not going to allow themselves to be voluntarily reclassified according to ideological bent into a cleanly divergent party system. Those millions who refuse to admit to any party identification, proclaiming instead their political independence, are not going to permit that personal decision to be flouted merely because someone desires a neat pyramidal party system. The party system in America is not static, but in structure and membership it is still essentially as it was in the beginning. Therefore we do not propose to make sweeping recommendations to reform the party system. We do have some suggestions which we believe would improve the lot of the congressional candidate but which will fall far short of meeting the demands of radical party reformists.

In making these recommendations, we assume that some of the imbalance in congressional districts will over the years be undone as court edicts are enforced to require balanced, contiguous districts based upon the principle of one man one vote, as laid down in *Wesberry* v. *Sanders* (376 U.S. 1, 1964). There is already evidence to suggest that some progress has been made along these lines since 1964. If a more favorable balance in district composition is achieved, it logically follows that a more competitive political balance will develop within individual districts. If this happens, many of the problems of the nonincumbent candidate in the noncompetitive district could be overcome by natural political evolution.

Another force at work which may help to develop greater competition between the parties within the congressional districts is the obvious tendency toward a two-party system in previously one-party areas. The widespread election to office of Republicans in the South and Democrats in the New England and midwestern states bears witness to far-reaching change and suggests that greater competition for congressional seats may develop in some areas as a natural consequence of two-party growth.

The suggestions we make are less ambitious. For the most part they require no changes in the law or the party structure. With one exception they are within the scope of authority now possessed by the established party organizations. Some of them will cost money, but conversely should save as much as they cost if they are successful and result in greater competition at the congressional level. Furthermore, though the benefits to democracy cannot be measured in monetary terms, the ratio of costs to results should be favorable.

We do not intend these recommendations to be taken as criticism of the existing national party organizations. We have seen, at first hand, the work expended by them on the congressional races every two years and particularly in nonpresidential elections. We believe that incumbent congressmen in particular fail to give the national party committees their just due. This lack of recognition comes largely from a failure of communications between the congressman and the committee staffs. The incumbent relies heavily upon his own staff during a campaign for reelection, and most of the contacts between the professionals who man the national headquarters and the congressman's campaign are at the staff level. We checked several contests at random to trace the amount of candidate criticism of the party committees against the actual contribution of the party groups to those particular campaigns. We found that in most cases the party contribution from the national committees was far greater than the incumbent winner was willing to admit.[2]

The nonincumbent tended to be less critical of the national-level committees and more critical of the state and local party organizations. In this he was entirely justified in most cases. Some challengers were nevertheless critical of the national party committees and often with some justification. The committees were often frustrated in their efforts to assist the challenger candidates in solving problems

---

2. We have noted the lack of coordination and cooperation between the various national party agencies which is due in part to inherent differences in function assigned to various committees and in part to the difficulties involved in coordinating activities between organizations spread throughout the city of Washington. The Republican party has taken steps to increase coordination and cooperation between the party units. In mid-1970 the Republican National Committee became the first occupant of the new Dwight D. Eisenhower National Republican Center on Capitol Hill. Upon completion in 1971, this building will house, in addition to the National Committee, the Congressional and Senatorial Campaign Committees, the Young Republican Federation, the Federation of Republican Women and the Capitol Hill Club. This will mark the first time that the national units of an American political party have been jointly housed and should maximize contacts between party leaders, whether or not the party is in control of the presidency. The Democratic National Committee has moved to new headquarters space near the Potomac in downtown Washington. There are no known plans for the DNC to construct its own building. It would seem advantageous for the Democrats to consider such a move, not only to strengthen coordination between the various party committees, but to possibly encourage a revitalization of the Democratic National Congressional Campaign Committee, which has never lived up to its potential or to the important place in party affairs enjoyed by its GOP counterpart.

of personnel, finances, and communications. The suggestions which follow are meant as an attempt to breach the gap—real or imagined —between the two groups of candidates and the various organizational levels of the party.

PARTY ORGANIZATIONS

An overriding consideration which permeates the party system over much of the nation is the general weakness of the state and local party organizations. This weakness extends into every section, is bipartisan, and does not discriminate between large and small states. When dealing with 100 separate party organizations at the state level, it is difficult to generalize; but in order to offer any constructive criticism at all, general statements are necessary. It is also difficult to be objective because of the lack of objective criteria against which to measure performance. The subjective judgments which follow are based on candidate comment and tempered by our own firsthand experiences in off-year national campaigns.

For the most part in 1962 those state parties with full-time state chairmen and full-time staff assistance carried out the most professional program of campaign assistance to congressional and state and local candidates. Those states and parties with part-time chairmen and little or no staff were often those most severely criticized by the candidates for lack of campaign assistance and understanding. Therefore, we propose that each party in as many states as possible elect chairmen who can devote their full time to the party organization. These officers should receive salaries commensurate with their abilities and the demands of their position. That does not mean a minimum living wage but rather a professional-level salary, to enable the chairman to really devote full time to his job.

The implications of this simple proposal are far-reaching. The chairman can work to develop strengthened and viable party organizations at the local level in his state. He can engage in more meaningful and more fruitful recruiting efforts, not just for congressional candidates, but at all levels. He can maintain crucial liaison with the national party organizations and should have a better chance to put into effect some of the tested or experimental campaign techniques developed by them. He should have an opportunity to employ innovative techniques developed in other states and locales. If, as innumerable textbooks have proclaimed, one of the benefits of the federal system is the use of the states as laboratories for experiments in government, there is no reason why the same principle should not apply to state party systems.

An important corollary to the full-time chairman is the full-time paid executive director for those party systems which are unable, for one reason or another, to elect a full-time paid chairman. An executive director can achieve the same gains as can a chairman, except that the chairman's command carries more authority. Yet to make a real contribution, the executive director must be retained for a period of years in order to take full advantage of experience, establish desired rapport with party stalwarts, and make full use of new campaign techniques. Therefore, his salary must be maintained at a level which will permit his remaining in the position in the face of competitive pressures. One of the authors recalls arriving in mid-campaign in a state capital in 1962 to be met by a newly hired executive director of the party who had just graduated from college and had no political experience whatsoever. The state party was burdened with a long-time chairman who was paid expenses but devoted almost his full time to his own business. The state head-quarters consisted of one room with a desk, filing cabinet, and waste basket. There was no secretary, although a volunteer reported twice a week for half a day of typing duty. Fortunately the party in question controlled all major state offices, but that truth belied the fact that the state was a truly competitive one. The executive committee of the state's party was courting disaster. It struck in 1966, when two of the six constitutional executive offices and one house of the legislature were captured by the opposition. No party, however successful momentarily, can survive in a competitive system without some effective organization at the top. Unfortunately that party in that state more or less exemplified many of the state party organizations in the United States.

FIELD WORK

It would be financially impossible to furnish a trained field man for every congressional district in the nation. Not only would the cost be prohibitive, but the recruitment of experienced field men would be virtually impossible. Either party could afford, however, to fund and staff a reasonably large number of regional party headquarters, each responsible for twenty-five to forty congressional districts. We are not suggesting that these be operated only at campaign time. On the contrary, they should be maintained full time in election years as well as others. If, as numerous authors report, the congressman truly does begin his next campaign as soon as he is sworn in, the party organization can hardly do less. Even if the regional offices consisted only of a field man and a secretary, the necessary continuity would be maintained and the planning essential to the next campaign could remain constant. These party agencies would represent a new formal level of party organization. There is little question that these offices would represent a true liaison between the national-congressional campaign committees, the congressional districts, and the state headquarters. With full-time state organizations, as proposed earlier, it is not difficult to imagine a whole sweep of pre- and post-campaign activities which could be the responsibility of these regional party agencies. Campaign postmortems could be held; campaign schools could be organized, with the necessary leisure time allocated to realize their full potential; recruitment could be enhanced; and party finance could be regularized. Obviously the problems of funding and staffing would have to be solved, but the parties have proven repeatedly that there is political money available and that there is a reservoir of talent which, with proper training and remuneration, would be politically effective. Any political-science professor can recall occasional students who wished to work full time in politics upon graduation but could not find a salaried position in the parties. These proposals could go far toward providing the niches in politics which could be filled by such individuals.

STAFFING

The problems of staffing in politics are monumental. The national committees have been known to go for months without filling top-level positions because of lack of personnel who are both experienced and can afford to move into full-time politics. The problem is no less severe at the state and local levels, where money is often even harder to accumulate in noncampaign years and where trained or experienced personnel are virtually nonexistent. The problem is twofold. First, those who have the experience in running campaigns or organizing parties are in private nonpolitical jobs, which they cannot afford to leave. And second, those who can afford to work for the meager salaries provided are often either young and inexperienced or old and tired. The remedy to both problems would seem to demand that enough money be provided to pay competitive salaries, so that experienced men and women can afford to leave private employment to work for the party, and to provide formal training in practical politics to young people who wish to make politics their profession but have no way to enter the field and cannot afford to stay once there.

To solve these dual problems is no easy task. However, we believe that they can be solved with a minimum expenditure of money and a maximum return on the investment. We propose that each party, through the coordinated efforts of its national, congressional, senatorial, and state committees, establish a Political Academy in Washington through which formal training sessions could be combined with on-the-job internships for selected "classes" chosen from throughout the nation. These classes might be composed of 50 or 100 interns, each chosen by the state central committees and/or the national party organizations, with salaries (or fellowships) provided by a fund pool collected from all party sources. The class might last for a year—or longer—with some specified number of months devoted to attending actual training sessions in Washington, with instruction provided by professionals in politics, elected officials, administration officials (in the case of the party in power or former officials for the party out of power), outstanding state and local political organizers, spokesmen for interest groups, and others who may have a contribution to make. At the end of the formal training sessions the trainees might be assigned to political offices in Washington or across the nation, in order to get some number of months of on-the-job training. At the end of the entire training period the trainee would be returned to the sponsoring state or placed in an employment pool from which the staff needs of the expanded state or regional headquarters could be met.

This proposal is not a radical one. Both parties have for years run election-year campaign schools of a few days' duration for candidates and managers. The usefulness of the political internship has been proven beyond question by the programs of the National Center for Education in Politics, the American Political Science Association, and other university-run internship programs across the nation. This proposal merely expands and combines these programs to formalize them and, presumably, to make them more successful. Instead of short ad hoc training sessions at campaign time, this proposal would provide long-range in-depth training to prospective or inexperienced party officials on a regularly scheduled and formal basis. Over a period of years a reservoir of political talent could be built up to meet those deficiencies in party organization which we have found to exist. The simple fact is that campaign strategy does make a difference, but its effectiveness depends upon the availability of experienced campaign strategists.

FUNDS

The two American parties seldom end a campaign with a surplus of money. Anyone who has engaged in fund raising for a political party in a noncampaign year will testify to the difficulties. To accomplish the internal changes we have recommended will take money. We are in no position to estimate how much will be required, but the amounts will be substantial. We think that the availability of trained specialists and permanent staffs in the various regional and state party headquarters will eventually result in more careful and less wasteful expenditures. Nevertheless, the necessary expenditures to accomplish these long-range savings will be substantial.

If these proposals are to work, money will need to be forthcoming in reasonably steady amounts throughout each year. We therefore support those, including the President's Commission on Campaign Costs, who have called for legislation to provide a system of tax credits for small contributions to bona fide national or state party organizations. As noted in Chapter 6, experiments in raising large sums through small contributions have been highly successful in the Republican party in recent years. There is every reason to believe that expanded programs, encouraged by tax credits, would provide the necessary funds to put into effect the recommendations we have made with reasonable guarantees that the flow of money would not be interrupted.

Here, then, are four proposals for change. None of them is revolutionary, and none of them alone can solve the problems which beset congressional and other party candidates. Organizational change alone is not going to increase competition between the parties. There will remain great variation in the political viability of the parties from district to district and state to state. It is our contention, however, that within the parameters laid down by the district system the best hope for the nonincumbent congressional candidate lies in a strengthened organization below the national level.

In a two-party system approximately one-half of the candidates will always be defeated. The politics of defeat, however, should be written in terms of better-matched and more equitable contests, not as a final response to an uneven and cruel inevitability.

Appendix A

Candidate Questionnaire
1962 Congressional Election

Research Division   1730 K Street, N.W.
Democratic National Committee   Washington 6, D.C.

1. a. When did you first decide to run for Congress? (month)   (year)
   b. Was this your first campaign for Congress?   Yes   No
   If "no," when did you run before?
   (Specify if in a different district or state.)
   c. Check those who urged you to run for Congress:
      Family, relatives   It was my own idea
      Party leaders   Other:
      Friends, associates
   d. When did you publicly announce your candidacy for Congress?
      (month)

2. a. At the time of your decision to run for Congress, what chance of
      winning did you feel that you had?
      No chance   Good chance
      Remote chance   Certain victory
      Fair chance
   b. Explain briefly some of the reasons why you assessed your chances
      in this way.
      (For those who believed they had a remote chance or no chance at
      all of winning:) Why did you decide to run?

3. Did you have a primary or convention contest for the nomination as
   Congressional Candidate?   Primary   Convention   No
   contest
   If "primary"   Did you know when you first announced that you
                   would have primary opposition?   Yes   No
                   Did you announce before or after the other candi-
                   dates?   Before   After
   If "convention" Did you have opposition at the convention for the
                   nomination?   Yes   No
                   Did this arise before or after your announcement
                   of candidacy?   Before   After

4. Most counties in the U.S. have active party committees. (In some
   urban areas the major political committees may represent precincts,
   wards, or districts.) To what extent did the announcement of your
   candidacy receive the encouragement of these committees or their
   leaders?

Very much   Little
Some   None

5. a. Did you receive encouragement from other party officials to seek election to Congress?   Yes   No
   If "yes," which officials? What office did they hold in the party?
   b. At what point in your considerations did you discuss it with them?
6. How did your family respond to your candidacy?   (choose one)
   Enthusiastic   Unenthusiastic but agreeable
   Indifferent   Opposed
7. What problems did you have in organizing your primary campaign?
   a. Securing voting lists
   b. Drafting volunteers
   c. Raising money
   d. Finding campaign manager
   e. Finding finance manager
   f. Finding time for personal contact work
   g. Other (specify):
8. From whom did you receive the best advice during your primary campaign?
   a. Manager
   b. Finance chairman
   c. Personal friends (specify):
   d. Relatives (specify):
   e. Business or occupational associates (specify):
   f. Professional party workers or groups (field agents, National or Congressional Committees, local party officials, etc.)
   g. Other (specify):
9. a. Did any private interest groups or organizations at the state or local level encourage you to run for Congress?   Yes   No
   If "yes," please name the groups (AMA, ABA, AFL-CIO, C of C, etc):
   b. After your nomination, did you seek or receive endorsements of any such groups?   Yes   No
   If "yes," list the:
   Endorsements sought by you from such groups   Received?
   Endorsements volunteered by such groups   Accepted?   Rejected?
10. FOR THOSE CANDIDATES WHO HAD PRIMARY CONTESTS FOR THEIR NOMINATIONS:
   a. Were there "scars" remaining from your primary campaign which contributed to your defeat in November?   Yes   No
      Explain.
   b. Did the nature of your primary campaign influence your style of campaigning during the general election campaign?   Yes   No   Explain.
   c. Did your defeated primary opponent(s) publicly or privately

support your candidacy in the general election? Yes   No
Specify:
If "no," would such support have enhanced your chances of victory?
Explain.

11. What was the major source of campaign funds for your *primary* campaign?

12. a. What efforts were made to organize "volunteer," "independent," or "citizen" groups outside the regular party campaign structure?
   b. What were the titles of these groups in your campaign?
   c. Was your organization instrumental in setting them up?   Yes   No
   If "no," who organized them?
   d. Were they effective?
   e. What was the relationship of these groups to your campaign staff?
   Excellent   Poor
   Fair   Hostile
   Good

13. a. Who served as your campaign manager for the general election? (name)
   b. What was his relationship to you? (Friend, relative, business colleague, etc.)
   c. Did you continue with him for the entire campaign?   Yes   No
   If "no," why not?
   d. Approximately how many volunteers contributed a substantial amount of time to your efforts at campaign headquarters?
   e. Did you employ any paid campaign workers?   Yes   No
   If "yes," how many?
   What jobs did the paid workers perform?

14. a. Did you hire an advertising or public relations firm to assist you?
   Yes   No
   If "yes," at what stage in your campaign?   Early   Middle
   Late
   b. FOR THOSE WHO EMPLOYED AN ADVERTISING OR PUBLIC RELATIONS FIRM:
   How would you evaluate the shortcomings and strengths of your public relations services?   Explain.

15. a. Was a public opinion poll taken in your district at any time before or during your campaign?   Yes   No
   If "yes," what effect did this poll have on your campaign effort insofar as the following items were concerned?   (Briefly explain each answer.)
   Allocation of money for radio, TV, advertising:
   Organizational efforts:
   Staffing of campaign organization:
   Selection of issues:

Cooperation with other candidates:
Others (specify):
b. How was this poll financed? (Solely by you or jointly with others?) Specify.

16. To what extent did you and your organization use the following campaign techniques? Please estimate the percentage of your campaign efforts devoted to each of the following activities:

REMARKS

Radio talks	%
TV talks	%
TV debates	%
Door to door	%
Billboards or signs	%
Cards, pamphlets	%
folders, etc.	%
Other: specify	%
	100%

17. In what ways was the staff of the *State* Central Committee headquarters useful to you during your campaign?

very much somewhat little not at all

Research assistance
Speech preparation
Candidates Conferences
Speakers
Women's Activities
Nationality or minority groups
Personal advice
Young Democrats
Other: specify
Remarks:

18. In what ways was the staff of the *Congressional* Campaign Committee helpful to you during your campaign?

very much somewhat little not at all

Research assistance
Legal advice
Film spots, radio tapes, etc.
Personal advice
Field support
Finance
Your opponent's voting record
Other: specify
Remarks:

19. In what ways was the staff of the *National* Committee headquarters useful to you during your campaign?

very much somewhat little not at all

Research assistance
Speech materials
Candidates conferences
Published materials
Field support
Speakers
Women's activities
Nationality or minority groups
Young Democrats
Personal advice
Your opponent's voting record
Other: specify
Remarks:

20. Do you feel that there was a "turning point" in the campaign at which time you believe that your chances of election became noticeably lessened?   Yes   No
    If "yes," what was it?

21. Were there any apparent difference between the campaign which you waged and that carried on by your opponent?   Yes   No
    If "yes," what were they?

22. a. Did your personal campaign organization include any type of research assistance? (i.e. compiling material on your opponent, providing up-to-date clipping files, analyzing census data, voting records, position papers, etc.)   Yes   No
    b. Where did you go to get assistance of this kind if you did not have it within your personal organization?
    c. In retrospect, how important do you feel research is in a Congressional campaign?
       Very important
       Somewhat important
       Not important at all
    d. Which of the following National Committee publications were of most use to you during your campaign? (Please rank in order of importance.)
       "The Democrat"
       Fact sheets
       Suggested speeches
       Speech cards (of the Democratic Study Group)
       "The Fact Book of 1962"
       Press releases
       "Federal impact" material for your district or state

23. Would you rank, *in order of emphasis,* the five issues in your opponent's campaign which were most damaging to you?

    1.

    2.

    3.

    4.

    5.

24. Would you rank, *in order of emphasis,* the five issues in your own campaign which caused the most damage to your opponent?

    1.

    2.

    3.

    4.

    5.

25. Did any nationally-known Democratic leaders come to your district to campaign for you?   Yes   No

    If "yes," please list them by name.

26. a. Since the decision to run for Congress involves rather extensive financial commitments, to what extent did you have financial backing for your candidacy? (Please indicate approximate percentages.)

    From: Personal friends

               Party leaders

               Your own funds

               Other groups (labor, farm, business, civic, etc.) Specify.

    b. Which of the above had originally encouraged you to run? Specify.

    c. Which came to your support financially only after you announced your candidacy? Specify.

27. Approximately what percentage of your total campaign expenses were paid by:

    Congressional Campaign Committee   %

    Your own resources and savings   %

    Your own borrowing or family lending   %

    Borrowing on a note with others   %

    Private contributions from friends and supporters   %

    State, district or county committees   %

    Volunteer, citizens or independent groups   %

    Other   %

28. Do you believe that your campaign was adequately financed? Yes   No

    If "yes," what would you estimate the total cost of all campaign efforts on your behalf to be?

                    $

    If "no," how much additional financing do you feel you would have needed to win?

                 $

29. In analyzing your defeat, what factors do you feel were your greatest obstacles to victory?

	little importance	*considerable importance*	*great importance*
Lack of money			
Inadequate organization			
Lack of local party support			
Lack of state party support			
Lack of national party support			
Inadequate knowledge of the issues			
Your own qualifications as a candidate			
Lack of newspaper support			
Other (specify):			

30. In analyzing your opponent's victory, what general factors do you feel contributed most to his success?

	little importance	*considerable importance*	*great importance*
Ample money available			
His campaign organization			
Support of his local party			
Support of his state party			
Support of his national party			
His grasp of the key issues			
His ability to put himself across (showmanship)			
Endorsement by General Eisenhower			
Other (specify):			

31. If you had it to do all over again, what changes would you make in your campaign staff, organization, or effort? Explain.
32. Do you feel your candidacy made a positive contribution to the party in your district, state, or in the nation? How? Please elaborate.
33. Do you intend to try again for national office?   Yes   No
Undecided
Do you intend to run for another public office?   Yes   No
Undecided
If so, when?
What office?

Below you will find some questions concerning your personal and professional background. Some of this material you have already given to the Democratic Congressional Campaign Committee or to others at the National Committee. Since the results of that survey were incomplete, we would appreciate your giving the information requested with the understanding that your name will not be associated with it, and it will be kept in complete confidence.

1. Year of birth
2a. Place of birth   (state or foreign nation)
2b. Place of parents birth
3. Present occupation
4. Former occupations
5. Education: *Level*   *Place   Graduated*
                                                       (state)   (yes or no)

        Grade school
        High school
        Trade school
        College or university
        Graduate school
        (including law or medicine)
    College degrees held:
6. Length of residence in state   In the district
7. What governmental posts had you held before running for Congress?
    Position   *Dates held*   *Appointed or elected*

Appendix B

November 16, 1962

Dear:

The Republican National Committee is conducting a survey of 1962 congressional candidates to secure information which will help us to improve our services to future candidates.

This year Dr. Robert Huckshorn, Director of our Arts and Sciences Division, will be conducting this survey among both the winners and losers of congressional contests. The results will aid in making a meaningful evaluation of the effectiveness of our campaign in both issues and organizational efforts.

Your cooperation in completing the enclosed questionnaire will be of great help to us. The results will be kept strictly confidential. Any information which is made public will be totally in statistical form with no names attached.

A prompt return of the questionnaire in the enclosed stamped, self-addressed envelope will be appreciated.

Very truly yours,

William E. Miller

December 21, 1962

TO: 1962 Republican Congressional Candidates

FROM: Dr. Robert J. Huckshorn, Director
        Arts and Sciences Division

This is a note of inquiry concerning the questionnaire which was sent to you several weeks ago. The response has been gratifying and I am preparing to draft a report on the Republican campaign for Chairman Miller.

To date I have not received a completed questionnaire from you. This might be due to delay in the Christmas mails or the press of your personal affairs at this busy time of year. But while the memory of your campaign is still fresh and before the postage rates go up in January, I would appreciate your taking the time to complete and return the form.

In case you have mislaid the questionnaire, please advise me and I will send you another copy immediately. If you have lost the self-addressed stamped envelope which I sent in the original packet return the question-naire to me here at headquarters.

Best wishes for a happy holiday season and a prosperous New Year.

Index

Agar, Herbert, 138 n
Age: as a campaign issue, 205; of
  congressional candidates, 22,
  23, 44, 205; and relations with
  constituency, 23, 205
Agel, Jerome, 106 n
Agriculture Committee, 203
Agriculture, occupation of candi-
  dates in, 26, 31–32
Alabama, 73 n, 171 n
Alaska, 33, 34, 171 n
American Bar Association (ABA),
  68
American Federation of Labor-
  Congress of Industrial Organi-
  zations (AFL-CIO), 68, 69,
  70–71, 217. *See also* Committee
  on Political Education (COPE)
American Medical Association
  (AMA), 28, 68, 109, 218;
  Women's Auxiliary of, 217. *See
  also* Medicare; American Medi-
  cal Political Action Committee
  (AMPAC)
American Medical Political Action
  Committee (AMPAC), 109,
  217–18
American Political Science
  Association, 238
Americans for Constitutional
  Action (ACA), 70
Americans for Democratic Action
  (ADA), 71, 80
Anderson, H. Dewey, 24 n
Arizona, 33, 34, 171 n
Arkansas, 171 n
Armed Services Committee, 205
Ash, Vera, 171 n
Auxiliary candidate services: field,
  157, 163–66, 173–74; of na-
  tional party committees, 15,
  108; research and publications,
  157–62; speakers, 157, 167–72;
  special groups, 157, 174–79;
  speech materials, 157–62; train-
  ing programs, 157, 163–66;
  voting records, 157–62

Bailey, John M., 145
Ballot design, 17, 18, 46

Bankers, as candidates, 26, 30
Battle Line. See Republican
  National Committee, News-
  letter of
Benham, Thomas W., 186
Berelson, Bernard, 193, 194 n,
  209 n
Bibby, John, 140 n
Bills, authorship of, as an issue,
  203
Binkley, Wilfred E., 138 n
Bliss, Ray, 140, 145
Bone, Hugh A., 11, 67, 92 n,
  118 n, 138 n
Bossism, as a campaign issue, 206
Bryce, James, 179
Buchanan, William, 194 n
Burns, James MacGregor, 6, 194 n
Businessmen, as candidates, 26,
  29, 30, 31
Butler, Paul, 142, 159, 161, 178

Cabinet, President's. *See* President's Cabinet, as campaign
  support
California, 33, 34, 62, 148, 171 n
Campaign: administration of, 89–
  133; management, 90, 93–100,
  163–66, 229; managers, midcampaign resignations of, 95,
  104–5; managers, qualifications
  of, 93–100; managers, selection
  of, 93–100; professionalism of,
  92–100, 133, 163–166; purchasing for, 93
Campaign financing: candidates'
  own contributions, 119–20, 127;
  candidate responsibility for
  debts, 105; definition of, 118;
  difficulty of for non-incumbent
  candidates, 105, 117–30; for
  nomination, 119–20; legal
  limitations on, 118, 121–22;
  sources of, 119–23, 127, 129–
  30, 239; state public disclosure
  laws, 118–22; support by nonparty groups, 119–20, 127,
  129–30; tax deduction for contribution to, 131–32, 239;
  variation in costs, 121